Dave ~

To Ray Perman

Very impressive venture,
very appreciated.
Hope you enjoy it.

Cheers

The Strategy-Led Business

The Strategy-Led Business

STEP-BY-STEP PLANNING

FOR YOUR COMPANY'S FUTURE

Kerry Napuk

McGRAW-HILL BOOK COMPANY

London · New York · St Louis · San Francisco · Auckland
Bogota · Caracas · Lisbon · Madrid · Mexico
Milan · Montreal · New Delhi · Panama · Paris · San Juan
São Paulo · Singapore · Sydney · Tokyo · Toronto

Published by
McGRAW-HILL Book Company Europe
Shoppenhangers Road, Maidenhead, Berkshire, SL6 2QL, England
Telephone 0628 23432
Fax 0628 770224

British Library Cataloguing in Publication Data

Napuk, Kerry
  Strategy Led Business: Step-by-step
  Strategic Planning for Your Company's
  Future
  I. Title
  658.4

ISBN 0-07-707775-X

Library of Congress Cataloging-in-Publication Data

Napuk, Kerry
  The strategy-led business: step by step strategic planning for your company's
  future/Kerry Napuk.
    p.   cm.
  Includes bibliographical references and index
  ISBN 0-07-707775-X
  1. Strategic planning. 2. Corporate planning. I. Title.
  HD30.28.N383   1993
  658.4'012—dc20   93–982
                                                                  CIP

1234   CUP   9543

Typeset by Goodfellow & Egan, Cambridge
and printed and bound in Great Britain at the University Press, Cambridge

Contents

Preface

*It is planning not gambling that produces
profit and security.*

MARCUS AURELIUS[1]

Thus wrote Marcus some two thousand years ago. His words are as appropriate now as they were then. The underlying assumption behind this book is that companies that create and implement strategic plans, as part of their management discipline, will produce 'profit and security'. The corollary is that firms that fail to plan will not.

Implicit in the assumption is the belief that management teams can change their companies dramatically and thereby, to a great extent, create their own destinies. Management teams can direct change by planning their own future and taking responsibility for their company, not passively letting outside forces shape their existence or being dependent on outsiders for solutions. *If the management team cannot think and plan its way to the future, who can?*

While any human enterprise can achieve great things if properly led, managed and resourced, managers still need tools to produce results. Strategic planning is a very powerful tool to create a future of your choosing and transform your company by managing the process of change in a positive way.

This book is about strategic planning and how you can use it to change your company and produce results. Strategic planning is an effective vehicle to take your company where you want it to go. You will provide the destination, this book will show you how to begin and end the trip. In this way, the book will guide your company through choppy waters until it arrives on chosen shores. My approach to strategic planning involves a mechanism to focus your energy and resources on achieving specific ends. This mechanism is in fact *a universal model*, because it has been validated in several companies of various sizes at different stages of development across many different industries and in various countries. This is no real surprise, as the fundamental problems faced by all businesses in most developed countries are basically the same. (These problems eventually will be experienced by new companies in the emerging market economies of Eastern Europe and the Commonwealth of Independent States.) Such problems inevitably deal with survival and growth. There is nothing more important to any business than these twin issues. Again, the universality of the model arises from the way it deals with common problems and issues confronting every business.

While this book is entitled *The Strategy-led Business*, strategies cannot be produced in a vacuum. *Strategies are means, not ends. If strategies are to be successful, they must be given direction in the beginning and implementation in the end. In other words, a company's future direction needs to be established before strategies can be created. You need to know where you are going before deciding how to get there. And there is no point establishing direction and creating strategies if you cannot successfully implement the plan in your company.* Thus, strategies are very much the middle of the exercise, the filling in a sandwich.

The strategic planning model consists of a framework and process for you to follow in planning your company's future. It may seem pedantic at times but there is a reason for the design and presentation of each segment. Each step is integrated with the one before and the one following. The process cascades from one point to the next, building an integrated approach in which your business can be managed consistently to achieve your objectives. It is analogous to a funnel, wide at the top and progressively narrower at the bottom which reflects the exercise's focusing and refining action.

Strategic planning, therefore, is very much a means for achieving your ends, a vehicle for arriving at a selected destination. It is a method to think through a way to *the* future you want by concentrating on key internal and external factors affecting the life of your company.

The world is ruled by chaos. Uncertainty abounds in every corridor of human existence. At the same time, technological and economic change is bombarding commercial organizations in a fashion unknown to past generations. Moreover, the outlook is for even more turbulence, not less. The calm certainty of the 1950s is gone, probably never to return. Change is a constant of life and business is no exception. Management's most fundamental task is to manage this change. Recognition and acceptance of this fact of life raises the next central question: does management take the initiative or merely react? As Sir John Harvey-Jones, former chairman of the British chemical giant, ICI, said: 'one wishes to lead change rather than having to follow it'.[2]

Not all change is welcomed. Most people resist change because it is disruptive and threatening. Today's paradox is that people resist or have difficulty adjusting to change but there is no escape from change. We are all victims of the old Chinese curse: 'may you live in interesting times'. Change can be invigorating and challenging or it can be threatening and unnerving. Either way, change is here to stay. The issue, therefore, shifts from change recognition to management of the change process for specific outcomes. Strategic planning provides a framework to manage change within your direct control and thereby deal more effectively with external change that is not within your ambit.

Change always means opportunity to those people who can see, understand and respond appropriately, using rather than fighting it the way martial arts use an opponent's energy and momentum to advantage. New opportunities abound on a global scale, offering large rewards but at the same time raising more complex questions. Opportunities can be identified and converted if a company gets its act together internally and proceeds externally with a coherent plan.

My model deals with change by helping you to focus on the most important objectives and make decisions with continual reference to those objectives. In this way, your team stays on the right path, refusing to be diverted into side roads away from the most direct route to the chosen destination.

Financial aberrations like the 1980s come and go. In fact, such distortions have been coming and going at intervals since the Industrial Revolution. The business cycle has been with us for as long as anyone wants to remember. Fashions come and go in management and finance but fundamentals stay forever. The fundamentals in running and growing a business remain the same. It may be more complicated than before, but the well-led team focusing on its plan and staying close to the marketplace is a formidable force to deal with problems.

Above everything else, this book is about fundamentals. It focuses on a management tool and discipline for you to survive and prosper in turbulent times. In addition, the book looks at the latest management practices and trends, such as the revolutionary success of the Japanese and the belated Western response.

The future is an exciting one, regardless of the current economic climate, because there are so many possibilities. One of the most important is finding a way to unlock the immense potential in human resources which can help realize the future you choose for your company. And strategic planning should become your most effective and important tool to realize that future. As always, there are choices. But the first and most important choice is whether you choose to have forces wash over you like waves or to swim for it. In other words, the most basic choice is simply to be active or reactive. Companies without plans are reactive animals, they are shaped by outside forces. Companies with plans respond to outside forces within the context of their plan.

My strategic model grew from direct experience working with companies, medium and small, in a variety of roles: company doctor, venture capital packager, professional non-executive director and, above all, strategic planner. In the beginning my approach sprang from the need to look at something beyond next year's budget. Later it matured into more sophisticated requirements such as deciding where to position a business in the marketplace and how to create strategies for rapid and sustainable growth. The challenge was to create a means that would work for a range of ends and to develop a universal model that could apply to all companies. As will be discussed later, this model's greatest application is to medium sized companies.

References

1. Sidney Bloch. *Money Talk: A Lucrative Cocktail*, Buchan & Enright, London, 1986.

2. John Harvey-Jones. *Making it Happen: Reflections on Leadership*, Fontana, London, 1988.

About the author

What has the author done with his life as preparation for writing this book? Kerry Napuk, 52, holds a BSc degree in Business Administration and a MA degree in Economics from the University of California at Berkeley. From 1963 to 1972 he held various posts in economic organizations and managed research projects. Upon leaving graduate school, Kerry was selected in national competition to become the Research Intern at the AFL-CIO, the American equivalent of the British TUC. Following a year in Washington DC, he joined the research department of the United Packinghouse Workers, AFL-CIO in Chicago, where he became Research Director. Kerry left the trade union movement in 1968, to join an applied research 'think tank' in San Francisco and managed the Rankine cycle alternate propulsion programme for the California State Assembly. In addition, he was consultant to the Joint Committee on Economic Conversion in the California Legislature, which investigated ways to lessen California's dependency on defence spending.

Since arriving in Britain in 1973, the author has held part-time directorships in ten companies across such diverse activities and industries as wholesaling textiles, publishing and catering and manufacturing OEM components, laboratory equipment and speciality chemicals including pharmaceutical intermediates and biotechnology. He also acted as a company doctor on a regional basis for a major clearing bank in the United Kingdom and was active in funding and creating four start-up companies in new technology fields. Kerry has concentrated on strategic planning since 1989, leading seminars in Scotland, America, Hong Kong and Singapore. He has focused on planning, because it pulls together all aspects of his commercial experience.

The author manages his own vehicle for strategic planning, Nap Associates Limited, in Edinburgh. He and his associates deal with planning assignments at companies and among non-profit organizations.

Acknowledgements

I would like to thank the following people for their contribution, for better or worse, towards making this book happen: my associates John Carney, who urged me to write a book in the first place, and James Watters, who painstakingly read it and offered critical comments and suggestions. And, last but never least, my editor, Kate Allen whose support and encouragement was gratefully received and highly valued.

Introduction

*If you don't think about the future, you
won't have one.*

Forsyte from THE FORSYTE SAGA[1]

Introduction

Defining strategic planning is like trying to describe a giraffe to a farmer. The old story goes something like this: a stranger describes a giraffe in great detail to a farmer who has never been to a zoo. After listening intently, the farmer concludes 'there is no such animal'. Let us try to describe this animal called strategic planning anyway, by approaching the subject from different directions in the hope of getting a better response than the one provided by our farmer. In this way, you should acquire a flavour if not a taste of the subject at hand.

In the commercial world, most small and a lot of medium sized companies are reactive animals. They usually operate in one type of business, responding in various ways at different times to change and outside events. Others are opportunistic and actively seek growth. Some companies run out of energy with one good product or one type of service, others try to diversify. Some win, some fail and many stagnate.

Enter strategic planning. Strategic planning is a management tool to deal with the commercial environment by thinking your way *to* the company you want. This management tool is designed for use by the management team. And the most important single factor that distinguishes one company from another and one company's performance from the other is its management team and its ability to think and act, in other words, to manage. *Strategic planning is a powerful technique for leading from the top by mobilizing all the resources of a company behind an agreed plan.*

Every country's economic history is littered with examples of individuals and teams who have built organizations with personal formulas for success. Such success stories are usually too tied to a particular company for easy application elsewhere. Moreover, the personal success story rarely yields a complete approach that others can understand and use. If it was so easy, there would be only one way to run a company and everyone would be doing it. In truth, there is no one way.

On the other hand, strategic planning is a *proven and practical tool for all managements* to achieve results across a range of different businesses. As a management tool, strategic planning creates a coherent integrated framework in which companies can prosper by *focusing energy and resources on common ends*. It is this *single-minded focus* which is crucial for success, not being diverted or buried in detail and failing to decide where the company should go.

Nobody said it was easy to run a company. Rather, it is one of the least understood and most complex activities in the commercial world. Legions of business schools teach and billions of trees are converted into management books on all aspects of company life. Yet, relatively little is written about the life of the company and what kind of life it can choose. Hopefully, my approach will make sense to you and will allow you to make your company's future happen. Rather than tell you what you must do, the model asks *key questions* and leaves *you to find the right answers* for your business. There are no short cuts, you have to do the work.

Strategic planning may travel under different names such as strategic management and corporate planning. However, it is not just marketing, writing business plans, resourcing or budgeting. While it touches on all these things, it is different in one very important and basic way: *a strategic plan deals with the most fundamental questions in every company's life—where it goes and how it gets there*. This basic concern differentiates strategic planning from all other aspects of business activity.

Strategic planning is a recent management development. It originated in America during the 1960s and spread to Europe in the 1970s and 1980s. The use of planning increased as the business environment changed. As two academics noted:

> 'The business environment for most organisations has been characterised by increasing uncertainty, complexity and volatility. It is not simply the magnitude of changes in areas like legislative change, technological developments, industry structure and so on, that are causing problems for organisations, but the increasing *rate* at which these changes are occurring. It was the climate of change and complexity that led to the rapid rise of the importance of strategic planning in the USA.'[2]

Why plan?

'But why should we bother to plan? It is too much hassle to go through all this effort and detail. We are far too busy doing the business to waste time on useless plans. Plans are never any good anyway, because they always change. Why should I plan, then?'

I have heard these statements and more from executives under pressure. If you examine each one, they all say the same thing: 'we do not want to think about our business and what it is, where it is going and what we can do about it. We spend all our time reacting to what life throws our way and have no time to think about possibilities and make them happen.' This approach often becomes a self-fulfilling prophecy. *You have to make the time to consider the really big questions or they go unanswered.*

Sometimes I suspect that executives would rather not face fundamental questions about their business, because they fear what the answers and consequences might be. This becomes another reason not to face reality. The irony is that a company gains strengths when its executives debate the basic questions and realize that any problem short of receivership can be resolved with a strategy. Let us stop right here to make the following point: the *fundamental issue* is whether your management team will be active or reactive, that is, seek to choose a future of its making or allow the future to shape it.

There are several excellent reasons why every company needs to plan and why medium sized firms need to plan even more than smaller ones. Here are some of the reasons why companies should start strategic planning:

1. *Rate of change.* Change is accelerating, driven by new technologies that impact on one another. New technologies with ever expanding applications are revolutionizing some markets and shaping many others. For example, the shelf life for new products in some parts of the electronics industry is down to 16 months! In these market niches and segments, new products have to be developed and introduced in less than a year and a half or they will not be competitive in features or performance. Can you imagine how your business would deal with that rate of change? While this is an extreme example, you must be aware that change is accelerating and know you will have to respond sooner or later. The question becomes how do you deal with change: do you forever respond or do you attempt to lead change?

    A consultant expressed this trend as follows: there 'has been a dramatic reduction in product lifecycles, forced by the pace of technological innovation and more aggressive marketing. This has widespread implications for manufacturers, who are faced with a stark choice between a proactive, competitive strategy or an inactive, negative-growth, defensive position.'[3] Donald Trump said it somewhat more succinctly: 'The 1990s sure aren't anything like the 1980s.'[4]

2. *Complexity.* Business is getting more complex, demanding more formal responses to the outside world. Legislation, regulations and directives have become a major growth industry in themselves. Moreover, most products and services are getting more complicated to manufacture or provide and face difficult marketing and

distributing problems. Commercial life is not getting simpler. On the contrary, governmental requirements increase and international factors spread.

3. *Uncertainty*. Change and complexity create uncertainty. Do you think your way through the uncertainties or let them determine your actions? Do you anticipate and prepare for the uncertainties you have identified or wait for them and then react?

According to Sir John Harvey-Jones:

> 'Management is about avoiding surprise. Management is about having thought in advance of what's going to happen to you, so that your plans are ready, so that you're not taken aback, you've thought what's likely to happen, you've thought of the three or four actions you could take and you're ready. It's about both looking at the outside world, looking at the sort of things that can happen to you, and planning and thinking in your own mind how you are going to react to them.'[5]

Sometimes a reactive style is appropriate. Igor Ansoff noted this behaviour was appropriate in a climate that required 'standardized low-cost products or services'.[6] While that environment prevailed in the 1950s, it did not exist in the 1980s and certainly will not in the 1990s. Hardly any industry enjoys a predictable outlook today, not even the public sector! The external world is hallmarked by turbulence and upheaval and reactive companies rarely do well in the face of widespread uncertainty. Moreover, as Tom Peters and others have observed, customers are more demanding and are coming to expect products and services will be tailored to their specific needs, not just things that will serve everybody.

4. *Global interrelationships*. There is a knock-on effect as the global economy gets more interrelated economically. Consider the impact of currency movements on your business or the creation of large economic blocks like the European Economic Community. How does your commercial world look if you are inside the Community? How does it look if you are outside it?

For most of the time since the Second World War, America has enjoyed a huge internal market without real outside competition and an insurmountable lead in technology and productivity. As a result, management in some large national corporations became insular and arrogant. But look at the world today. America faces serious competition in all world markets especially in its home market. Do you wait for these effects to hit you or do you take the initiative and meet the competition?

Things change. They change on the micro and macro scales. Is the world that Clinton faces anything like the one Reagan confronted? Is your country's economy the same as it was ten years ago or even five years ago? Things change and now things change faster.

5. *Efficiency.* Strategic planning is efficient because you first determine where you are going and then focus all your resources on getting there. Thereafter every action is a step towards the end point, eliminating wasteful and counterproductive actions.

6. *Common aims.* Once you decide on your desired destination, everyone in the business is able to adopt common aims and pull together in the same direction. In this way, you avoid confusion over objectives and goals.

7. *Resource allocation.* Once a plan is agreed, resources are allocated behind the plan to achieve the objectives. This ensures that your resources are applied where they should go, not squandered or misallocated.

8. *Better management.* Management teams find that a strategic plan simplifies and improves the resource allocation process. A plan creates the framework in which important decisions can be taken with a clearer understanding of their impact on agreed objectives. Before any important decision is reached, managers can ask: Does this help achieve our objectives? Will it get us closer to where we want to go?

9. *Risk.* There is an implied risk in *not* planning, because you will be left at the mercy of change. As Harvey-Jones remarked: 'The reality of life is that while staying put is without doubt the most comfortable for the short haul, it is in fact the highest risk strategy of all.'[5] He also noted another risk related to the lack of planning: that businessmen too often run into action before preparing and deciding what to do.

   As the founder of one British company commented: 'I felt very vulnerable without a plan.'[7] A divisional managing director of a medium size company said that the strategy process made them 'aware' of each part of the company's strengths and weaknesses, which enabled management 'to agree a clear direction for them'. Management was able to recognize opportunities and devise a plan to convert them and was 'no longer purely reactive'.[8]

   When interviewed about planning, a chief executive of a diversified manufacturing company in America replied as follows: 'I can't conceive of doing business without a strategic plan. Every company has to do it. Either you get to be good at it or do it poorly and suffer the consequences.'[9]

Definitions

'OK,' the reader might say, 'you have convinced us. Now what is strategic planning all about?' One way of understanding the concept of strategic planning is to look at a few definitions.

John Argenti sees it as *'plans for the organisation itself'* dealing 'with *a small number of decisions and their great impact* [italics added]'. Accordingly, strategic planning is about 'identifying what these few decisions are and then finding strategic answers for them'.[10]

Barrie Pearson believes it is about identifying and focusing on the key issues for success, keeping them simple and acting with a sense of urgency.[11]

Another consultant observed that 'strategic planning for businesses is profoundly important, since it goes to the heart of what a business does and why it does it. At its lowest level, it can be thought of as a competitive reaction; at its highest, it can transform a business and ensure its future.'[12]

My definition

I define strategic planning as *a total concept of the whole business involving a framework and a process that guide its future.*

Strategic planning is *holistic* in the sense that it deals with the whole organization, differing from other business practices which usually look at one aspect of a company. The planning approach deals with *the* most fundamental and basic questions, ones that involve the very existence of the whole organization. You cannot get more fundamental than asking about where a company wants to go and how it is going to get there.

This distinction must be understood by any management team if it wishes to start a planning exercise or improve an existing one. *If a strategic plan is to work, it must concern the entire organization and guide the whole company's future.* Strategic planning is a *continual* process to understand your complete business: what it is now, what it can become in the future and how you will make it happen. It is definitely not a one-off exercise.

The commercial world is stuffed full of companies whose boards have written a plan, put it on the shelf and thought the planning process was over. Needless to say, such companies derived no benefit from their exercise except a short-lived bout of self-deception. The first stage of the process begins with the creation of a plan but it does not end there. You have to make it work outside the boardroom. My approach relies heavily on the Socratic tradition, *asking leading questions and seeking appropriate answers. While the questions may be the same for all businesses, the answers are unique because no two companies are the same.* Answers will differ for similar sized companies in the same industry and in the same market, because each company is different. Each company's management and employees have different personal histories and views of the world and they have different resources at their disposal. So, you would be surprised if two companies created the same plan. As Argenti has remarked: 'The only correct strategy is the one that comes out of an analysis of the company's total strategic situation—a situation that will be different for every company.'[10]

The framework

My model starts with a framework of four basic questions:

1. How did you get here?
2. Where do you want to go?
3. How will you get there?
4. How can you make it work?

These basic questions need to be answered by every management team. *The questions are universal because they are relevant to every organization that seeks to do something in the world. On the other hand, the answers will be different because every organization is different. Questions are the keys to exploration and understanding.* As Charles Handy said: 'when we have no questions we need no answers [and] other people's questions are soon forgotten'.[13]

The process

The process takes the questions raised by the framework and finds the most appropriate answers for your company.

The aim of the process is simple: to find the right answers to the basic questions for *your* company. That is it. There is no more. The entire model revolves around you getting the right answers to these four fundamental questions. Of course, there is more to it than this, but in general terms that is what it is all about.

The process forces you to seek answers through a rigorous intellectual exercise. As the basic questions are fundamental to the very existence of your company, they should spark considerable discussion and debate in the management team. Moreover, you might be surprised at the views expressed and the way in which consensus emerges.

While my framework raises the right questions, you have to find the right answers. And so it should be. It is your company and you have the obligation to find the best way forward. Moreover, if you find your own answers, you will take *ownership* of the plan. And it is essential for the success of the plan that it is your plan, not somebody else's. If your team does not participate in creating the plan, the team will have difficulty in owning it. Ownership is vital in the implementation phase and for the commitment required to achieve the plan.

It is highly unlikely that any outsider will know more about your business, market and industry than your management team. You should have most of the answers stored away, waiting for someone or some process to let them emerge and take shape. So, it is clearly correct for your team to do the work, find the answers and take ownership of the plan.

The right answers mean the ones that are appropriate for your business. You will know if they are appropriate by the results they bring. That is one good thing about strategic planning: *there are easy ways to keep score and measure progress.* You will know how well you are doing as you go along. It is very important to measure progress in order to improve your focus and performance. Even before results are known, however, you will know if the answers are right. You can use your judgement to feel their 'rightness' and you will know they represent the team's collected and balanced view.

Strategic planning is a continual process, calling for management commitment, discipline and formal review and monitoring and measuring progress. Periodical reviews take time to measure progress, evaluate new problems and face new challenges. In this way, the plan becomes a living document that improves with experience as the experience is incorporated and becomes the basis for the next plan.

Strategic planning has to be a continual process, because things change and your plan has to change too. On the other hand, while it can be exhausting, it is also fun and rewarding and is a practical and user-friendly process. Moreover, a strategic plan enables you to look at your company with a clear and concise format and allows you to monitor progress towards your objectives. The company's progress, *therefore,* is measured against the plan, *not just management accounts.*

Whether or not you undertake strategic planning depends to a large extent on whether your company is inward or outward looking. It also depends on your management team's style, especially that of the chief executive, that is, whether he or she is active or reactive. Another factor involves the way your organization views the outside: do you look at what really works in the world and search for role models to improve your own performance?

The systematic search for examples of corporate self-improvement is embodied in company and industry success factors and bench-marking, which will be discussed later. Nevertheless, the learning company approaches the outside world with a strong sense of enquiry, hoping to find useful concepts, mechanisms and techniques to use or adapt or improve upon. This is perhaps the only useful short cut in planning, to learn from other companies what works and if you can use it in your own company's situation. Even here, however, you need an established framework, process and discipline to absorb effectively other role models and useful programmes.

Characteristics

Probably the best way to understand strategic planning is to look at characteristics of the process. The following characteristics best describe that giraffe mentioned at the start of this chapter.

1. *Dynamic*. Strategic planning must deal with the outside world, because it seeks to get you where you want to go and the 'where' is out there. It is not a theoretical exercise, but rooted in the marketplace, market segments and niches. As markets are changing and perpetually in flux, strategic planning has to be a dynamic process in order to reflect these changes. A strategic plan failing to respond to these changes, would change quickly from a giraffe to a white elephant.

2. *Continual*. Strategic planning is a continual process, because it must deal continually with the dynamics of the market. As a management tool it demands discipline in the form of periodical reviews and updates. Reviews are essential to test assumptions with market responses. The more experience that is incorporated in your plan, the more effective it becomes over time. The world does not stand still and neither can your corporate plan.

3. *Flexible*. If the conditions upon which the plan is based change, you will have to change the plan. No strategic plan is written in stone: it must be flexible. If events require changes and if your plan needs to change, you have to be flexible enough to allow it to change. The only good strategy is one that works. The only way you know a strategy works is by what it does in the marketplace. So, do not get attached to strategies unless they work and keep on working.

4. *Responsive*. Your ability to respond is the key to flexibility. In this context, responsibility means the ability to respond. In order to respond, you need to be close to the market where change occurs. Responding is quite different from reacting, because responding means adapting an existing strategy for a specific objective. Reacting means trying to respond but without a strategy, which is like eating soup without a spoon.

5. *Analytical*. Strategic planning is analytical but not mired in detail. However, there is no substitution for doing your homework and learning all you can about a marketplace. As Kenichi Ohmae has observed: 'No proper business strategy can be built on fragmentary knowledge or analysis.'[14] This involves a commitment and willingness to devote management time and resources to collecting and evaluating information about your commercial world. Planning cannot exist in a vacuum. It needs input upon which decisions can

be made. You can look at these inputs as indirect experience which complements the direct experience to be gained through new strategies in the market.

6. *Creative.* Strategic planning is a creative process, because it depends on the intuition and judgement of the management team. After all the analysis and data collection are over, you have to think about how you feel. One practical rule-of-thumb is first look at the data, then see how you feel about them. Do not be reluctant or embarrassed about considering if a plan feels right, checking your gut reaction is as appropriate as collecting the data. You should ask yourselves, as a team, do the direction and plans feel appropriate? Are they right for us? Can we really achieve them? It has to feel right as well as look good.

7. *Action orientated.* Strategic planning is about taking actions, not just making plans. The basic purpose of planning is to decide what to do and then go out and do it. In fact, the process by its very nature is action orientated, because it involves thinking followed by implementing. If your plan never sees action, the exercise has been wasted. Think, then act, then review and think and act again.

8. *Focused.* Strategic planning deals with the whole company by deciding where it will go in the future and how it will get there. In order to work, therefore, all major decisions must be made with reference to the plan. Otherwise, the management team will be diverted and the company will stray from its chosen course. By referring all major decisions to an agreed framework, it provides the most effective focus. Discipline is essential for this focus to be realized and sustained. Managers have to ask themselves: Will this decision help achieve an objective? Will it get us closer to where we want to go?

9. *Resource allocation.* Strategic planning is efficient, because it allocates the company's resources to common ends. The process allocates resources in the most efficient way by ensuring that resources are put where they will achieve the most impact on agreed objectives. If resources are allocated behind priorities tied to objectives, resources will be focused where they can have the greatest impact. In this way, leakage and misallocation of resources is reduced if not eliminated. As long as you continue to measure results, resources will be re-allocated for maximum impact.

10. *Change.* Last but not least is the ability of planning to deal with change. Planning gives management 'a framework within which to make decisions in uncertain conditions'.[12] The planning process itself can be a very effective vehicle for dealing with change inside

and outside the company. It offers an excellent opportunity inside the company to bring to the surface issues in a constructive problem-solving atmosphere and arrive at a consensus which people will respect and honour. In the planning process, the key questions become: What is best for the company? Will it achieve our objectives? Moreover, if you have dealt with change inside the company, you are in a much better position to handle change outside.

And change is everywhere. Just consider the landscape after the corporate feeding frenzy in the last decade. During the 1980s, ten industries in America lost nearly two-fifths of their companies. Furthermore, 187 companies in the *Fortune* top 500 disappeared, including almost half of the top 50 retailers and 29 of the top 50 transport companies![15] Nor was Britain immune to corporate extinction. Between 1986 and 1991, one-quarter of the 2525 quoted companies were taken over.[16]

Planning is not a military exercise

Some people ascribe military dimensions to the planning process. While there are parallels and common language, strategic planning is first an internal struggle then an external one. Strategy originated within a military context but over-emphasis on militarism can be misleading. If business was like warfare, there would be more successful military men running companies and West Point and Sandhurst would be more prestigious than Harvard Business School.

End point

Strategic planning has a definite end point, because it is not a theoretical exercise. The end point is to gain a competitive edge by strategically positioning your company in the right markets at the right time, securing rapid and profitable growth during good times or survival in bad times until you can catch the next upswing in the business cycle.

If we break down this end point into its constituent parts, the outcomes are easily stated:

1. Strategically position your company.

2. Right markets at the right time (with the right product/service).

3. Secure rapid and profitable growth.

4. Survive until next upswing.

5. Gain a competitive edge over competitors.

On the upside, strategic planning is all about maximizing profits. There is no real argument about whether or not companies should make profits or what level of profit they should make. Of course, there are legitimate issues concerning how profits are made and spent and these are often considered to be corporate social issues.

Companies must make profits or die because there is no other way to accumulate or attract sufficient capital. You cannot borrow all your capital, because the interest burden would crush you. You have either to accumulate capital from profits over years as retained earnings or to attract expansion capital other ways. In addition, profits have to increase over time to absorb inflation and, even more important, to fund the company's ambitions. As Mack Hanan has stated: 'There is no other way to accumulate sufficient capital. Either it will come from internally produced growth profits or it will not come at all . . . It is hard to argue against the need for growth when the alternative is capital starvation.'[17]

On the downside, strategic planning can make the difference between survival and corporate death, because it forces management to think through the difficult as well as the good times. Strategies for survival are different from those for expansion but strategies are still needed. Almost all core businesses are capable of being shrunk and kept intact for expansion when conditions are more favourable. The point is simply that planning is useful for growth *and* survival.

The nutshell

The nutshell is that strategic planning is the best vehicle you have to get where you want to go. If you do not plan, you can only react. If you plan, you become active. If you do not plan, you remain reactive. *In the end, we plan for the future to have a future of our own choosing.*

Strategic plan or business plan or both?

Some managers wonder what the difference is between a strategic plan and a business plan. The easiest way to distinguish one from the other is to think of one as general (the strategic plan) and the other specific (the business plan). The strategic plan deals with the whole company while the business plan deals with detailed implementation of one specific aspect of the strategic plan.

A strategic plan is concerned with the entire company: what it produces, where it competes and how it allocates resources. It deals with fundamental choices that will affect the entire organization—choices about the future.

Business plans are concerned with the details of implementation after the big choices are made: you first need to decide where you want to go and how you are going to get there. Business plans, therefore, are involved in the last stage of strategic planning: the implementation process.

Medium sized companies

Why is strategic planning most suitable for medium sized companies? Here medium sized means companies with 150 to 2000 employees and sales between $20m (£10m) and $500m (£250m). Medium companies have enough resources to make an impact on the market or markets in which they compete. On the other hand, they are small enough to manage directly, that is, to decide what they are going to do and go out and do it. Medium companies also have management resources to create and implement plans.

These three factors (sufficient market presence, direct management ability and enough resources) distinguish medium companies from small ones at one end of the spectrum and one factor (direct management ability) distinguishes them from very large international corporations at the other end.

Tom Peters recently extolled the virtues of Germany's 'astonishing economic—and managerial—success: the Mittelstand, or middle-sized companies'. Peters went on to list the following traits among the best examples:

- Focused

- Small equals strong

- Symbiosis with the end user

- Customer wishes pervade every nook and cranny

- Big spenders where it counts, i.e. for the customer

- On the leading edge, where it matters

- The world is their oyster

- The long haul

- Obsessed with improvement (small and large), not competitors

- A disciplined but flexible workforce

- Quality shoppers, quality producers

- Little bureaucracy

- Product, product, product[18]

One chief executive of an American medium sized company highlighted the following advantages over large competitors:

1. Action and reaction speeds, moving with a sense of urgency.

2. Effective communications inspiring customers and employees.

3. Motivated employees.

4. Minimal central overheads.

5. Flat organizations facilitating management contact with customers and factory works.

6. Management focus on the important priorities like quality and productivity.[19]

The whole issue and notion of size is changing, as well as the scale needed to produce or service. Peter Drucker commented on this point, saying: 'the period of just being "big" is over. Now it's deciding which size is best. Elephants have a hard time adapting. Cockroaches outlive everything.'[20]

Corporate planning, the predecessor to strategic planning, was attacked and discredited in large corporations over the last decade and for very good reasons. An often voiced complaint was that the planning function was located in far away, insensitive headquarters which forced unrealistic, unwelcomed or unacceptable plans on to operating units. Such efforts were doomed, because plans did not derive from the operating conditions of each division or subsidiary. Consequently, nobody in operating companies really took ownership of the plan. Major international headquarters around the world might have spent the time more productively by concentrating on issues within their spheres as holding companies, such as setting financial performance criteria and corporate-wide goals.

Strategic planning is very suitable for medium sized operating companies that have the necessary preconditions for effective planning. In that regard, my model has application for divisions and subsidiaries of large corporations if they are medium sized operating units.

On the other hand, small companies with fewer than 150 employees and sales less than $20m face other problems. Often management teams have not been formed or lack sufficient capacity or resources to create and implement strategic plans. Many smaller companies are driven by single-minded individuals called entrepreneurs who are unable to create a balanced management team required to build a medium sized company. Sometimes the entrepreneur fears an intellectual debate about the future and the strain it can place on his or her leadership and ability. Usually, the management has no formalized strategy, and the entrepreneur carries everything around in his or her hat!

Often the small company is too busy reacting to events to take the time to plan, and ends up focusing on survival, not growth. Usually small companies exploit one product or service and cannot get beyond their opening act. Many times a small company starts life as a dedicated subcontractor to larger companies and never gets beyond that relationship. These are some of many reasons why small companies fail to plan.

Occasionally, however, small companies do plan and achieve corporate objectives and goals. When they do, they become medium sized organizations with a built-in competitive advantage—strategic planning as a management discipline.

The management pendulum swings once more

While many large international corporations started life as small companies, there is a dearth of case studies of medium sized companies. Very little is known about the growth and development of these vital businesses which, in some cases, will become the major corporations of tomorrow.

Moreover, the pendulum now is swinging back towards strategic planning in major corporations but with a clear difference: central planning is being devolved to strategic units. In other words, corporate planning has given way to effective strategic planning at subsidiaries and divisions which, in many cases, are the equivalent of medium sized companies.

Michael Goold at Ashridge Strategic Management Centre noted this change as follows:

> 'In most large, multi-business companies, the trend today is towards decentralisation . . . The essence of decentralisation is to locate primary responsibility for proposing strategy and achieving results with the general managers of individual profit centres or businesses, not with central management. The purpose is to ensure that strategies are based on detailed knowledge of specific product-markets, increase business level 'ownership' of strategy and reduce the overload on the chief executive and his team.'[21]

The strategic planning model

My approach to planning starts with a framework of four fundamental questions. First, we look at how you arrived at this point in your company history, identifying what made you successful and what requires more attention. Second, we deal with where you want to go from here by creating your vision, listing your objectives, conducting an internal evaluation of strengths and weaknesses and setting your goals. Third, we determine how to get where you want to go, devising strategies and dealing with external opportunities and threats. Finally, we look at how to make the plan work in your company, reviewing structure and implementation and concentrating on action programmes. This model can be summarized as follows:

NAP ASSOCIATES: STRATEGIC PLANNING MODEL

1. **How did we get here?**
   1.1 Successful factors
2. **Where do we want to go?**
   2.1 Vision
   2.2 Objectives
       (1) Internal evaluation:
       Strengths and weaknesses
   2.3 Goals
3. **How do we get there?**
   3.1 Strategies
       (1) External evaluation:
       Opportunities and threats
4. **How do we make it work?**
   4.1 Structure
   4.2 Implementation
       (1) Action programmes
   4.3 Review

In diagram format, the model is as follows:

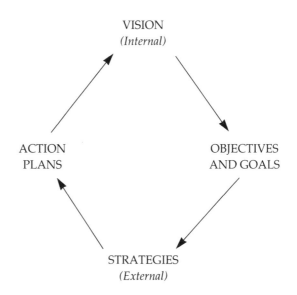

Summary

1. Strategic planning involves a total concept for the business as a whole.

2. Strategic planning consists of a framework in which universal and fundamental questions are asked and a process in which the right answers are sought for your company.

3. The framework deals with four basic questions: How did we get here? Where do we want to go? How do we get there? How do we make it work?

4. The process involves finding the right answers to these questions for your company. No one strategy may be appropriate for two companies, even ones operating in the same market.

5. The planning process is dynamic and action orientated, requiring flexibility and responsibility. Because markets change, planning must be a continual process, requiring periodical reviews and iterations to become effective. Plans evolve over time and get better by becoming more focused.

Now that we have had the first taste of what strategic planning is, we can start the exercise by looking at the first basic question involving where your company is today.

References

1. R. S. Tricker, 'Strategic management: the management accountant as strategist', *Management Accounting*, December 1989.

2. Nigel Piercy and Neil Morgan, 'Strategic planning and the management accountant,' *Management Accounting*, November 1989.

3. Stephen Young, 'Manufacturing under pressure', *Management Today*, July 1988.

4. *Forbes Executive Calendar*, 1992.

5. John Harvey-Jones, *Making It Happen: Reflections on Leadership*, Fontana, London, 1988.

6. Igor Ansoff, *Corporate Strategy*, Penguin, London, 1987.

7. Charles Batchelor, 'Strategy: the value of planning ahead', *Financial Times*, 13 June 1989.

8. Christopher Lorenz, 'The analytical paradox: forget the plan—have a strategy', *Financial Times*, 30 March 1988.

9. Daniel Gray, 'Uses and misuses of strategic planning', *Harvard Business Review*, **64**(1), January/February 1986.

10. John Argenti, *Practical Corporate Planning*, Unwin Hyman, London, 1989.

11. Barrie Pearson, *Common-Sense Business Strategy Workshop*, 1990.

12. Richard Vaughan, 'Think before you plan: a sound strategy', *Accountancy*, September 1989.

13. Charles Handy, *The Age of Reason*, Arrow, London, 1991.

14. Kenichi Ohmae, *The Mind of the Strategist: Business Planning for Competitive Advantage*, Penguin, London, 1983.

15. John Forbis and William Adams, 'Corporate victims of the eighties', *Across the Board*, December 1990.

16. Maggie Urry, '25 per cent of companies taken over', *Financial Times*, 26 March 1992.

17. Mack Hanan, *Fast-Growth Strategies: How to Maximise Profits from Start-up Through Maturity*, McGraw-Hill, New York, 1987.

18. Tom Peters, 'The mighty minnows: Germany's best kept secret', *Quarterly Enterprise Digest*, February 1992.

19. *Directors and Boards*, 'Being a global leader', **16**(1), Autumn 1991.

20. *Forbes*, 19 August 1991.

21. Michael Gold, *Strategic Control Process: A Research Paper*, Ashridge Management Centre, England, December 1989.

How did we get here?

We learn from history that we do not learn from history.

GEORGE FRIEDRICH HEGEL[1]

Introduction

The first step in creating your strategic plan is to reach a clear understanding of where you are now. This understanding is reached by reviewing and evaluating your corporate history in the most objective way possible.

There are three very good reasons for looking at the past before turning to the future. First, you review the company's history in an evolutionary context which highlights previous changes and accomplishments. Second, you identify and appreciate the strengths and success factors which brought the company to this stage in its development. Third, you establish an understanding of the historical position which gives a clear departure point from which to discuss the future.

Examining your company's history enables you to recognize what the management team accomplished to get where it is now. You can assume that it did something right or it wouldn't be here. But, what specifically worked for you? What did you do poorly? What is there left to do? These are some of the questions that will concern us in this chapter.

What you did right

The first step towards corporate self-evaluation is to look at what you got right in building the type of company you have today. How will you know what you have done right? There are several ways to identify and validate successful features of your business. Invariably, proof comes from the marketplace and can be measured in satisfied repeat customers and a well-earned reputation. Sometimes managers are not clear about what the company actually does and what impact it has on customers. Perceptions may be based on *ad hoc* impressions and defined by the exposure level of a manager's particular function in the company. An open discussion of what the company actually does and the results of its actions should reach a general understanding of what is done right, as well as what is done wrong.

Exercises

Each exercise is listed in detail through the book as it would emerge in sequential order during a planning exercise. All exercises are summarized in a step-by-step guide to a strategic planning session in Chapter 15.

EXERCISE 1 SUCCESSFUL FACTORS

Here is a useful exercise for your management team at this stage in a strategic planning session. Every manager should record the points he or she feels contributed to the company's past success. Each point should be listed and discussed until all are fully understood and accepted or discarded. The surviving points should be placed in order of priority, reflecting a consensus over the importance of each item. You need to concentrate on the most important factors in your success to date, limiting the list to no more than six points.

In the next chapter we will review these points to determine if they are significant success factors upon which you can build for the future and use to differentiate your company from others in the marketplace.

What you do well

It is important to identify clearly those things that you really do well. This evaluation starts with the internal view: What does the team believe the company does really well? Internal views, however, need to be validated by the external world, which in this case is a marketplace composed of customers and suppliers. In this context, therefore, what does the outside world think you do well? You may have to ask customers, suppliers, shareholders, financiers, media and even competitors to find out. Otherwise, without external validation you may fall victim to your own self-delusion.

After discovering what the outside world thinks about your company, is the internal view compatible with the external one? If so, you have identified and validated features of your business that you do well. If not, there could be a conflict between views and you need to understand what that difference is all about.

External views will embody comparisons with competing products and/or services. While you can compare your products/services with the competition, the market makes the most objective determination and provides the ultimate validation in the form of sales. Seeking views of people outside the company provides you with a lot of useful information on where the company stands against competition, as well as on its own in performance terms.

Identity

Another part of the self-examination process is to ask, as honestly as possible, what kind of people you are. Do you have a clear sense of corporate identity? Is this view compatible with what you do well? How do you feel about who you are? Are you comfortable with this feeling?

These successful factors are called 'strengths' and are discussed in more detail in Chapter 3.

Intangibles

Searching questions about identity, feelings and other intangibles are difficult for many management teams. Executives tend to be extroverts who are used to dealing with external matters and solving problems. Yet intangibles are at the heart of the 'feel' or 'buzz' in any organization, especially in people companies where the very product is creativity and thinking. Some examples of intangibles are impressions, style, relationships, chemistry and handling outsiders. These 'soft' factors are becoming very important in the new ways of doing things and will be discussed throughout the book.

People instinctively recognize intangibles—customers consciously note them when first contacting a company and visitors often comment on them. Why is this so? One answer is that people respond to human signals. Another possibility is that people are affected by first impressions when sensitivity often is heightened and everything they see and hear is recorded.

Management needs to be aware of human intangibles in the strategic planning process, because it is always people who achieve results and attain goals. Moreover, the right intangibles can make the difference between realizing the plan and falling short, i.e. between success and failure. Intangibles also are the centre of 'corporate culture', which is discussed in Chapter 13.

Even more important is the need for the management team to 'feel comfortable' with its view of the company. This intangible, the feeling, will play an important part in the confidence necessary for building the future. While success cannot depend merely on feelings, they are a necessary and vital element and need to be recognized as such.

Management teams and employees who 'feel good' about themselves can accomplish much in the world. Positivism and morale are powerful forces when coupled to leadership, analysis and action. Too many organizations ignore these 'soft' factors and behave as if their people were not their most important asset. W. Edwards Deming, a founder of the movement for Total Quality Management, fervently believes that people always have been the key to performance and that success flows from cooperation between people.

What is left to do

After identifying the positive factors in your success, it is equally important to look objectively at the areas where you are not doing the right things or where things could be done much better. If you are honest with yourselves, there always will be things that can be improved. Hopefully, they will be down on your list of priorities, reflecting the need for incremental improvements and fine tuning. If something requires significant improvement, however, it will require urgent attention. If you fail to identify your shortcomings, you will not address them and they might interfere or even cripple your strategic plan. We call these shortcomings 'weaknesses' and they also will be dealt with in more detail in Chapter 3.

Another important reason for recognizing problems is to create a balanced view of the company. If the management team dwelt only on the successful features of the business, it could lead to an unrealistic plan which failed to acknowledge, let alone address, any weak points. *An important element in the planning process is to reach a balanced view of the company*, warts and all, which allows a management team to create a *realistic* plan that is based on strengths but recognizes and addresses weaknesses.

Foundation

If your answers to the questions above are positive and consistent, you have a solid foundation upon which to start planning. If they are not, you should mark the differences for future attention during the rest of a planning exercise.

External Factors

Having looked at internal factors leading to your present position, what about external factors, 'things' outside the company? How do key outsiders view you? What do your important customers really think about you? What would your suppliers say? Do you know? Do you care? *Have you ever asked outsiders what they thought about you?*

By 'things' we mean issues of product or service quality, customer care, pricing, innovation and other elements which create an impression or feeling about what you do in the marketplace and regulate relationships with customers. Moreover, do these external views support your internal understanding? In other words, do you have evidence that people outside your company feel the same way about you as you do about yourselves?

The external view is another vital piece of *reality checking* along the road of self-evaluation. All through my approach to strategic planning, we take several 'time outs', breaks in the process, to check that we are being realistic, that we can do what we want to do and that we are not fooling ourselves about our capability. Again, it is very important to establish a balanced view of your company and to build on that knowledge. *You need to avoid a trap that managements often fall into, regardless of company size, believing what they choose to believe without validating those beliefs outside the company.* This is the way managements get 'out of touch' with employees, customers or suppliers.

In order to prevent this from happening, managements need to create 'feedback loops' which provide a regular flow of information from customers and suppliers on the company's products and/or services. Such loops are created between field representatives and customers and between managers who go out and visit different customers and suppliers. They are also created by listening to employees who talk directly with customers. This commitment to validation and feedback is critically important. Yet how many companies do you know that regularly obtain and assess feedback from the marketplace? *If you do not ask, you will not know. If you do not know, you cannot change.*

Management teams are quite capable of fooling themselves into believing their company is something that it is not. And, if the team's views are not based on reality, the strategic plan will be built on false assumptions and the result will be more distortion and even greater eventual problems.

These twin themes, the internal and the external, flow in and out of this book as of course they do in each of our lives. You need to recognize the difference and reach a balanced understanding of both. *The good news is that you can influence your internal behaviour and performance which can change the external response.*

You should check periodically, therefore, that your house is in order and your team has got its 'act together'. No belief or assumption should be allowed to become dogma. While these statements make obvious common sense, how much lip service is paid to them? How many adjustments, rationalizations, compromises and allowances have been made for individual as well as company performances? *Never forget that a balanced and effective management team is the most important prerequisite for building a future.* Moreover, building a competent and balanced management team is within your control.

What business are we in?

Another obvious but rarely asked question is: what is your real business? What business are you in? You must be kidding, you might say, I'm in such and such business. That is what it says on the letterhead and in our product literature.

This is a funny question, often a tricky one. It is human nature to define, to label. Such treatment enables us to understand something and feel comfortable with it. By our very act of defining and labelling, however, we often restrict the subject to the most easily understood terms. For example, if Europe's largest automobile service company, Kwik-Fit, stuck to selling and installing tyres, it would not have expanded its product line to exhausts, brakes, suspension systems, batteries, radiators, lubrications and child safety devices. In other words, Kwik-Fit decided it offered a convenient service to motorists and, consequently, it was in the automobile parts business, not just the tyre trade. In so doing, it opened up a number of new products and services to offer to the customer calling for tyres and was able thereby to expand far beyond its original activity in Scotland.

By labelling, we can narrow our view of an activity and exclude a whole range of possibilities. Of course, these possibilities might be irrelevant to the future but, on the other hand, one or two might not be. *If we do not ask ourselves the question, we will never know the answer.*

Another related question is should we stay in this business? Michael Walsh, as new CEO at Tenneco, a Houston conglomerate with six major businesses, touched on this issue by saying:

> 'If you have lousy businesses and run them well, you are still going to have poor returns. So you have to know whether you are in the right businesses and be unsparing about ones that don't have good prospects. If you followed purely strategic studies, everybody would want to be in high-growth, high-margin businesses like pharmaceuticals or consumer products. But you have to work your way from where you are to where you want to be.'[2]

Do you really know who your customers are? Silly question isn't it? But for some businesses it is not easy to know who the *real* customers are. And until you do know how can you be sure you are meeting their needs? One way to explore this question is to ask your customers what they do with your product or service. How do they use it? This is often a difficult question for many new technology ventures, especially ones offering a new way of doing something.

Summary

1. You need to understand your company's history in order to identify its successful features, the strengths, and to recognize any important weaknesses.

2. This understanding, or self-evaluation, starts by asking the following questions: What have you done right so far? What do you really do well? What kind of people are you?

3. If the answers to these questions are positive and consistent, you have a solid foundation upon which to plan the future. If there are inconsistencies, you note them for future attention.

4. You want to reconcile the internal view with the external by asking other questions: What do your customers and suppliers really think about you? What kind of business are you really in? Who really are your customers?

Now the decks are cleared for the start of the planning exercise. We can start to look at your company's future by asking the second basic question about where you want to go.

References

1. Jonathon Green, *The Cynic's Lexicon: A Dictionary of Amoral Advice*, Sphere, London, 1986.

2. Michael Walsh, 'Success depends on leadership', *Fortune International*, 18 November 1991.

Where do we want to go?

*Man is limited not so much by his tools as
by his vision.*[1]

Introduction

We begin the structured planning process by addressing the single most important question: *where* do you, the management team, want to take your company? This is a critical question for several reasons. First, you need to select a destination upon which you all can agree. Second, you have to communicate the destination clearly to your employees and by various ways to outsiders. Third, everything else in the planning process flows from this declaration.

The direction your management team selects for the company will *shape* all the major actions taken under a strategic plan. *Everything in the strategic plan flows from this decision.* For that reason alone, it is essential you take the time to decide the right future direction for your company.

What about missions, etc.

American companies are fond of creating mission statements. Some mission statements are useful if they successfully answer the following question: what are we, the management, trying to do for whom?[2]

Mission statements need to be readable. They have to make immediate sense to people who read them. Brevity is important, clarity is essential. More importantly, people should be able to remember the mission, especially if they are expected to make major decisions by referring to it.

Unfortunately, most attempts to publicly state a mission result in ambiguous declarations that become meaningless for management, employees and public alike. Such mission statements would never do in wartime because they lack clarity. Often they are so vague that any well-intentioned troops would get bogged down or permanently lost. One observer noted that 'mission statements tend to provoke cynicism and confusion rather than clarity and commitment'.[3]

Many mission statements appear to have lost the message. Perhaps this resulted from too many rewrites by too many hands. Let us assume that mission statements have a bad press and a poorly deserved reputation and it is better to ignore them than try to reform them.

Vision

Vision, on the other hand, has much more going for it. Warren Bennis, a leading management light in America, wrote that leadership could be defined as 'the capacity to create a compelling vision and translate it into action and sustain it. With a vision, the leader provides the all-important bridge from the present to the future.'[4] Perhaps Sir John Harvey-Jones put it best by simply stating: 'The business that is not being purposefully led in a clear direction which is understood by its people is not going to survive.'[5]

The creation of a powerful vision is not easy. It needs to be 'real' for the people creating it, that is, they have to feel it has meaning and significance. If they do not believe it, who will? Also, it needs to be definite to have impact. Often vision is ascribed to leaders after they have achieved it. Before the vision is realized, the visionary risks being labelled a revolutionary or an eccentric. Yet, when people cry out for leadership, the best leader sees into the future and offers a compelling vision to share. The process involved in this type of mass visionary appeal is not clear, although it is best understood after the fact. Hindsight, as always, 'is an exact science'.[6]

When I used the concept of 'vision' in a seminar, there was a general unease among participants signified by shuffling of papers and clearing of throats. Perhaps such reactions stem from meeting the biggest intangible in the planning process. After all, vision is not something a manager can sit down and solve. It requires inspirational thought and motivational power. Whether we like it or not, therefore, we are stuck with 'vision', because there is no other word with the same depth and breadth. I will try, on the other hand, to make it as tangible as possible.

Vision statement

A vision statement is a clear declaration about where the management team wants to take the company. It needs to send a clear message to employees and the market regarding what the management intends to do.

Accordingly, the vision needs to be inspirational but realistic. If a vision does not inspire people, they will not be motivated. If a vision is not realistic, it will never be realized and people will become disillusioned. One business leader commented that 'above everything, I am sure that clarity—clarity of ambition and aspiration—is the absolute key to vision'.[7]

Many large, decentralized and international companies use a vision to unite their workforce, linking employees with a shared sense of direction. For example, Merck, a major American health group, has a 'Statement of Corporate Purpose' that declares 'we are in the business of preserving and improving human life. All of our actions must be measured by our success in achieving this.' On the other hand, Disney's vision is simply 'To make people happy'.[8] Walt Disney was reputed to have gone to artists for his vision, steering well clear of accountants and business people.

While Singapore Airlines is the fifteenth largest airline in the world, it is number one in profitability. Chairman Joseph Pillay defined the company's vision in the following words: 'offer the customer the best service that we are capable of providing; cut our costs to the bone; and generate a surplus to continue the unending process of renewal'.[9]

Timeframe

How far do you look into the future? *Strategic plans usually are made for a five year period.* Sometimes companies choose three years, others select four. One reason for selecting a five year horizon is because it may take that long to change fundamental attitudes and alter direction. In any event, your plan needs to look beyond the annual budget cycle. However, the time horizon should be within reasonable control of the management team. Given the present rate and pace of change, five years may be testing the outer limit.

Remember, the plan is not written in stone and, therefore, you are not making inflexible commitments for five years. On the contrary, the plan is reviewed annually and, in reality, becomes a rolling five year plan that goes on until the vision is realized or the business changes ownership. Progress is measured during these periodical reviews and reported to shareholders, employees and any important third parties. While the long view may be for five years, formal reviews each year look at the entire plan and make changes where necessary. Most progress is incremental and cumulative, but occasionally it can be startling and dramatic.

Conflicts

The company's destination also needs to be compatible with the individual aspirations and ambitions of each member of the management team, otherwise the exercise can be counterproductive. If one team member's personal agenda is in conflict with the corporate vision, there will be dissension and division and performance will be affected. It is very important, therefore, to make sure that each team player's personal agenda is compatible with the company's agenda.

Can a single vision serve a whole company? Some planners believe that vision statements are needed for each separate and definable business and even major departments. It really depends on the size and composition of the operating units. It can be confusing if there are several visions within a company, but it could be too restrictive trying to fit all activities under one umbrella. You have to make a judgement. However, in order to justify its own vision, the activity would need a separate identity and management team with its own view on where the business should go in the future.

One way to deal with this problem is to create a vision for the company as a whole, leaving individual divisions or separate businesses to adopt their own mini corporate plans with compatible visions. In one company, for example, it was useful to adopt a company vision, which helped define separate visions, objectives and priorities for individual product groups.

EXERCISE 2

HOW TO CREATE YOUR VISION STATEMENT

How do you create your vision statement? There is a very simple exercise devised by Barrie Pearson.[10] Each member of your management team sits down and writes two statements of vision: the existing one which brought your company to its present position and the one which will be needed in the future. Each manager should express his or her statement in one paragraph with no more than three sentences. If possible, managers should be encouraged to express their vision in one sentence. Emphasis on brevity forces each participant to focus on core points, leaving diverting fringe subjects on the sidelines.

After completing the exercise, each team player should read his or her statement. After each statement is read, discussion should lead to a consensus on the future vision of the company. Consensus will emerge when certain key words are repeated and common themes become self-evident. Consensus is very important, because it allows everyone involved in the process to 'take ownership' of the vision. As Dwight Eisenhower expressed it: 'I would rather persuade a man to go along, because once he has been persuaded, he will stick. If I scare him, he will stay just as long as he's scared, and then he is gone.'[11]

It is mandatory that all senior members of the management team participate fully in this exercise. There are two good reasons why this is necessary. First, if everyone participates they will spark off one another and produce a better result through the creative process. Second, everyone will 'own' the vision, because it will be a collective decision in which everyone participated. Remember, if you are chairing the planning exercise, a thorough discussion in which openness, honesty, cut-and-thrust occur inevitably will lead to a more solid agreement.

Invariably, *vision statements are about becoming something different in the future, about leaving one place now to go to another place later.* Wherever possible, *your future direction should be expressed in one crisp, concise sentence.* You are trying to establish a lasting impression that will guide the company towards its new future. Accordingly, the clearest impression will be the briefest. It will also remain in people's memory longer. A business leader underscored this point by stating that a vision needs 'to be able to be expressed in a single, understandable, clear and unambiguous sentence'.[5]

Vision takes time. It is not the sort of thing that becomes reality overnight. People need to know that it will take some time to realize the vision. According to Warren Bennis, 'putting a vision into practice is a long-term process'.[4]

Inspirational but realistic

Vision statements are about future direction. Your team is searching for the right inspiration to motivate people to take the company through its next stage of development. Accordingly, the direction needs to contain ambition, something to strive towards and, hopefully, achieve. On the other hand, it would be overly ambitious to court too high a level of achievement, failure to attain which would discourage everyone. The exercise can be regarded as *applied imagination*.

In short, the vision statement needs to inspire and motivate employees, but it must be achievable to be believable. Let us divide this point into its key components:

1. Inspirational

2. Motivational

3. Achievable

4. Believable

In other words, the vision statement must be realistic but still visionary, reflecting what the company wants to become, where it wants to go and striking the right note between inspiration and credibility.

Stark failure awaits a management team so overly ambitious that its plan is scorned by employees or a team whose plan is so turgid and conservative that it fails to ignite a spark anywhere. So, you need to be conscious about balance when creating your company's vision statement. The balance is struck when your vision inspires your people but is real enough to be achieved. *Vision statements should have a major impact on employees.*

Charles Handy makes the following comments on vision:

1. 'A leader shapes and shares a vision which gives point to the work of others.

2. The vision must be different.

3. The vision must make sense to others [and] stretch people's imagination but still be within the bounds of possibility.

4. The vision must be understandable.

5. The leader must live the vision.

6. The leader must remember that it is the work of others.'[12]

Sun Tzu wrote the following words more than 2500 years ago: 'Those who have Direction can arouse like charging waters, Uprooting boulders along the way.'[13]

Examples

Some examples of corporate vision statements might help illustrate this step in the process. These examples were adopted by real companies as statements of future direction but references to specific industries and special circumstances have been removed for reasons of confidentiality. Unfortunately, the need for confidentiality has eliminated much of the excitement involved in creating the following visions:

1. 'To become the leader in providing quality service and innovative technological solutions to problems in selected market segments and geographical territories.'

2. 'We will become a nationally recognised, innovative supplier of high quality products which are leaders in selected niche markets.'

3. 'To become the market leader in America for our specialist products.'

4. 'To dominate selected markets and to become the market leader by providing the best product for the job, solid field support and continual innovation to meet customer needs.'

5. 'To become the leading professional force in the world market designing and manufacturing innovative systems and servicing systems and selected equipment in overseas markets.'

EXERCISE
3

REALITY CHECKS

Because the company's future direction is so important, it is essential that the management team confirms the corporate ambition. Confirmation is achieved through reality checks, which are tests that the corporate vision is appropriate and realistic for your company.

Here are some tests in the form of questions to check the reality of your vision statement:

1. *Personal ambitions.* Is each team member's personal ambition compatible with the company's statement? The team should deal with any conflicts that might arise between one team member's personal agenda and the future

direction of the company. If the planning exercise is led properly, such conflicts ought to emerge and should be handled in an appropriate manner.

If such a conflict exists, it is much better to deal with it at the beginning of the process rather than letting it interfere down the road when real damage can be done. This problem most often arises when a medium sized company is privately controlled by a few owner managers or dominated by one owner manager.

Note: personal agendas need to be compatible with the company's agenda or problems may arise which could detract from future progress or, if serious enough, might even split the organization. An important part of the planning process is to unite and bond the management team behind a future course of action. Union begins with the vision and needs to be carried through the company and into the outside world.

2. *Individual disagreements*. Another variation that could affect the plan's impact is a substantive disagreement among team members about the future direction. Such differences need to be ironed out in the vision exercise, but sometimes a disagreement is more fundamental and cannot be resolved quickly. If this occurs in your company, the majority in the team need to convince the person or people who disagree. If the majority cannot convince the minority, it may be necessary for the minority to leave the company.

Dissenters at best will give lukewarm support for the plan and at worst will form a nub of dissent which, one way or another, will work to undermine the plan. It is far better that all senior managers openly and honestly embrace the future direction and take individual as well as collective ownership than have even one person half-heartedly go along to avoid confrontation or leaving.

3. *Comfort level*. Is the team really comfortable with the direction? The team needs to feel relaxed about its vision, because it needs to be inspired and motivated along with the rest of the employees. They also need to believe the vision can be realized.

If the team cannot believe in the future direction, how will it convince other managers and employees? This is the reason why the debate over direction must occur at the beginning of the planning process. All doubts and dissents need to be aired and differences resolved, presenting a united front to employees and outsiders.

Senior executives should create an atmosphere in which all team members feel free to raise their doubts without attack or embarrassment. Airing opposing views is the way consensus and balanced decisions are reached. It also is the way in which commitment is forged and respect is engendered.

In order to achieve this, you need an atmosphere in which frank and open discussion can occur. The right atmosphere and tone during the planning process is critical to forging unity and can be inspirational in itself. Accordingly, the chairman or chief executive should be sensitive to this human factor and take responsibility for creating an open and trusting atmosphere.

4. *What kind of people?* Does the future direction fit comfortably with the kind of people you really are? Does it recognize and build on your qualities?

    If you ask people for something they cannot deliver, it is unrealistic and will not be achieved. Moreover, it will be demotivating and counter-productive, diverting resources to the unrealizable. Even worse, employees will lose confidence watching the management team fail to realize the company's future.

5. *What we do well.* Does the future build directly on what the company already does well? Is it a logical extension of your strengths? Again, if you are asking the impossible, the team will fall short with all the other problems associated with going public and failing.

Strengths and weaknesses

The ultimate reality check on your vision is whether or not it is realizable given the company's strengths and weaknesses. Is the future direction achievable given existing strengths? Can your weaknesses be identified and corrected with available resources and within the timeframe dictated by the plan? Will any remaining weaknesses cripple the plan?

The best way to declare confidently a future direction that sustains commitment and belief is to conduct a realistic and detailed assessment of your strengths and weaknesses. You may have heard of this exercise before. It is usually described by the acronym of SWOT, standing for the first letters of the following words: Strengths, Weaknesses, Opportunities and Threats. Another name for the exercise is WOTS-UP: weaknesses, opportunities, threats and strengths.

While SWOT and WOTS-UP are useful, these exercises are limited because they do not ask where a company is going nor look at how to make a plan work inside the company. In this sense, they are like an animal without a head or tail. Moreover, some managers mistakenly assume that these shorthand exercises are for strategy creation or constitute a strategic plan.

The strengths and weaknesses exercise constitutes an internal evaluation. It is supposed to be a critically hard self-examination. It needs to be critical and hard in order to work. The most difficult part is being ruthlessly honest about your real strengths and weaknesses. With regard to weaknesses, much of the difficulty arises from avoiding critical assessments of people in important positions and sweeping problems under the proverbial carpet over long periods. This is the time to empty all the cupboards, look at the contents and find constructive ways to deal with the problems. With regard to strengths, some managers shy away from recognizing what the company really does well. Sometimes you need to pat yourselves on the back, take credit for the good things and find ways to exploit these strengths.

After the internal evaluation is completed, it is worth while to validate the exercise externally, that is, confirming your strengths and weaknesses with key customers and suppliers. Checking your internal view outside the company is another way of checking the reality of your assessment, as well as obtaining useful feedback on the experience and perception of key players in your world.

As John Argenti suggests,[14] the internal evaluation focuses on what your company does outstandingly well or badly, what special abilities or disabilities it has and where its advantages and disadvantages are compared to direct competition. Let us divide the internal evaluation into the following parts:

1. What is done outstandingly well or badly?

2. What are the special abilities or disabilities?

3. What are the advantages and disadvantages compared with direct competitors?

How do you identify the most important strengths and weaknesses? You should be looking for things that impacted on past performance or will have a major impact in the future. Also, you should consider whether or not these factors distinguish you from direct competitors. The question you need to ask is will the strength or weakness help or hinder realization of the vision? Specifically, will it help achieve our objectives or will it hinder them?

Perhaps some examples will help identify what is meant by strengths and weaknesses. Here are some typical statements from management teams:

1. 'Our factory is outdated, the layout has not changed basically in 20 years and our costs are one-third higher than the competition.'
   Comment   Clearly a weakness with major impact on profitability.

2. 'We are proud of our product line, our products are market leaders and attract premium prices.'
   Comment   Clear strengths.

3. 'Customers tell us we have the best service in the market even though our prices always are the highest.'
   Comment   Another strength.

4. 'Company debt is too high and interest payments absorb most of our profits.'
   Comment   A fundamental weakness that saps profits and starves future investment.

5. 'Our team barely copes now but we can't handle any more growth.'
*Comment   A cry for help with future implications and a clear
weakness.*

One authority[15] lists the following categories 'for assessing strengths and
weaknesses':

1. Organization

2. Personnel

3. Marketing including sales force, knowledge of the customer's
   needs, breadth of the product line, product quality, reputation,
   customer service

4. Technical

5. Finance[15]

Other areas worth examining are pricing, quality, customer care, the
competition and the nature of the business. Argenti suggests the following
items are worth examining for strengths and weaknesses: finance, production, purchasing, products, marketing, distribution, R&D, employees,
management, industry position and profit centres.[14]

EXERCISE   STRENGTHS AND WEAKNESSES EVALUATION

4   **Background**

One approach to an overall assessment was developed by Kenichi Ohmae. His
Critical Success Factors (CSF) analysis asks the following questions:

1. What were the factors that brought you success in the past?

2. What does it take to succeed in your industry? What are the success factors
   utilized by the successful companies in your industry or market?

3. How do your success factors compare in detail with those of the industry?[16]

Differences arising from this comparison will indicate weaknesses that need to be
examined. On the other hand, similarities indicate strengths upon which to build.
The two key questions to ask, according to Argenti, are as follows:

1. 'What are the CSFs for our business and will they be different in five years
   time?'

2. 'What would our abilities look like if they were ranked in each CSF?'[14]

On the other hand, Mack Hanan believes there are only three indispensable success
factors:

1. Entrepreneur management

2. Marketing skills

3. Emergent technology[17]

A company may have unique or innovative success factors which help differentiate it from competitors in the marketplace. These special factors need to be cultivated and exploited before competitors try to copy them. If a special factor is proprietary, your company may have a finite lead depending on the security of the factor.

In any event, success factors need to be reviewed periodically, because they may lose their success with changes in the marketplace. As markets continually change, new features may become more important. *The rules of the game continually change and you need to find the new ways to play.*

The exercise

My approach involves the team participating in a reality exercise which ends with a detailed appraisal of strengths and weaknesses.

Each team member should list the strengths of the company in one column and the weaknesses in another. Sometimes a strength is also a weakness and crossovers are common. Each list should be read aloud until a composite one can be created. You need to focus on important items and avoid creating an enormously long list of points which will take an excessive amount of time to evaluate. Accordingly, you should concentrate on up to six items only in each column.

Strengths and weaknesses need to be ranked by importance, that is, by impact on the vision, objectives (see Chapter 4) and goals (see Chapter 5). After listing in order of importance, each one should be discussed in terms of how the management team will enhance or build on strengths and how weaknesses will be reduced if not eliminated. Specific comments and responses should be noted for each item requiring attention.

It is particularly worth while analysing the strengths and weaknesses of each major product or service. Too often companies fall into the trap believing that their offering to the market is vastly superior to any and all competition. It rarely is. However, you will not know that unless you check out the competition by examining what they are doing. And the best way to understand the competition is to conduct a strengths and weaknesses evaluation of their company, products and service.

How does your product/service compare on price, performance, longevity and other factors? How do the unique selling points of your products or services compare with the competition? What about foreign competition? Is anyone producing a superior offering? If so, how and why? Can you apply any of their success factors? Can some of their success rub off in your direction? You won't know unless you go out and see and ask the hard questions.

Throughout the internal evaluation process you can use the following rule-of-thumb: *lead with your strengths and contain your weaknesses until they can be minimized or eliminated.* If your weaknesses far outweigh strengths, you have a serious problem. If resources are not available to correct the problem, you should be looking for another way to overcome the imbalance, such as bringing in a new management team or even merging with a stronger company.

Obstacles

Sometimes weaknesses take the form of internal obstacles. Occasionally these problems are masked and are difficult to identify clearly. Often managers are reluctant to deal with obstacles even when identified. These problems have been labelled 'the enemy within' by Barrie Pearson,[18] who lists the following commonplace obstacles:

1. 'Procrastination over poor performers in key jobs.' If you do not remove such people, you condone mediocrity and show others that promotion is not based on merit but on loyalty. You do not do the poor performer any favours either, because he or she would be better off somewhere else doing something more suitable.

2. 'Lack of personal accountability for outstanding results.'

3. 'Inadequate salaries and incentives. Get the best people, get the best out of them and pay for results.'

4. 'Tolerating loss makers.'

5. 'Excessive interference by head office.'

6. 'Organization structure.'

Obstacles need to be dealt with when they have been clearly identified. Otherwise, obstacles lead to things getting worse and they hardly ever resolve themselves. Sometimes the obstacle involves an individual in a key position (see Changing an individual in Chapter 12).

Misleadership

Management should never forget that employees are perfectly capable of committing their time, energy and resources to the wrong things. Economic history is replete with examples of major commitments and efforts behind plans that did not work. It is management's task to make sure the company's direction is the right one and that human and financial resources are allocated in the best way to the right ends.

Summary

1. It is critical to get the future direction right, because everything else in the plan will be devoted to realizing the company's vision.

2. The vision should be clear and concise and if possible expressed in one sentence.

3. The direction needs to be inspirational and motivational as well as achievable and believable.

4. Personal agendas of individual managers should not conflict with the vision.

5. Individual disagreements need to be aired and resolved.

6. The management team needs to be unanimously behind the vision statement.

7. The vision should reflect what kind of people you are.

8. The vision should extend from what you do well.

9. The vision should be based on your strengths after acknowledging your weaknesses and what can be done about them.

Now that you know your future direction, where you want to go, we can look at the role of objectives in realizing your vision.

References

1. Richard Pascale and Anthony Athos, *The Art of Japanese Management: Applications for American Executives*, Warner, New York, 1981.

2. Arthur Sharplin, *Strategic Management*, McGraw-Hill, New York, 1985.

3. Andrew Campbell, 'A mission to succeed', *Director*, February 1991.

4. Stuart Crainer, 'Vision and leadership', *Director*, October 1988.

5. John Harvey-Jones, *Making It Happen: Reflections on Leadership*, Fontana, London, 1988.

6. Arthur Bloch, *The Complete Murphy's Law: A Definitive Collection*, Price, Stern, Sloan, Los Angeles, 1991.

7. John Harvey-Jones, 'Heroes, captains, lookouts and managing growth', *Accountancy*, February 1991.

8. *Economist*, 'Management focus: the vision thing', 9 November 1991.

9. *Economist*, 'Singapore Airlines: flying beauty', 14 December 1991.

10. Barrie Pearson, *Common-sense Business Strategy: How to Improve Your Profits and Cash Flow Dramatically*, Mercury, London, 1987.

11. *Forbes Executive Calender*, 1992.

12. Charles Handy, *The Age of Reason*, Arrow, London, 1991.

13. R. L. Wing, *The Art of Strategy: A New Translation of Sun Tzu's Classic The Art of War*, Aquarian, London, 1989.

14. John Argenti, *Practical Corporate Planning*, Unwin Hyman, London, 1989.

15. Howard Stevenson, 'Defining corporate strengths and weaknesses', David Asch and Cliff Bowan (eds), *Readings in Strategic Management*, Macmillan, London, 1989.

16. Kenichi Ohmae, *The Mind of the Strategist: Business Planning for Competitive Advantage*, Penguin, London, 1983.

17. Mack Hanan, *Fast-Growth Strategies: How to Maximize Profits from Start-up Through Maturity*, McGraw-Hill, New York, 1987.

18. Barrie Pearson, *Common Sense Business Strategy Seminar*, 1990.

Objectives

*Asking dumb questions is easier than
correcting dumb mistakes.*

LAUNEGAYER'S OBSERVATION[1]

Introduction

Objectives are things that must be achieved in order to realize the vision
and arrive at the chosen destination. *We set objectives to break down the
vision into parts that can be identified, measured and achieved.* In this
way, the vision becomes more tangible and accessible. Objectives are also
criteria by which success or failure is determined. After implementing the
strategic plan, you can measure your company's progress by how far you
move towards achieving specific objectives.

Objectives can also be regarded as the ends, and strategies as the means
to those ends. If objectives are the parts, the vision is the sum of those
parts. Objectives are also useful guidelines or bench-marks for management to define and describe what needs to be done in order to succeed.
Invariably, these guidelines involve qualitative business and management
issues.

Progress towards most objectives can be measured. Accordingly, you
should not be setting objectives that are all incapable of measurement,
qualitatively or quantitatively. If you cannot measure in some way the
progress towards an objective, how will you know if it has been achieved?

Characteristics

If objectives are to play a proper role in the planning process, they must be
specific, easily understood and widely communicated. While they should
be challenging, they also must be attainable.[2]

Let us break down this point into its key parts:

1. Specific

2. Easily understood

3. Widely communicated

4. Challenging

5. Attainable

6. Measurable

It is not enough to have one objective or to make the only objective generating profits. Companies are composed of people and people usually have a mixture of objectives, sometimes even conflicting ones. Charles Handy has made the following comment: '"To make profits" or "the bottom line" is not, by itself, a useful way of describing the purpose behind an organisation. It does not begin to tell you what to do or what to be. It is akin to an individual saying that he or she wants to be happy.'[3]

What objectives?

A number of people have indicated areas where objectives are needed. In this regard, it is useful to look at a few selections, because they reflect what is most important to achieve in a company.

Peter Drucker writes that management should set objectives in the following areas:

1. Market standing

2. Innovation

3. Productivity

4. Resources

5. Profitability

6. Employee participation

7. Public responsibility

Barrie Pearson suggests objectives are set for the following items:

1. Broad commercial rationale

2. Direction and priorities

3. Philosophy, policies and values central to the way a company will develop

4. Qualitative goals crucial to success[4]

I believe that management teams may wish to set objectives for the following subjects:

1. Profitability

2. Return on investment

3. Meeting real market needs

4. Product quality

5. Customer service

6. Market share

7. Growth

8. Competition

9. People and the working environment

Setting your objectives

Your vision may not involve any of the above objectives. You have to tie your objectives to your vision. You accomplish this by asking the following question: 'What do we, as a management team and company, have to do to realize the vision?'

Another way to set your objectives is to examine each element in your vision to see what specific objectives are needed to achieve it. In other words, *you break down the vision into its major parts and look at what objectives will be required to realize that part.* In addition, you may wish to consider separate objectives for the organization as a whole, which might involve operational issues as prerequisites for achieving the other objectives.

Examples

Another way to understand objectives is to look at actual examples. Again, the following extracts are taken from real strategic plans without reference to the particular company involved.

Objectives of an engineering company

1. Recognize and understand real market and customer needs.

2. Respond to these needs with specific actions.

3. Operate professional management systems incorporating extensive use of information technology.

4. Establish profit and share option schemes for all employees.

5. Make the working environment like an extended family where all employees feel involved and committed.

Objectives of an equipment manufacturing company

1. To attain and maintain the highest product quality to specific national and international standards.

2. To identify and meet customer needs and respond quickly and correctly to any changes and trends in the marketplace.

3. To anticipate and incorporate technological improvements based on sound engineering, good design and reproducible quality.

4. To achieve higher levels of productivity with new equipment and better layout.

5. To bring greater managerial professionalism, imagination, style and prestige to markets worldwide.

6. To become the market leader in selected niche and geographical market segments.

7. To achieve a positive corporate culture where people work and play hard but always perform and receive commensurate rewards based on performance including profit share for all employees and share options for key managers.

Objectives of an international company in a service industry

1. To always put the customers first by meeting their needs.

2. To maintain integrity at all times in customer relations.

3. To recognize and respond to national feelings where needed.

4. To become opportunistic and market orientated without changing the house style.

5. To be different and to build on that difference.

6. To establish measurable standards for service and quality.

7. To monitor and continually improve those standards.

8. To create a mechanism to identify problems in the market which can be solved by technology.

9. To develop, adopt and market the best technological advances before the competition.

10. To monitor competitive technology in order not to fall behind.

Objectives of a publishing company

1. To continually improve the quality of publications.

2. To produce high quality, high margin publications meeting defined criteria for payback, sales, margins and risk and reward.

3. To create a working environment where people are stimulated and enjoy work.

4. To attract and retain high quality people.

British Gas established the following vision, which they call a Statement of Purpose and which was sent to every customer by mail: 'We aim to be a world class energy company and the leading international gas business.' Their vision will be realized through the following eight objectives:

1. 'Running a professional gas business providing safe, secure and reliable supplies.

2. Actively developing an international business in exploration and production of oil and gas.

3. Making strategic investments in other energy-related projects and businesses worldwide.

4. Satisfying our customers' wishes for excellent quality of service and outstanding value.

5. Constantly and energetically seeking to improve quality and productivity in all we do.

6. Caring for the environment.

7. Maintaining a high quality workforce with equal opportunities for all.

8. Cultivating good relations with customers, employees, suppliers, shareholders and the communities we serve.'

Toyota Manufacturing (USA) Inc. set the following four objectives which they call 'principles':

- 'To produce America's No. 1 quality car based on "customer first" philosophy.

- To contribute to the quality of life, as well as to the economic growth, in the communities we serve.

- To promote stable employment and improved well-being of employees through steady growth of the company.

- To develop unique, innovative production and management systems by combining the best ideas of two countries.'

Toyota also stresses that its future depends on the 'respect for the individual worker and the success of good team management'.[5]

In their annual reports, HP Bulmer Holdings, a British cider company, publishes a list of objectives relating to such areas as profits, quality, worker participation and conditions and the environment. While admitting there are priorities and not all objectives are equal, Bulmer's recognizes that its success depends on employee understanding and support for each objective.

YKK is the world's leading zipper manufacturer with plants around the world. It created competitive advantage through fast service, high quality and keen prices. At its home base in Japan, YKK maintains a philosophical objective entitled 'Cycle of Goodness', parts of which are implemented elsewhere in the world. The cycle involves employees investing some of their pay in the company to improve production and quality and participating in working practices that keep costs under control. The company, in turn, reinvests profits which finance growth and increase employment. The Cycle benefits society, as well as employees.[6]

Levi Strauss manufactures the world's best known denim jeans. Some observers have paid it a high compliment indeed, saying that it resembles a Japanese company. Chairman Haas believes in making Levi Strauss an 'empowered' company based on six aims set in 1987: ethical management, diversity, different behaviour, recognition, communications and empowerment. As a result, the company focuses on the long term and stays committed to its aims.[7]

Paul O'Neill, the President of Alcoa, set an objective that every business unit 'begin sharing information and working together more closely'.[8] A similar objective was established at General Electric and other large companies which have come to realize that benefits will flow if parts of their empire talk to each other. Other companies, such as 3M, have taken communication further by creating inter-functional teams between business units to create new products.

The objective of quality

Often managers feel the need to say something about quality without fully understanding what is involved. I regard quality to be such an important objective that it warrants separate treatment in this chapter.

After watching Japanese companies strike success after success, Western companies are becoming aware of the vital importance of quality. Market leadership increasingly is becoming dependent on three factors: developing new products quickly; producing products of consistent high quality; and delivering products on time. In the rush to achieve these results, management is being compressed and brought closer to the factory floor and quality responsibilities are being spread throughout the company.[9]

There is a clear and measurable benefit from better quality. Most experts estimate that quality improvements can achieve savings up to 30 per cent of manufacturing costs. Or, looking at the opposite effect, poor quality can add up to 30 per cent to manufacturing costs. Quality is rapidly becoming a universal objective. Several countries are following Japan's lead in establishing prestigious national awards for outstanding quality. Having created the legendary Deming prize in the early 1950s, the Japanese have seen the Americans follow suit with the Malcolm Baldrige National Quality Award in 1987, and the Dutch based European Foundation for Quality Management made its first award in 1992.

The Baldrige Award may reshape American managerial attitudes, fostering, in the hopes of Ford's chairman, Donald Peterson, 'rediscovery of cooperation as a national strength'. Quality forces responses on a number of fronts. If your company accepts that the customer is the final judge of quality, management should establish clear quality values, the workforce needs to get fully involved and everyone then strives for continuous improvement. But quality does not stop at your factory door. You need to get involved with outsiders too, such as suppliers and the local community.[10]

In order to reach the right attitude, however, managers need to clearly define quality, establish a structure to realize improvements and measure progress at specific points. And as one leading exponent, W. Edwards Deming, preaches, *quality is a continuous process of continual improvement*. Once you start, you never stop.

Henry Casley, Managing Director at Britain's Southern Electric Company (SEC) believes in quality and getting it right the first time. His philosophy is simple and straightforward: if your customer is satisfied, your business will be profitable. Satisfied customers are created by identifying what the customers want and making sure they get it. Casley regards quality as just another, but more acceptable, name for productivity and efficiency. Using quality as a lever, management forces employees to make contact with customers and their needs.

SEC is structured into six operating divisions. Each management team was asked to find ways to overcome staff attitudes. Team building exercises were started and quality managers appointed who set up Quality Improvement Groups (QUIGs). So much for internal actions, what about the customers? Actions were taken to improve the quality of service, such as taking all customers' names and calling them back to ask if they were satisfied with the service and ensuring that service engineers telephone customers if they are going to be late for a call.[11]

Quality is a very serious issue at Motorola, the American telecommunications and electronics company. Richard Buetow, Quality Director, feels that quality has to 'do something for the customer'. As quality is in the eye of the beholder, Motorola seeks out its most demanding customers and questions them about quality needs for each product. The company also follows Genichi Taguchi's concept for 'robust quality' which demands that robustness is designed into a product rather than setting tolerance levels and trying to hit targets within those levels. As a result, Motorola's foldable cellphone has one-eighth the number of parts it had in 1978 and components snap together rather than being screwed or fastened. The pressure is on for getting it right the first time, because products have shorter and shorter shelf lives.[12]

Like Motorola's cellphone, higher quality invariably means designing products that are simpler and have fewer moving parts or are easier to use. For example, the Sony Walkman has half the parts of the original model and is four-fifths cheaper in real terms; and Toyota's cars have about half the moving parts of cars made by General Motors. Designing quality in helps considerably to reduce the problem of measuring it out after the product is made.[13]

William Wiggenhorn, Motorola's corporate vice-president, said that 'in the 1980s Motorola Inc. thought that quality meant meeting the customers' expectations. Then we changed that definition to say exceeding expectations. Now we say that quality is anticipating customers' expectations—in all products and services.'[14]

Product quality is much better if designed in and not inspected out. This is a cardinal principle about quality. Another cardinal principle is that quality pays for itself. In fact, it more than pays for itself in reduced manufacturing costs, fewer after-service costs and return business from satisfied customers.

An in-depth study by McKinsey of the machine-tool-making industry in West Germany identified the following success factors among the top performers:

1. Simplicity. The top firms made a narrow range of products using less than half the parts of their less successful competitors, which meant they were faster, simpler and cheaper to manufacture. Most importantly, it meant that quality was built-in, resulting in fewer defects and lower waste.

2. Improvements. The better firms had continuous, incremental improvements which were passed on to customers. Product development was a joint effort with customers and suppliers.

3. The best companies had fewer managers, short communication lines, a greater proportion of skilled workers and spent six times more on education and training. The result, not surprisingly, was much higher levels of productivity.[15]

How did this mania for quality get started? It is ironical that the movement started in America but the leading experts went unheralded in their own country.

The modern quality movement had its roots in statistical process control techniques developed in the 1930s at Western Electric's Hawthorne plant, a part of AT&T. Statisticians were trying to understand the small variations in products caused by mechanical processes. These slight variations were measured and the processes were modified in order to reduce variations. As a business issue, quality intrigued two young statisticians at the Hawthorne plant, W. Edwards Deming and Joseph Juran. Other gurus emerged in different companies, such as Philip Crosby at ITT, Armand Feigenbaum at GE and the late Kaoru Ishikawa in Japan.[9]

Paralleling the saga of the unsung poets in their own land, Deming and Juran went to Japan as part of the post-war reconstruction exercise. In the early 1950s, the Japanese had a poor reputation for quality. As a result of this concern, Japanese executives started attending Deming and Juran seminars. By 1980, more than 150 000 people including 2000 senior managers had attended these courses. According to Juran, the impetus for quality must come from the top. Deming agrees, saying that 85 per cent of quality problems are not the fault of workers but of management. The fault lies with management systems that produce bad quality. That is why top management must take the lead.

The Japanese kept telling visitors that quality was a people issue, but nobody would listen. Now the message is getting through. The vehicle for change is management teams. Teams need to be formed and given projects and the power to manage. If this is done, they will take ownership of the problem and do something about it.[14]

The famous American company, Mack Trucks, is a classic example of how poor quality tied to a bad culture almost ruined a company. During the 1980s, management failed to invest in manufacturing and quality suffered. Poor quality control resulted in badly finished vehicles which hit Mack's reputation. An egocentric management refused to acknowledge the problem and a 'parochial culture' almost put Mack under. Renault, the French vehicle manufacturer, rode to the rescue and rapidly cleared up the mess after a takeover.[16]

Even hospitals are getting in on the act. In America, hospital managers are focusing on quality as the number two priority behind cost containment. Why? *Experience has shown that 25 to 30 per cent of operating budgets go towards correcting mistakes.* Quality experiments also are being undertaken in Britain's national health system. Quality initiatives range from shortening waiting times, better response times from ambulances to reducing recovery time from serious operations.[17]

Dr Juran estimates that about one-third of industry's time is spent correcting mistakes which could have been avoided. Improvements need to be incremental and realized project by project. Nor can a company rely on quality circles as the answer, because most problems are inter-departmental. Cross-functional teams are very important.

American companies tried to copy the Japanese success by creating quality circles, but the problem was much wider. Americans are finally paying closer attention. It is certainly about time and there is a lot at stake. Juran guesses there will be higher returns from quality than from selling products.[18]

Big Ed Deming is 92 and still going full tilt, working six days a week and preaching 12 hours a day on the importance of quality. *He teaches that the more quality you design and build into products, the less it costs. It is far cheaper to design it in than inspect it out and the customer is more satisfied too.* Again, Deming stresses that quality is a process of continuous improvement requiring a major commitment from top management and involving everybody in the company. While the responsibility for quality starts in the boardroom, everyone must be involved in the process of change. According to Deming, there is 'no instant pudding'. Quality is a way of thinking. Piecemeal approaches do not work. You have to consult and involve people on the factory floor.

Quality is about continuous improvement and continuous improvement means continuous measurement and self-assessment. Quality is ruled by cause and effect. You have to identify variations and determine if they are significant or not. Cooperation between people is the key to success, not competition which is divisive. Deming abhors performance related pay, because it fosters pernicious competition and destroys cooperation. His philosophy is embodied in the famous 14 principles.[19] Deming explains this philosophy as follows: "All people ask for is a chance to work with pride and joy. Management has taken all of it out. Then you take quality out. Instead of working for the company, people all compete with each other. . . . The Japanese top management were willing to learn. They were willing to live by cooperation, not competition.'[14]

Deming fears it will take a crisis before Western companies really come to grips with quality. When customers came to regard Japanese products as cheap imitations of dubious worth, the Japanese turned to quality as a way out. They understood the problem, according to Deming, because they were in a crisis.

The objective of innovation

Many fast growth companies have adopted innovation, the constant creation of new products and services, as a primary objective. There are several examples of companies that have adopted innovation as a corporate objective. One of the leaders is America's 3M (Minnesota Mining and Manufacturing) Corporation. It stated an objective to generate 25 per cent of sales from new products which did not exist five years ago. This is quite a challenge in a corporation with 1990 sales of $13 billion and a product line of 60 000 items, but 3M is well on target.

The 3M Corporation uses two methods to foster innovation: first, it created something called 'bootlegging', which allows technical staff to work on projects of their own choosing. Second, the company uses, as so often is the case, cross-functional teams. Their experience showed that collaboration between scientists with different disciplines led directly to the creation of new products. It also added considerable knowledge value and less material cost to new products—and knowledge value attracts a premium. A clear system of priorities, however, rules this activity. Each business nominates a few things that will change its fundamental nature. From this pool, 3M picks up to 50 potential future products for fast track development.[20]

What about the Japanese? Japan's most effective weapon, often dazzling competitors in other countries, is 'rapid innovation'. One way this is accomplished is through something called 'product covering', which involves rushing out an instant product to compete with somebody else's innovation. The process is rather simple: the innovation is feasible technically, because it exists. Using reverse engineering, the product is disassembled and short cuts discovered. Japanese often get involved in product covering for a purely domestic reason, i.e. they want to stop distributors and retailers from moving to competitors.

Product covering is part of a more powerful process known as 'product churning'. Western companies tend to use a 'rifle' approach to product development, testing the market, revising the product and finalizing the product until customer needs are met before the launch. Japanese companies do the opposite. They tend to 'shotgun' new products by testing the market through selling the first batch directly from production. Once a positive response is achieved, the new product can be refined and value added through new features over time. This approach hedges risk, because it builds on an initial positive market response.

Japan produces new products in 30 to 50 per cent of the time taken in the West. It is able to do so for several reasons. First, Japan has a large pool of well-trained engineers, 5000 to every million people compared to 3500 in America and 2500 in Germany. Second, most products are designed with off-the-shelf components which may require only 10 per cent new inventions and already build in cheaper costs and reliability. Third, Japanese work closely with suppliers, exchanging a free flow of information. There are good reasons why rapid innovation is a way of life there: Japanese companies are driven by special factors in their country, including, for example, rigid distribution networks and an insatiable appetite for new products.[21]

There may be an irony in the rush of Western companies to copy the many successes of Japanese firms. Much Japanese commercial behaviour appears to exist in order to meet the requirements of distributive and industrial structures in their domestic market. Accordingly, some Japanese practices might not be applicable in the West because the Japanese methods evolved from different market characteristics and pressures.

There is another aspect of product innovation—the need to get information and ideas to flow within an organization and then translate them into action and competitive advantage. Thus, time becomes an important factor in innovation. Time compression, the time taken from idea to product in the marketplace, allows a company to widen the range and increase the technical depth of products and services. Viewed another way, time becomes the cutting edge, the lever against competition and the ultimate competitive advantage.

In order to achieve time compression, companies need to run design and development processes in parallel, as well as the production capability to make the new products. Project teams, therefore, are required from marketing, design, engineering, production and other functions to work closely together to meet specific deadlines.[22]

Sometimes companies have to change their way of doing things to achieve innovation. Several key factors for success have been identified: first, there is a need to make specialists into generalists and pool knowledge; second, hierarchies have to be broken down because traditional structures put the emphasis on control rather than experimentation and creation; third, information needs to flow through the company, not get stuck in laboratories and individual departments; fourth, time needs to be created just to think. These factors concern process, not product. If you change the shape of the company from reaction to creation, the thinking goes, new products ought to follow.[21]

The objective of customer care

Another objective of increasing importance, especially in service companies, is customer care. In adopting this objective, companies have re-enthroned the customer as 'king'. Like quality, customer care is rapidly becoming a competitive factor in manufacturing and service companies. But what is involved in adopting customer care as an objective?

The first principle in customer care is getting, and staying, close to your customers. Companies seeking to reach their customers have to find new channels of communication, such as customer surveys, customer interviews and follow-ups, test marketing, focus or panel groups, complaint hotlines, field audits and other means of access. The primary objective is to create contact points and establish feedback loops.

All this effort has a definite payoff—customer loyalty. Listening to customers and responding to what they tell you is the key, not developing 'attitudes' that you know best or that the customer can always be taken for granted. Training sales staff is also a critical factor, studies have shown that two-thirds of ex-customers left because of unsatisfactory service.[23]

Increasingly, people are doing business based on how they *expect* to be treated. In the arena of expectations, reputation for service and quality is a distinct competitive advantage. Why? As Tom Peters points out, the negatively treated customer rarely forgets. In fact, ten times more people remember a bad experience than a good one. On the other side of the coin, a customer who is pleased will bring in five or more new customers.[24] Moreover, loyal customers who are not abused are worth a lot of sales over the life of the relationship. There is a ring of inevitability in the statement 'that retaining customers is cheaper than acquiring new ones'.

In some industries, service is the only differentiating factor. For example, an American survey in 1987 discovered that 42 per cent of people who switched retail banks did so because of service problems. Another study indicated 68 per cent of customers left car dealers because of 'indifference' shown by sales or service people. Nor will you always hear directly from disaffected customers. An A. C. Nielsen survey discovered that only 2 per cent of dissatisfied shoppers complained to a manufacturer, but 34 per cent switched products.[25]

A basic problem is that *too few companies look at the transaction from the customer's point of view*. Do you ask yourself the following question: 'what does my customer want from this transaction?' For example, does the customer want a complete package of products and services or is he or she more interested in lower prices? Does the relationship involve after care or is it a one-off transaction? Moreover, do you ask these questions to customers at regular intervals and respond accordingly? Unfortunately, too often the internalized view prevails: 'we know what the customers want and how to give it to them'. Such dated views are very risky in today's marketplace where information, awareness and expectations are much higher than ever before. Moreover, the most important element in expectations remains 'word of mouth'. And bad mouthing, negative word of mouth, carries hefty penalties because the disaffected are much more vocal than the satisfied.

Some companies suffer because of national characteristics. For example, customer service is an accepted way of life in Japan although less so in America, because market share is built on customer loyalty. Over a long period, loyal customers spend more and are cost effective to retain. They may tell eight other people about the good service received. Yet, in Britain, customer service often gets mixed up with servility and the class system.

Xerox UK is a British company that is actively pursuing customer satisfaction. Since 1985, it has spent a lot of time trying to understand its dissatisfied customers, who are estimated at 7 per cent of the total. Xerox's goal is to reduce this number to zero (nil) by 1993. During 1989 and 1990, it worked on role clarification, employee involvement, training, reward, recognition and measurement. Company incentives are tied to customer satisfaction, ranging up to 30 per cent of pay for directors.[26]

What do your customers say about your products and/or services quality and care? When was the last time you asked them? More importantly, what have you done about the answers? Is customer care one of your primary objectives?

Summary

1. Objectives are things that must be achieved to realize the vision.

2. Objectives are what it takes for you to succeed with the plan.

3. Objectives are the ends which provide useful guidelines and benchmarks for management on what must be achieved. They usually deal with qualitative business and management issues but many can be measured.

4. Objectives need to be specific, understood, challenging but attainable.

5. Objectives should be set by asking what needs to be done to realize the vision.

6. Companies should look closely at objectives for quality, innovation and customer care.

Now that we have looked at objectives, we will turn our attention to goals for your company.

References

1. Arthur Bloch, *The Complete Murphy's Law: A Definitive Collection*, Price, Stern, Sloan, Los Angeles, 1991.

2. Arthur Sharplin, *Strategic Management*, McGraw-Hill, New York, 1985.

3. Charles Handy, *The Age of Unreason*, Arrow, London, 1991.

4. Barrie Pearson, *Common-Sense Business Strategy: How to Improve Your Profits and Cash Flow Dramatically*, Mercury, London, 1987.

5. *Directors and Boards*, 'Being a global leader', **16**(1), Autumn 1991.

6. John Thompson, 'Strategy, profit: a means or an end?', *Accountancy*, August 1991.

7. *Economist*, 'Business: a comfortable fit', 22 June 1991.

8. *International Business Week*, 'The corporation/strategies: the recasting of Alcoa', 9 September 1991.

9. Simon Holberton, 'An idea whose time has not only come but will prevail', *Financial Times*, 20 March 1991.

10. Martin Dickson, 'Total quality: bouquets and barbed ire', *Financial Times*, 3 February 1992.

11. Paul Taylor, 'Customer care: plugged into the quality circuit', *Financial Times*, 20 January 1991.

12. *Economist*, 'Management focus: future perfect', 4 January 1992.

13. *Economist*, 'Business: surviving the deluge', 13 October 1990.

14. Gerald Michaelson, 'The turning point of the quality revolution', *Across the Board*, December 1990.

15. *Economist*, 'Manufacturing: less is more', 25 May 1991.

16. Martin Dickson, 'Mack's long haul back to health', *Financial Times*, 20 March 1992.

17. Alan Randall, 'Hospitals get the quality treatment', *Financial Times*, 6 March 1992.

18. Geoffrey Foster, 'The Juran quality cure', *Management Today*, November 1987.

19. *Business Matters*, BBC Television Channel 2, 20 August 1992.

20. *Economist*, '3M: 60 000 and counting', 30 November 1991.

21. *Economist*, 'Management focus: create and survive', 1 December 1990.

22. Christopher Lorenz, 'Accelerated product development: competition intensifies in the fast track', *Financial Times*, 28 June 1991.

23. Guy de Jonquieres, 'Wrong choice from the menu', *Financial Times*, 6 September 1991.

24. Tom Peters Seminar, *Business Matters*, BBC Television Channel 1, 23 February 1992.

25. William Davidow and Bro Uttal, 'Coming: the customer service decade', *Across the Board*, November 1989.

26. Simon Holberton, 'In pursuit of repeat business', *Financial Times*, 13 May 1991.

Goals

The farther away the future is, the better it looks.

FINNIGAN'S LAW[1]

Introduction

Goals provide clear evidence that objectives have been achieved. Actually, goals are quantified objectives. They measure the distance required to achieve qualitative objectives. In other words, they are milestones on the way to achieving objectives.

How to set goals

Goals can be established by using three different criteria:

1. *Historical.* Use your company's actual financial experience over the last five years as a guide to future performance. In this regard, it is particularly important to examine budget versus actual performance. Another approach is to look at your results compared to the industry average over the last five years.

2. *Competitive.* Make a detailed comparison between your performance and that of direct and indirect competitors.

3. *Normative.* Adopt standards derived from literature surveys, rules of thumb or the opinions of outsiders such as consultants and journalists.

It is important to agree on the criteria you will use to evaluate overall performance, because the agreed criteria will become the yardstick to measure performance.

Targets versus goals

The art is to set targets that stretch people but goals that are achievable. In this way, targets and goals produce satisfaction and rewards while advancing the company towards its vision.

What is the difference between targets and goals? Targets are numbers beyond goals. They are set to extend people. You strive towards targets, which should be greater than goals. Goals, on the other hand, should be achievable. Progress is measured and communicated against goals, not targets. Another distinction is that targets can easily be set for individuals but goals are established for the whole company. Targets can be moved upwards and downwards depending on experience. Goals are set for a longer time period than targets and should be adjusted much less frequently, if at all.

EXERCISE   REALISM

5

Like the vision and objectives, goals have to be realistic. It is counterproductive to set goals too high and fall short. People become demoralized by failure and management looks foolish for setting unobtainable targets.

You can determine how realistic your goals are by asking the following questions:

1. How realistic are your goals compared to industry averages?

2. How realistic are your goals compared to the market leader or fastest growing company in your industry?

3. Is your market growing fast enough to allow you to reach your goals?

4. Will you have to win more market share to achieve the goals? If so, how realistic is this? Where will the new share come from? Will you be able to win it within the projected timeframe?

5. How will higher profits be achieved? What is the scope for price rises or cost reductions?

6. Is the time allowed realistic?

7. Are you fully exploiting existing products, services, customers and markets?

Whatever figures are chosen, they must be based on a logical build-up from year to year, not plucked out of the sky. The logicality of your figures is the ultimate reality check in setting goals. Can you justify the figures? Are the assumptions valid in building the figures? Does everyone agree with these assumptions?

When making assumptions, it is useful to recall *Wethern's Law of Suspended Judgment*: 'Assumption is the mother of all screw-ups.'[2] Also, the compounded growth rate needs to be realistic in order to maintain that all-important credibility, internally and externally. In short, your *goals need to be based on defensible assumptions and calculations.*

Remember, you want to set realistic goals and realism is based upon defensible logic and past performance. An additional point worth making is that *goals are set to be reached. Targets are made to stretch people beyond goals.* Be careful not to confuse the two points.

What goals to set

The most common goals are ones for sales and profits to be achieved over time, usually in the third and fifth years. For example, your company may set twin goals of sales within three years of £20m ($40 million) and within five years of £32.5m ($65 million) with profits, respectively, of £2m ($4 million) and £4m ($8 million).

During its major restructuring programme, Tenneco, an American conglomerate, reported the following goals to its shareholders: first, a 20 per cent return on shareholder equity; second, a 15 per cent annual improvement in earnings per share; and third, a pledge to generate cash for capital investment and dividends.[3]

Other goals can be set for diversification. You might be seeking a large proportion of sales from new markets within the planning period. For example, Hanson Trust set a goal, which was achieved, to generate half its sales from North America within five years. Other goals can be set for quality, number of employees and any other measure that is important to your company. In fact, quantitative goals can be created for almost every objective. If an objective is adopted, you should have some idea when it is achieved. Interim milestones are an excellent way to measure progress towards achievement.

One international company with which I worked set the following goals: 'Achieve in real terms within five years sales of £100 million and net profits of £4 million before tax. A further goal is that half of sales will be generated in North America within this time period.'

Alcoa's president, Paul O'Neil, set his 50 senior executives from around the world the goal of closing the gap with world competitors in all their various businesses by 80 per cent within two years.[4]

The 3M Corporation set several specific goals in 1991:

■ Generate half its sales revenues outside America.

■ Reduce the manufacturing cycle time by 50 per cent.

■ Create $5 billion sales from products developed within the last five years.[5]

■ Maintain R&D at high levels (running at 6.9 per cent of sales which is double American average).

■ By 1995, cut by one-third the time taken to get innovations to market.

■ By 1995, reduce unit costs by 10 per cent in real terms.[6]

In 1987, Motorola set a quality target of 3.4 defects per million units manufactured against the prevailing rate of 40 defects. In 1982, the rate was 6000 per million. Motorola estimates the improvement over that five year period saved $700 million in manufacturing costs which was equal to 6.4 per cent of 1990 sales. Its goal in the 1990s is to reduce manufacturing defects by 90 per cent every two years until it hits a target of one defect per billion units.[7]

Summary

Let us review the main points:

1. Goals measure the distance to achieving objectives and are the tangible evidence that objectives have been achieved.

2. Goals are quantified objectives and they need to be achievable and realistic to be credible. Targets should stretch people.

3. Goals can be established using three criteria: historical, competitive and normative.

4. Goals are usually set for sales and profits over time but they can also be established for other factors such as diversification, quality, number of employees and any other critically important aspect of your business.

Setting your company's agenda

By now you will have created your company's *agenda* through taking the following actions:

1. Declaring your future direction through the vision statement.

2. Establishing objectives that must be achieved to realize your vision.

3. Setting goals to measure the distance to achieving the objectives.

Vision, objectives and goals are the company's agenda for the future—the future of your choosing.

You should try to express the company's agenda on one page or less, conveying in a clear and concise way what your management team wants to do over the next three to five years. If you have a more complex company structure with other entities such as divisions, subsidiaries or product groups, you may wish to create mini-agendas for each significant unit. If the unit has its own management team, which controls the unit's future, it might benefit with its own vision, objective and goals. Any mini agenda, however, needs to be compatible with the company's agenda.

Taking the process down into the organization also allows operational people to participate and take ownership of the plan for their unit. Many management teams find this is a very useful way to establish clear objectives and set priorities in each operating group.

When you look back on this part of the planning exercise, you will come to appreciate the amount of creative effort that went into shaping the company's agenda.

You have established the framework for strategy formulation. Now you can look at the plans necessary to achieve the objectives. In Chapter 6 we concentrate on how your company gets to where it wants to go.

References

1. Arthur Bloch, *The Complete Murphy's Law: A Definitive Collection*, Price, Stern, Sloan, Los Angeles, 1991.

2. Arthur Bloch, *Murphy's Law Book Two: More Reasons Why Things Go Wrong*, Price, Stern, Sloan, Los Angeles, 1980.

3. Charles Leadbeater, 'Corporate restructuring: why Tenneco sold its foundations', *Financial Times*, 5 September 1990.

4. *International Business Week*, 'The corporation/strategies: the recasting of Alcoa', 9 September 1991.

5. *International Business Week*, 'The corporation/strategies: 3M run scared? Forget about it', 16 September 1991.

6. *Economist*, '3M: 60 000 and counting', 30 November 1991.

7. *Economist*, 'Management focus: future perfect', 4 January 1992.

Strategy Part I— How do we get there?

*Those who understand Strategy
Move without delusion and progress
without tiring.
Hence the saying:
'Know the other and know yourself.'*

SUN TZU[1]

Introduction

Now that you know where you want to take the company, the emphasis shifts to getting there. And how you get there depends on plans. These plans are called strategies and their purpose is to achieve the objectives.

It is worth remembering throughout the strategy creation exercise that *strategic planning is about identifying and dealing with the really significant issues facing the company.* You need to agree what these major issues are and then decide what to do about them. Obviously, you only can deal with a few major issues with any sense of urgency. Therefore, you cannot afford to be diverted into less important areas, nor can you take on too much.

Strategic planning is about focusing on the important questions and taking the appropriate actions that will achieve the objectives and realize the vision. Accordingly, strategies should be tied to specific objectives while being based on opportunities in the marketplace. Strategies involve doing, i.e. taking actions. Strategies are not remote ivory tower exercises. On the contrary, they grow from the realities of the marketplace and the company's interaction with the market.

Characteristics

You will obtain a feel for strategies by looking at the following characteristics:

1. Strategies deal with the external world, unlike previous exercises which looked internally, i.e. vision, strengths and weaknesses, objectives and goals.

2. Strategies are rooted in the outside world which means you have to understand markets, opportunities, changes, trends and external threats.

3. Strategies are concerned with the product or service mix to be produced or offered and the markets in which the products or services will be sold.[2]

4. Strategies often involve complex decisions that deal with a high degree of uncertainty, usually requiring an integrated approach, which mean major changes in a company.[3] As a result, strategies differ considerably from other decisions.

5. *Strategies must be flexible, requiring you to be sensitive and responsive to market changes. The first overriding imperative about markets is that they change. The second imperative is that you must try to know what is going on out there all the time or you will not know what is changing. The third imperative is that if you do not know what is changing you cannot respond. The fourth imperative is that if you cannot respond to changes your strategies will be unrealistic and will not work.*

6. Strategy is not about making a single document but rather *it is a continual process of adapting to an ever-changing environment.*

7. Strategies 'deal with a choice of resource commitments among alternatives'.[2]

8. Strategies usually result in incremental improvements over time. Occasionally there is a masterstroke strategy representing a major breakthrough and turning point for the company.

9. Strategy can also be defined as an action plan to deal with the commercial environment. For example, Ohmae says that 'strategy is really no more than a plan of action for maximizing one's strength against the forces at work in the business environment'.[4]

10. Strategies are devised within definite restraints. For example, Bowman suggests that a firm's strategy 'is influenced and constrained by the existing structure, culture, values and resources'.[5] Bowman indicates only one hard restraining factor, i.e. resources. The other 'soft' factors are discussed in Chapters 12 and 13.

11. According to the controversial Canadian Professor Henry Mintzberg, strategy 'can just as easily be conceived as a pattern that emerges. . . . Nor does strategy have to aim at achieving a particular position, such as a dominant market share. It can equally well be about the purpose and self-image of the business. . . . The biggest job of planning is stimulating strategic thinking.'[6]

What are strategies?

Strategies are specific plans to achieve the objectives you set after creating the vision. *Objectives are the ends, strategies are the means.*

Unlike the agenda which emerged from an internal evaluation, strategies are created by an external process directly tied to markets. Having looked inside with your management team to set the agenda, you now look at the external world to develop strategies. Kenichi Ohmae defines strategies as the process of matching 'corporate strengths to customer needs'.[4] Arthur Sharplin sees 'the job of the strategist in the planning phase to develop strategies which take advantage of the company's strengths and minimize its weaknesses in order to grasp opportunities and avoid threats in the environment'.[7] Strategies are plans that identify and convert opportunities on one hand and respond to changes on the other. *Strategies manifest themselves as market plans.*

What about strategic management? What is the difference between planning and managing? The easiest way to distinguish between the two is to look at planning as the process of making strategic choices while managing is about producing the results from those choices. As Peter Drucker has said: 'strategic planning is management by plan, while strategic management is management by results'.[2]

Strategies are unique to your company. It is highly unlikely that two companies will have the same strategy. As every company has a different culture, management, mix of strengths and weaknesses and products and services, strategies are bound to be dissimilar. As Argenti points out: 'there is no strategy that is right for every company. . . . The only correct strategy is the one that comes out of an analysis of the company's total strategic situation.'[8]

End point

The end point of strategic actions is deceptively simple: *the right combination of new products, markets and technologies that produce the right results.*[2] You create this combination by expanding the present position, adding new products or services, penetrating new markets and dropping old products and markets.[2] The search for the optimum combination is continual and dynamic.

Let us look at each part of the end point as follows:

1. Expanding present position.

2. Adding new products or services.

3. Penetrating new markets.

4. Dropping old products and markets.

The end point involves a dynamic journey without a real end. It involves continual change, reflecting the movement inside markets. While the end point is simply stated, it is not so easily achieved.

The centre-piece of all strategies is your product or service portfolio and the markets in which you sell. Successful strategies are about optimizing the product mix to maximize profits, creating the largest share in markets which brings further benefits in higher margins and more security.

The ultimate point is to become market leader of your niche or segment. Why? Because studies have confirmed what senior managers already knew, the largest player in any market enjoys the highest prices and best margins. Moreover, market leaders are more secure because they are more difficult to dislodge.

Accordingly, strategists look carefully at how to increase market share and achieve leadership. General Electric in the United States openly adopted the objective of becoming number one or two in selected markets. If GE could not reach those leadership positions, it got out of the industry. GE's Chairman, Jack Welch, did just that when he radically restructured his company, selling billions of dollars worth of activities and buying even more if it helped achieve leadership positions.

Change, change, always changing

The one thing you can say about markets is that they change and keep on changing. And that is why you need to stay close to the market, to see and understand what the changes are and what they mean to your company. In other words, 'since the environment is continually changing for all organisations, strategic decisions necessarily involve change'.[3]

Mack Hanan paints a vivid picture of dynamic markets:

'From the 1970s on, markets have been undergoing dramatic change. They are becoming smaller, and based on highly specialized needs. Their demand for customer-tailored benefits has become the key to their segmentation. At the same time, pressure from new technologies has acted to telescope product life cycles and drive them down towards their break-even points.'[9]

Another example of markets in ferment can be found in Britain and America's retail sectors. The 1980s were a retailer's dream, because everybody made money by just being there. Now several changes are reshaping retailing in an unparalleled fashion. First, the twin driving forces of inflation in the 1970s and credit boom in the 1980s are gone, leaving very much reduced margins for error. Second, cost pressures continue to compress margins. Third, supply clearly exceeds demand and competition is stiff, leading to a state of almost permanent sales to attract fewer shoppers. Fourth, discount stores have brought value for money to the forefront. Fifth, an older population will demand different responses from many stores. Sixth, specialized stores called 'category killers' are adding to intense competition in niche markets. For example, the American Toys 'R' Us has taken 20 per cent of the British market with 33 stores over the last 7 years, and more category killers are spreading in furniture with Swedish retailer, Ikea and in computers with PC World.[10]

Even the market for commercial aircraft is changing. Boeing Aircraft Corporation is dropping its long held attitude of 'we know best' and is involving airlines, suppliers and subcontractors to help design their latest widebody twin-engine jet, the 777. Why this change in behaviour? New aircraft launches are high cost exercises involving enormous investments and greater market risks. Competition has increased from Airbus Industrie in Europe and McDonell Douglas at home. Also, Boeing is shifting away from a technology driven company towards one that meets real customer needs. As a result, there are 235 design and build teams with a range of specialists from inside and outside the company.[11]

According to Kenichi Ohmae timing is 'vital. . . . The most brilliant strategy will be useless if it fails to take account of the ever-changing trends of the market.'[4]

Key issues

The key issues in strategic planning are as follows:

1. What are the changes in today's marketplace?
   What is happening to customers tastes, attitudes and demands?
   What is happening to technology?
   What trends are emerging?

2. Where will you compete?
   What offers the best chance of results?
   Should you compete geographically? On individual products, by product lines, by customers, or what?

3. What will your customers want in the future?

4. How will you offer better products in the future?
   Can you offer better prices, features and/or performance?

5. Can you build your business on any clear success factors?

6. How will you generate the necessary resources?

7. How will you deal with competitors?

Shell Oil Company devised the following seven critical questions to ask managers during strategic planning sessions:

1. What are the critical issues?

2. If everything went well, how would the business develop?

3. If it went wrong, how would the business develop?

4. What changes are needed in the current culture to achieve the objectives?

5. What are the lessons from past successes and failures?

6. What are the important decisions over the next five years?

7. What would you decide if it was your business?[12]

Cardinal rules

There are a few useful guidelines in creating strategies which are important enough to call 'cardinal rules'. *The first cardinal rule of strategies is to select only a few strategies that must be done with a sense of urgency. The second cardinal rule is to arrange strategies in order of importance, because all strategies are not equally important. Remember: the most important criterion for strategy selection is that it achieves your objectives.*

Summary

1. You need to identify the major issues in your company and decide what to do about them. Therefore, you need to focus on the critical questions and take appropriate actions to achieve objectives and realize the vision. Each objective needs a strategy.

2. Strategies deal with the external world, markets that are continually changing. You must stay close to markets to respond to these changes.

3. Strategies take the form of market plans to convert selected opportunities.

4. The strategic end point is the best combination of new products, markets and technologies that produce optimum results.

5. You should select only a few strategies that must be handled with a sense of urgency. You also need to rank strategies by priority.

References

1. R. L. Wing, *The Art of Strategy: A New Translation of Sun Tzu's Classic The Art of War*, Aquarian, London, 1989.

2. Igor Ansoff, *Corporate Strategy*, Penguin, London, 1987.

3. Gerry Johnson and Kevan Scholes, *Exploring Corporate Strategy*, Prentice-Hall, London, 1989.

4. Kenichi Ohmae, *The Mind of the Strategist: Business Planning for Competitive Advantage*, Penguin, London, 1983.

5. Cliff Bowman, *The Essence of Strategic Management*, Prentice-Hall, London, 1990.

6. Geoffrey Foster, 'Mintzberg's strategic force', *Management Today*, April 1989.

7. Arthur Sharplin, *Strategic Management*, McGraw-Hill, New York, 1985.

8. John Argenti, *Practical Corporate Planning*, Unwin Hyman, London, 1989.

9. Mack Hannan, *Fast-Growth Strategies: How to Maximize Profits from Start-up Through Maturity*, McGraw-Hill, New York, 1987.

10. John Thornhill, 'Hardship in the high street', *Financial Times*, 26 March 1992.

11. Paul Betts, 'A revolution on the runway', *Financial Times*, 7 May 1992.

12. Bernard Taylor, *Strategy in the Boardroom Seminar*, 1987.

Strategy Part II—Opportunities

*If everything is coming your way, you're in
the wrong lane.*

LAW OF LIFE'S HIGHWAY[1]

Introduction

Strategies are tied to markets. You have to look critically at your markets
in order to identify opportunities that will achieve your objectives.

The fundamental questions

The Socratic tradition continues by focusing on six critical questions for
the formulation of effective strategies. The critical questions to devise
strategies are as follows:

1. What and where are the best business opportunities?

2. What are the market plans to realize these opportunities?

3. What resources will be needed to convert these opportunities?

4. How will you obtain these resources?

5. What are the critical risks, external threats and responses to your
   strategies?

6. What actions need to be taken immediately, in the short term and in
   the long term?

Let us explore each of these questions in some depth.

WHAT AND WHERE ARE THE BEST BUSINESS OPPORTUNITIES?

Basic criteria

Most objectives can be achieved if the business grows. Corporate ambitions require
funding. Growth will generate profits and profits will provide more funding. So,
you are looking for opportunities that will generate the highest return for the least

effort and risk. Or, in more technical terms, the most output for the least input at the lowest risk.

Let us break down the basic criteria as follows:

1. Highest return

2. Easiest to convert with existing capabilities, i.e. feasible

3. Less risky

When you list all your possible opportunities, *these basic criteria should be used for ranking possibilities by their attractiveness, i.e. by priority. Other criteria can be added later to the evaluation and ranking process.*

The search for opportunities

Before evaluating and ranking, however, all the possibilities need to be identified. As Ohmae says 'analysis is the critical starting point of strategic thinking'.[2] How do you go about exploring the range of opportunities?

Sun Tzu, more than 2500 years ago, recognized the importance of gathering information and evaluating it. In his classic work, *The Art of War*, he said: 'The Strategic Arts are First, measurements; Second, estimates; Third, analysis; Fourth, balancing; Fifth, triumph.'[3]

Choices

You should realize there are choices out there. Therefore, you need to explore many options in order to select the best opportunities for your company. Often a chief executive or management team may fix on one opportunity to the exclusion of all others, cutting off the exploration process before it even begins. If this happens, the team is left committed to only one course of action and nagging doubts eventually may emerge— was there a better opportunity to pursue?

Preselecting one opportunity without searching for others has the following inherent flaws:

1. The opportunity selected may be the wrong one.

2. All spare resources may get allocated to the wrong opportunity.

3. The resources remain committed as long as there are no alternatives.

4. There is no back-up strategy that can be selected if the first one runs into trouble or is proven wrong.

5. The team might not take full ownership of a course for action unless all options are explored and debated. It is very difficult for

any dissenter to challenge a single-minded chief executive or management team who demands acceptance by authority or weight of numbers.

Existing products and markets

There are good reasons why it is best to look first at possibilities in the existing product portfolio. First, you know more about your present products than new ones; second, you should know more about your existing market than a new one; and third, it should be more cost effective to realize these opportunities than it will be to convert new ones. Remember, you already have made a major investment in existing products, services and markets and, therefore, any additions will be incremental and usually at higher contribution rates. Thus, you should start the opportunities search in your own backyard. Looking at your existing activities, you can ask the following questions:

1. What does the customer really want from the product and/or service and can the customer be satisfied in 'a radically different and better way'?[2]

2. Can you expand existing sales?

3. Can you cut costs and generate more profits?

4. Can you add value (and hence margin) to existing products?

5. Are there new products or services that can be sold to the existing customer base?

6. Are there new applications for existing products?

7. Can new markets be opened with existing or modified products?

Another way to look for opportunities in existing activities is to ask if there are any other ways to increase profitability from sales. In this regard, you may wish to review the following possible actions:

1. Change the price.

2. Increase sales activity.

3. Generate more effective promotion.

4. Increase quality.

5. Broaden product line.

6. Expand territory.

Sometimes opportunities appear if you look at your activity in a different way. Look at what your product or service does, not just what it is. This may lead you to see other things that you can do for your customer, such as adding a maintenance package. Adding products or services is called 'bundling' and removing them is called 'unbundling'.[4]

Profitability also can be improved by reducing costs or increasing productivity. Some actions worth reviewing might be as follows:

1. Improve product and/or service quality.

2. Increase productivity through better work flow and self-managed teams.

3. Increase productivity through employee motivation.

4. Increase output and lower costs through new technology.

5. Redesign products to reduce raw materials and improve quality.

6. Change mix of labour and capital.

7. Review direct and indirect staffing requirements and assignments.

8. Contract out for specialist functions.

As you can see, there are many ways to re-examine the existing product and service portfolio for opportunities that may have been overlooked. This examination calls for an open mind and some lateral thinking. Is there something staring you in the face? What are the most obvious moves? Have you really optimized your market share? Is there more growth and profit potential in your existing activities?

The search for opportunities in existing activities requires discipline and honesty. It is human nature to seek the new as the most desirable, a version of the ancient adage: 'the grass is always greener on the other side'. The commercial corollary is that 'every new opportunity looks better than the old ones'. You might be surprised what is available from a fresh look at your existing portfolio. Resist the temptation to wander into new lands until you are convinced you have explored fully your own country.

Are you sure there is nothing more that can be done to produce results from existing activities? If so, you can consider new opportunities.

New opportunities

All new opportunities need to be identified. The identification process starts by taking a close look at markets. Sometimes opportunities jump out at you and other times you have to create them from things you see.

There is an old gambling story attributed to Damon Runyon that goes something like this: if you meet a man in a bar and he bets you that he has a deck of cards in his pocket with a jack of spades which will jump out and spit in your eye, then, son, you better get out your handkerchief before you make any wager. Well, the best opportunities are like that jack of spades, they jump out at you. On the other hand, you will not find the jack of spades unless you pick up the whole deck and start dealing.

The best way to identify opportunities is by breaking them down into the following components:

1. Market segments which can be demographic, behavioural or physical.

2. Geographical territory.

3. Product or service.

Market research

You need to look closely at a market to really understand it. By looking, I mean collecting and analysing data. And this means avoiding the NMRH (No Market Research Here) syndrome. You simply cannot rely on *ad hoc* impressions and fragmentary knowledge of markets, especially not on hearsay. There is no substitute for a formal and systematic investigation of your prime markets.

If you have an in-house marketing effort, competent external marketeers should validate internally generated data and, at the very least, conclusions. If you do not use professional marketing consultants, you should have a closer look at what they can offer. Professional marketeers can be very useful in profiling competitors, because they are able to ask questions and get answers that would elude you.

Outside marketing consultants are being used more and more. In Britain, for example, companies spend £300m each year on research. Many firms have eliminated in-house departments, preferring to buy in specialist expertise when needed.[5] A useful guideline to follow when employing outside marketing people is to provide them with a very tight brief. You must be very clear and detailed about the questions you want answered. Do not ask a marketeer to just 'have a look' at a market. If you commission a marketing consultant without specific instructions about the precise information wanted, the marketeer will generate unfocused material that may confuse you as well as waste your time. In fact, the best way to use any external professionals is to provide them with focus and direction. In that way, you get the results you want at the lowest cost.

Customers

The most important thing to remember about marketing is that it involves looking at your business from the customer's viewpoint. If you are serious about the customer's point of view, you must set aside whatever you *think* the customer wants and be open to talking *and* listening directly to him or her. You need to ask your customers what they want from you. You will never know until you ask.

The customer is the 'king'. As the Chief Executive of the Maytag Corporation in America said: '*In today's marketplace, the consumer decides who succeeds and who fails* . . . [italics added]. To be successful you must attract consumers, you attract consumers by giving them what they want and what they want are features, price and quality, and the most important thing is quality.'[6]

If you start looking at markets from the customers' point of view, you start asking the following questions: How do they use the product and service? What are the customers' needs? What do they want? As marketing consultant James Watters from Edinburgh, Scotland says over and over: 'There are no short cuts. You must get into the market to find out what customers want and ask a lot of questions. It's as basic as that. And it's not that difficult, because people generally like to talk about their business.'

Market segments

A market segment is a market with homogeneous or similar customer characteristics.[7] *The most important issue in selecting a market segment is whether or not there is a real need and if that need is sufficiently large and has enough potential to justify the investment required.* If you can identify a real need with potential, you have an opportunity. Opportunities are based on needs. 'Find the right ones and fill them' remains the most fundamental tenet in marketing.

When examining individual market segments, you need to analyse the following points:

1. History relevant to what you want to do.

2. Trends and future projections for growth.

3. Clear imbalance between supply and demand.

4. Changes in competition.

5. Opportunities for real price increases.

6. Opportunity to introduce a specialized product or service.[8]

When you are looking at market segments or niches, break the markets down to the most specialized and successful competitor. Having identified the segment leader, you need to understand, as best you can, the leader's product or service, cost structure and profitability. Is there room for you to improve on this performance? Has your competitor missed something in the marketplace? Can you beat existing competition, including the market leader? If you cannot answer these questions positively, you ought to rethink your plan to enter that segment. You have to see clearly how your company will succeed and win through.

Kenichi Ohmae suggests a strategist has two possible approaches: first, to use his or her imagination to dissect the market into its key segments; and second, to identify what makes winners different from losers and then analyse the differences. At the centre of this exercise is the challenge to find the industry's 'secret' for success.[2]

Cycles

What is happening in the segment or niche? What is the dynamic life cycle of products and services? What implications do these cycles have for you, a potential new entrant? What about your product or service's life cycle? How does it fit with the prevailing life cycle in the segment or niche?

An analysis of product and service cycles will highlight the requirement for introducing new products and hence the demands on innovation, research and development. Some markets place very strenuous demands on companies. For example, a recent study in America indicated that in high-growth markets with short product cycles delays in shipping of only six months might cut a product's overall profitability by one-third.[9]

Research indicates that products have a definable life cycle which moves through five stages and each stage impacts differently on profitability:

1. Introduction of the product in stage one.

2. Growth of the product in stage two.

3. Product matures in stage three.

4. Product starts declining in stage four.

5. Product disappears into extinction in stage five.

Accordingly, you should be asking the following questions: Where are our main products in this five stage cycle? What do our product cycles look like when transposed against the cycles of leading products in the segment?

Cliff Bowman goes further, noting there is an industry life cycle as well. Moreover, the industrial life cycle will influence the nature of competition. For example, in the early stage of a new industry, there are several competitors attracted to a market in which demand exceeds supply, providing enough customers for all the suppliers. During this initial stage, there are 'no rules of the game' and many products and processes are on offer.

However, as the industry matures, 'rules' start to emerge, i.e. 'consumer expectations about quality and performance are recognized and industry standards are established'. Competition heats up, because further growth is achievable only through stealing customers from competitors. As every supplier shares virtually the same ability (experience curves about equal), the competitive factor becomes price. In mature and declining industries, companies have to be very efficient to earn acceptable profits.[10]

Matrices

What happens if you have too many opportunities and have difficulty in choosing the best ones? Having examined all opportunities and thought about strategies, you may still have a problem selecting the best opportunity. In this event, marketing matrix 1 might be a useful tool for setting priorities.

Marketing matrix 1

	Opportunities				
Market	1	2	3	4	5
Opportunity					
Description					
Existing demand					
Potential					
Market route					
Timing					
Target sales (by milestone)					
profits					
margins					
Costs					
start-up					
direct					
indirect					
Assumptions					
Competition					
Risks					
Sensitivities					
Manager					
Personnel					
Priority					

Another very useful marketing matrix was provided by James Watters. It clearly highlights the first priority of looking for opportunities in your existing product portfolio and existing customer base before taking the risk of developing new products or entering into new markets (see marketing matrix 2).

Marketing matrix 2

Products

		Existing	New
Customers	Existing	Market penetration	Product development
	New	Market development	Diversification

Timing

Timing can be a critical issue in converting some opportunities. As we have seen, the Japanese pride themselves on innovating new products and rushing them to market, averaging less than two-thirds of the time taken in the West. Much of this time can be accelerated by identifying the need and responding quickly. One study revealed that half the time taken to get a product to market was wasted between need identification and start of design work.[9] Hence, when it comes to timing, *the critical issue is identifying and acting upon the opportunity, which in turn is a function of staying close to markets and responding quickly*. In any event, it is always useful during the process of identifying opportunities to recall Ducharme's Precept: 'Opportunity always knocks at the least opportune moment.'[1]

Competitors

Marketing also means how you differentiate yourself from competitors and, conversely, how they mark themselves from you. Product differentiation will take many different forms. It might involve product design including such things as features, quality and performance. It could mean service considerations over reliability, after-care support or credit terms. It might be intangibles like brands, images and fashion. In all cases, however, the objective is to differentiate the product by offering more perceived value.[11]

No market segment or niche can be evaluated without understanding the competition and no management team can know enough about the competition. A competitor should not be underestimated. If you survive in tough markets, you must be good at something. Moreover, no team should ever assume that competitors will stand back and let you take market share away from them. Sooner or later competitors will respond. Do you know competitors well enough to anticipate their responses and counter them?

You can begin to understand the competition by trying to profile each serious opponent in the following areas:

1. Product features and diversity

2. Geographical coverage

3. Market segment

4. Market share in each segment

5. Distribution channels

6. Marketing efforts such as branding

7. Product quality

8. Technological content or leadership

9. Research and development capability

10. Cost position

11. Pricing policy

12. Where they are developing future sales

13. Gearing, i.e. amount of borrowed funds in relationship to retained funds

14. Size

15. Type of ownership

Fortune magazine once ran an article on how to 'snoop' on competitors, i.e. collect data on the competition. Some of the novel techniques employed included the following items: milking potential recruits, picking brains at conferences, conducting phoney job interviews of people wanting to join or leave competitors, hiring people away, interviewing competitors, encouraging key customers to talk, getting customers to put out false bid requests, grilling suppliers, pumping buyers, studying aerial photographs, taking plant tours, taking competitor products apart and buying competitor's garbage.[12] Laughable, yes. Serious, yes. While amusing, the article stressed the importance of knowing your competition in order to anticipate their next strategic move.

A systematic search and analysis of competitors from conventional available sources is highly recommended. Among the possible places to look are your sales force, engineering staff, suppliers, distributors, advertising agencies, staff you take from competitors, conferences, trade journals, reporters, trade associations and stockbrokers, as well as all published sources open to the public.[13]

Service companies, too, are not immune from competition. Service is their primary means of product differentiation and the source of competitive advantage. In addition, customers are coming to expect more service which adds value. There is considerable pressure, therefore, continually to re-invent and re-present services.

Competitors have to be monitored continuously, because their actions can impact dramatically on your profitability and future plans. Accordingly, you need to create mechanisms to watch competitive products and services for performance, benefits, delivery, service, innovation and, most importantly, pricing. Moreover, information needs to flow freely from the marketplace to the appropriate senior managers.

What every company wants to be

What every medium sized company wants to be is *a niche player providing a specialist product or service at a premium price based on unique benefits.* That is certainly what every venture capitalist wants—the big return to make his or her portfolio attractive to future investors. This is about as close as you can get to describing their Holy Grail of venture.

What does this say to you? It clearly identifies the elements most attractive to outside investors. Let us break down this statement into its key parts:

1. A niche or segment player (avoiding major corporate attention and competition).

2. Specialist product or service (avoids competition from non-specialists).

3. Premium price (which means higher margins and, therefore, greater profitability).

4. Unique benefits (discourage the competition while retaining loyalty and dependency of customers).

Defend your segment or niche

On the other hand, if you exploit the Holy Grail it may attract competitors looking for the same combination of factors. In this case, competitors will be exploring your vulnerability, figuring how they can attack your privileged position. Michael Porter, the renowned authority on competitive advantage, commented on this point as follows: 'The key to growth—even survival—is to stake out a position that is less vulnerable to attack from head to head opponents, whether established or new, and less vulnerable to erosion from the direction of buyers, suppliers and substitute goods.'[14]

Again, the golden rule of market niches and segments is to lead them.

Market leadership brings measurable benefits. Research covering thousands of international products demonstrated beyond doubt that market leadership brought higher prices and consequently greater profits. While medium sized companies may not dominate major markets controlled by huge international corporations, they can aspire to rule selected segments in domestic and even international markets. Perhaps the most *important criterion* for ranking, therefore, is to ask if an opportunity has *the potential for you to become the market leader*. If so, what will it take to become market leader? Can you do it? How long will it take?

In this regard, Porter noted six classical barriers to entry which afford protection to existing players:

1. *Economies of scale*, but technology is fast changing this old stand-by.

2. *Product differentiation* remains an effective protection especially if you can brand the product or service.

3. *Capital requirements* still hold sway, although some flexible competitors like the mini steel mill have been proved to nibble away at even large-scale investments.

4. *Cost advantages* independent of size still exist in form of patents or know-how.

5. *Access to distribution channels* is proving a very potent leverage but is being challenged by specialist distribution companies who will warehouse and distribute products.

6. *Government policy* still creates protected positions but is subject to change albeit over a longer period.[14]

EXERCISE 7 WHAT ARE THE MARKET PLANS TO REALIZE THOSE BUSINESS OPPORTUNITIES?

After data collection and rigorous analysis, you have identified and ranked the possible opportunities. This is the first but critical step in formulating a market plan, which lists the actions you will take to convert the opportunity.

The market plan is the detailed strategy. The strategy is implemented through the market plan. No market plan—no strategy implementation. Michael Lawson writes that 'marketing . . . is the very essence of what corporate strategy is all about. Define a corporate strategy without a marketing plan and you have wasted your time.'[15] The market plan is implemented through a sales plan (see below).

As you might expect, marketeers have created some marvellous slogans. Here is a small sample:

1. 'The function of marketing is to plan, create, price, promote, and distribute goods and services.'[7]

2. 'Do it cheaper, do it better or do it different.'[13]

3. Marketing is all about the 4 P's—product, price, place and promotion.

Cliché or not, *marketing probably is the single most important aspect of business. The best compliment paid to a company is that it is 'market-led'. By that, people are saying the company succeeds by staying close to the market and providing a product and/or service to meet a real market need—and providing it in an innovative and effective way.* In one way, marketing is like the vision, everything important flows from it.

What is the difference between marketing and selling? A marketeer identifies the opportunity and determines the best route to penetrate the market. Identification is achieved through market research and the route is detailed in a market plan (see sample questions and format below). Selling is presenting the product and/or service to customers targeted by the market research and actually realizing the sale.

There are some principles of marketing that everyone should recognize and accept.

- You can never know enough about your marketplace. In order to know your marketplace, you must get into it and return to it on a regular basis. You must fight the tendency to stay inside your fortification because it is a 'safe' haven. There is nothing safe about staying inside your company, that is a false haven. The internal view is never real, because reality is out there, not in here.

- You need to know information about each relevant market segment.

- The key to unlocking market segments is to identify accurately the need(s) of common customers.

- Next provide a product or service that meets those real needs at a price customers will pay and which meets your financial requirements.

- Find the best route to the market at the most opportune time.

- Audit the market response and adjust the market plan based on customer and competitor responses and changes in the overall environment.

Market segments can be differentiated in at least five ways:

1. Using demographic data, such as family units, education, income, occupation, marital status and asset ownership.

2. Using behavioural traits, such as consumption, social classes, religion, etc.

3. Using physical characteristics, such as age, sex, health, physicality, etc.

4. Using special characteristics, such as intelligence, leisure habits, acquired tastes, etc.

5. Using market conditions, such as distribution methods, competition levels, etc.[7]

Business begins in markets. If you wish to stay in business, you need to stay close to markets. While there are numerous techniques and skills associated with marketing, *the fundamental prerequisite to becoming market-led or even market-driven rests with the commitment to understand and meet the real needs of customers.* The emphasis is on 'real' needs as distinguished from those that are illusory or artificially created. Real needs have a habit of staying around, while unreal needs can be fashionable and fickle. Real needs are tangible and capable of being recognized by your customers.

It is said that a management team is often surprised by what it discovers when systematically gathering hard facts about a marketplace for the first time.[8] But the process does not end there. In fact, it has just begun. As market segments and niches are continually changing, you must stay close to markets to respond to these changes. As Ohmae has commented:

'A farsighted entrepreneur does not forget for a moment which market segment he is servicing, what kind of service he is offering to what kinds of customers, or by what kind of mechanism he makes his profit. As long as he keeps all this clearly in mind, he will be highly sensitive to any changes in the market that may signal a change in the fundamental reasons for the existence of the business.'[2]

Key questions

What goes into a market plan? The best way to begin the market planning process is by looking at questions which should be raised. Here are some of the key questions for creating a market plan:

1. What is the market environment for your defined niche or segment?

2. What opportunities or threats are identifiable in that market environment?

3. How will you take advantage of these opportunities or threats? *Remember: any change can present an opportunity.*

4. Who are your customers? Will they change in the future?

5. What are their real needs? How do your customers use your product or service?

6. What are your product or service's characteristics? What are its strengths and weaknesses?

7. What are your product or service's unique selling points (USPs)?

8. How do you add value?

9. What does an analysis of your past sales and customer base reveal? Is Pareto's Principle applicable, i.e. that 20 per cent of customers will account for 80 per cent of revenue or profits? If so, what does this suggest?

10. What is your pricing policy?

11. What are the USPs of your main competitors? What are their strengths and weaknesses?

12. How do you compare with these competitors?

13. What is your target customer list?

14. How do they buy? When do they buy? Who does the buying?

15. What are the revenue, market share, growth or profitability targets?

16. How much is likely to come from the existing product portfolio and existing customer base including from price increases?

17. What is the 'revenue gap' between what is likely to come from existing products and customers and the amount projected?

18. How are you going to fill that gap, specifically, from new customers, new products and/or new markets? In other words, how are you going to generate the new business to fill the 'gap' between known and projected revenue?

19. Who makes the decision to buy within the target company?

20. What approach should be taken to each target company? Do you vary the approach with different types of customers?

21. What sales aids will you use?

22. What sales promotion will you employ?

23. Can you obtain editorial coverage?

24. What image are you trying to project?

25. How will you implement the market plan?

26. How will you monitor the market plan? Who should review progress against stated milestones, i.e. targets at specified future times?

27. How will you audit the market plan? Who should be informed of the audit results? *Note*: review progress, analyse market feedback and modify the plan accordingly.

28. When will you start the cycle again? *Note*: market plans need to be reviewed after the corporate plan review in order to adjust plans to changes in the company's vision, objectives or strategies.

Plan format

Once you have answered these questions, you can start creating the market plan. Market plans are made for a specific time period, usually for one year. After the year has passed, the actual experience should be compared formally to the projections. However, interim adjustments are made through use of the *market audit* (see below). In this regard, the following format is a useful guideline:

1.0 Introduction

    1.1 What you are trying to accomplish

    1.2 What assumptions you are making

    1.3 What revenue targets you have set

    1.4 What you anticipate will happen

2.0 Market environment

    2.1 Description of market environment for your defined niche(s) or market segment(s)

    2.2 What opportunities you identified, such as responses to pressure points, changes and trends

    2.3 What threats you have identified

    2.4 How you will take advantage of opportunities and deal with threats

3.0 Product or service

    3.1 Description of your product/service characteristics

    3.2 How your product/service is used

    3.3 Description of your USPs

    3.4 Your product/service strengths and weaknesses

    3.5 Specify what value you add

    3.6 How your product/service compares with the competition

4.0 Your market

    4.1 Description of target market niche(s) or segment(s)

    4.2 What strengths exist in the market that work for you

    4.3 What weaknesses exist in the market that work against you

5.0 Your customers

    5.1 Who they are

    5.2 What their real market needs are

    5.3 Analysis of past sales

    5.4 Analysis of customer base

6.0 Pricing policy

    6.1 How you set prices and whether you increase them

    6.2 What returns you require

7.0 Competition

    7.1 What their market segments are

    7.2 Who they are

    7.3 Their product/service characteristics

    7.4 Their USPs

    7.5 Their strengths and weaknesses

    7.6 How they sell

    7.7 Their environment, e.g. opportunities and threats

    7.8 How they develop their business

8.0 Marketing campaign

    8.1 Revenue targets

        8.1.1 From existing customer base, especially from price increases

        8.1.2 Revenue gap

        8.1.3 Amount needed from new customers

        8.1.4 Amount needed from new products

        8.1.5 Amount needed from new markets

    8.2 Target customer list

    8.3 Information required, e.g. financial profile, who buys, why, when and how

    8.4 Best approach

    8.5 New targets

    8.6 New approaches

    8.7 Product/service awareness and focus on target

    8.8 Image to convey

9.0 Sales campaign

    9.1 Sales aids

    9.2 Sales promotion

    9.3 Sales budget

The market plan audit

In order to stay close to market movements, a post-plan mechanism is essential. The device used is the periodical market audit which evaluates what has been done and what needs to be done based on actual marketplace experience. Market audits should become part of the management discipline and regular reporting procedures, especially at periodical reviews of the corporate plan (see Chapter 14).

A market audit is critical to the success of any market plan for the following reasons:

■ First, the market plan can become more effective if management analyses the elements of success through the market audit and understands how the plan has worked. This is achieved by comparing your assumptions with actual experience.

■ Second, markets are forever dynamic and changes may have occurred since the plan was devised and the audit is a mechanism to respond to the latest changes.

■ Third, the audit process looks at what is being done, evaluates it and then makes recommendations,[7] which puts the whole process on a systematic review basis which is good business practice (GBP).

■ Fourth, the market audit is a useful device for detecting future change and trends in the marketplace.

■ Fifth, the audit keeps management committed to what is happening in the marketplace and prevents people from saying the job is done once the market plan is formulated and agreed.

What distinguishes fast growing, successful companies from others? It will come as no surprise that the fast track companies have common success factors in marketing. Among the 30 successful medium sized companies in one study in the north-east of England, the following similar factors emerged:

1. Board members provided marketing expertise.

2. Marketing was highly regarded and fundamental to operations.

3. Customer and market information was selectively and quickly collected.

4. Senior managers were available to customers.

5. Customer care and quality were top priorities.

6. Customer problems were taken on board.

7. A positive corporate identity and culture were apparent.

8. Partnerships were formed with suppliers and distributors.

9. Key managers stayed in touch with customers.

10. Existing markets were developed before management rushed on to new products.[16]

Things were not fundamentally different in America. The top 100 fast growth companies were successful for two basic reasons: first, they put customers first by 'listening, understanding, serving'; second, they moved with 'relentless speed and adaptability'. The key remained quite simply to 'respond to customer wants and needs'. Michael Dell of Dell Computers, one of the fast trackers, said: 'our strategy puts us extremely close to our customer ... in stark contrast to the traditional IBM and Compaq approach of designing what they think is right and hoping customers will buy it'.[17]

Innovative marketing strategies

Some companies break new ground with innovative strategies that defy all the rules. In fact, unusual marketing approaches often differentiate a company from its competitors.

Body Shop International was founded in the United Kingdom by Anita Roddick and now operates in 37 countries with revenues of £116 million and profits of £20 million, selling its own products through franchise stores. Going against industry practice, Body Shop presents its products in plain packages and even gives a discount when the bottles are returned. Very little is spent on advertising, more resources go towards training people on product information and use. Consumers have responded positively to Body Shop's policies on the environment.

Marvin Lumber and Cedar Inc. in Warroad, Minnesota goes against industry practice by offering an enormous range of doors and windows in different sizes, panes and shapes. Chief Executive William Marvin will customize any order with a builder or architect's specification. Refusing to cut prices, Marvin Lumber has seen sales rise to $265 million over the last decade with 1 or 2 per cent better net margins than competitors.

Dubbed 'contrarian' marketeers, the leaders of these two businesses must have asked a lot of silly questions, such as 'why won't it work if we play the game the opposite of the way everyone else plays?'[18]

Another example of innovative marketing occurs when a company tries to reposition itself in the marketplace. In most cases, this involves going 'up market' to achieve higher prices and better margins for products and services.

The Churchill Group, a British manufacturer of pottery with 1992 sales estimated at £35 million and 1300 employees, decided to fill a need for 20-piece dish sets priced between £19.95 and £34.95. As the company operated 'down market' in price competitive items, the move to more expensive products placed considerable demands on the management. Accordingly, Churchill had to look hard at its markets and conduct its first market research into prices and features for middle market customers. This effort led to the appointment of the company's first marketing manager and, naturally, more market research. Churchill now stays close to trends in the home. Meanwhile, the up-market range is expected to hit sales of £6 million with margins three times higher at 15 per cent.[19]

Database marketing

A recent development is database marketing, i.e. selling goods or services to a preselected, highly targeted group of potential customers.

Dell Computers of Austin, Texas, innovated database marketing of computers directly to customers (see case study in Chapter 10). In so doing, Dell built up a detailed profile of its customers and used that database to sell other products. Marketing was done on the telephone, not in retail stores, with all the commensurate savings in overheads.

Databases enable a company to test-market new products and services very quickly and efficiently. They also allow companies to move fast into a marketplace with all the attendant advantages in manufacturing to order. The essence of database marketing is building an individual relationship with a customer. Computer technology and software developments have made this direct marketing technique possible and effective.

Database marketing has many distinct advantages such as repeat sales, customer loyalty, cross-promotions and developing and launching new products. All of these advantages impact favourably on sales and profits and save on costs. Database marketing is rapidly becoming a source of strategic advantage. When a company stays very close to a customer before, during and after the sale, a buyer is likely to be satisfied and will buy again.[20]

Direct Line Insurance Company (see case study in Chapter 10) and First Direct, a home telephone banking service launched by Midland Bank in the United Kingdom, are current examples of database marketing.

Strategies for service companies

While the above marketing comments are applicable to all companies, service firms have special circumstances and requirements. In developed countries, more workers are employed in services than in manufacturing. For example, more than 75 per cent of American workers are employed in service industries such as communications, transportation, health care, distribution, financial services, government and professional firms. In addition, between 65 and 75 per cent of people in manufacturing industries are performing service tasks like sales, research, logistics, maintenance, design and administration. More than 75 per cent of all costs are related to provision of services.[21]

The following observations are worth making about service companies:

1. Unlike manufacturing, services usually are 'consumed' at the same time they are produced. Their value to the customer is created at the instant of contact.

2. Economies of scale in service companies depend on the smallest service unit which can be made efficient and reproduced throughout the company, leaving automation and computerization to allow more time to be spent on customers and enabling less experienced staff to do complex things with much less training.

3. Some service businesses are turning their companies upside down to make everyone work on customer contact. As first impressions do last, everyone is urged to put what they can into every 'brief customer encounter'.[22]

4. Performance measurement is critical in service businesses. Therefore, you need to ask 'three questions. What has happened? Why has it happened? What are we going to do about it?'[23]

5. Quality of product and service are inseparable.

6. The same design, product and delivery are expected to be correct every time.

7. As innovation increases and competition intensifies, yesterday's 'excellent' service might not be as appreciated this year, because customers are demanding high quality in services like they have come to demand in products.[24]

8. Increasingly, product differentiation is becoming the key element in competition, making the way the product is delivered and maintained the source of market differentiation.

9. Successful quality and service delivery require a lot of painstaking efforts, such as market research, training and constant measurement.

10. Service delivery depends on employee attitudes and behaviour.

11. Companies need to measure customer satisfaction.

12. Companies need to find out what competitors are doing by buying their products and testing their services.[25]

13. Britain faces a particularly difficult up-hill battle for customer care. For various reasons, customer care remains an elusive experience. Explanations lie deep in entrenched attitudes, corporate cultures and national character. Change demands radically different attitudes and behaviour, starting with top management. It is all very foolish, because good customer care is not expensive but bad care can be costly spending 'a huge amount of staff time resisting complaints, refusing compensation and fending off customers'.[26] Many of these attitudes arise from the British class system where service is still considered a demeaning and subservient act.

14. If you want to provide a decent service, a European survey of 1000 managers listed the following nine questions for consideration:

   ■ Do you explain the company's customer service policy to all employees?

   ■ Have you agreed performance bench-marks with your staff?

   ■ Do you measure service regularly and discuss the results with employees?

   ■ Do you remind staff through discussions that customers always come first?

   ■ Do you ask employees for their views on customer needs and expectations?

   ■ Do you ask customers about their needs and if they are satisfied with your performance?

   ■ Do you set an example for staff when dealing with customers?

   ■ Do you work with your management team to remove obstacles to good service like poor facilities, delays and discourtesy?

   ■ Do you look regularly at service performance of competitors?[27]

A good example of concern over customer service is provided by London's Underground or 'Tube' system. Management has proclaimed a three-year programme to turn the Underground into a modern railway delivering customer satisfaction. The most important improvement will be to get train intervals right. If two-minute intervals are not maintained and trains run at one and three minutes instead, three-quarters of all passengers experience 50 per cent greater passenger loadings. In other words, the Underground's management is focusing on overcrowding as the main component in customer satisfaction. Maintaining the right intervals will require considerable discipline and training. The future of the Underground's management team hinges on this commitment to customer service.[28]

Summary

1. You start the strategy-making process by asking: What and where are the best opportunities?

2. Look for opportunities with the highest return and lowest risk which are the easiest to convert.

3. Start your search by first looking at opportunities among your existing products, services and customers.

4. New opportunities require data collection and analysis and need to be seen from the customer's point of view.

5. Marketing involves differentiating your product and service from competitors, therefore you need to profile and continually monitor the competition.

6. Most medium sized companies would like to be a niche player, providing a specialist product or service at a premium price based on unique benefits.

7. Leadership of market niches or segments brings clear benefits in higher margins, greater profits and security.

8. Market plans are strategies and need to be based on extensive market knowledge.

9. Market plans need to be audited on a regular basis and modified where appropriate.

10. As markets continually change, you must stay close to markets to respond.

11. Any change can be an opportunity.

12. There are special requirements for service companies.

References

1. Arthur Bloch, *Murphy's Law Book Two: More Reasons Why Things Go Wrong*, Price, Stern, Sloan, Los Angeles, 1980.

2. Kenichi Ohmae, *The Mind of the Strategist: Business Planning for Competitive Advantage*, Penguin, London, 1983.

3. R. L. Wing, *The Art of Strategy: A New Translation of Sun Tzu's Classic The Art of War*, Aquarian, London, 1989.

4. Thomas Stewart, 'The most fascinating ideas for 1991' *Fortune International,,* 14 January 1991.

5. Antony Thorncroft, 'Market research in the UK: a preoccupation with predators', *Financial Times*, 9 March 1989.

6. Daniel Krumin, 'Satisfying the customer is serious business', *Directors and Boards*, **13**(1), Autumn 1988.

7. Herbert Holtje, *Theory and Problems of Marketing*, McGraw-Hill, New York, 1981.

8. Barrie Pearson, *Common-Sense Business Strategy: How to Improve Your Profits and Cash Flow Dramatically*, Mercury, London, 1987.

9. Christopher Lorenz, 'The timing revolution', *Financial Times*, 21 August 1991.

10. Cliff Bowman, *The Essence of Strategic Management*, Prentice-Hall, London, 1990.

11. Stephen Young, 'Manufacturing under pressure', *Management Today*, July 1988.

12. Arthur Sharplin, *Strategic Management*, McGraw-Hill, New York, 1985.

13. John Argenti, *Practical Corporate Planning*, Unwin Hyman, London, 1989.

14. Michael Porter, 'How competitive forces shape strategy', David Asch and Cliff Bowman (eds), *Readings in Strategic Management*, Macmillan, London, 1989.

15. Michael Lawson, *Going for Growth: A Guide to Corporate Strategy*, Kogan Page, London, 1987.

16. Charles Batchelor, 'Secrets of marketing success', *Financial Times*, 14 January 1992.

17. Alan Deutschman, 'America's fastest risers', *Fortune International*, 7 October 1991.

18. Allan Magrath, 'Contrarian marketing', *Across the Board*, October 1990.

19. Charles Batchelor, 'Crossing the Ts on going up-market', *Financial Times*, 12 May 1992.

20. *The Journal on General Management*, 'Manager update', 3 (1), Autumn 1991.

21. James Quinn, Thomas Doorley and Penny Paquette, 'Beyond products: services-based strategy', *Harvard Business Review*, March/April 1990.

22. *Economist*, 'Management focus: serve them right', 5 May 1990.

23. T. J. Brignall, L. Fitzgerald, R. Johnston and R. Silvestro, 'Performance measurement in service businesses', *Management Accounting*, January 1991.

24. Christopher Lorenz, 'When service with a smile is missing by a mile', *Financial Times*, 10 January 1992.

25. Simon Holberton, 'The key to product differentiation', *Financial Times*, 26 June 1991.

26. Philip Sadler, 'Why do the British hate their customers?', *Director*, March 1991.

27. Michael Skapinker, 'Putting the theory into practice', *Financial Times*, 31 March 1989.

28. Richard Tomkins, 'It's our fault, we admit it', *Financial Times*, 11 December 1991.

Strategy Part III—Resources

There ain't no such thing as a free lunch.[1]

CRANE'S LAW

Introduction

Having looked at opportunities and selected the best ones, the emphasis now shifts to converting these opportunities. In order to realize opportunities you will need resources.

WHAT RESOURCES WILL BE NEEDED TO CONVERT THE OPPORTUNITIES?

How will you find the resources needed to convert these opportunities? Invariably, resources will fall into one of three groups:

1. Funds, i.e. money

2. People, i.e. new and/or existing staff with improved performance

3. Technology, i.e. new ways of doing things with hardware (plant and equipment) or software (know-how and processes)

Resources should be allocated 'to minimize the impact of weaknesses, avoid threats, and apply strengths to take advantage of opportunities'.[2] A clear list of resource needs should emerge as you examine each opportunity.

Strengths and weaknesses

Now let us return to our old friend, strengths and weaknesses. After the vision exercise, you made a realistic assessment of strengths and weaknesses. They should be considered again when dealing with resources. As a general guideline, *resources should be allocated to enhance strengths and address and correct weaknesses.* In short, play to your strengths but do not forget to deal with your weaknesses.

Often weaknesses take the form of obstacles which have accumulated over time. Some of these obstacles may be physical, such as production bottlenecks, insufficient space, outdated equipment and suchlike. Many obstacles, however, involve people or people-related issues. One common obstacle is the failure to deal with a key, long-serving employee who might be sitting reluctantly on the management team or strangling an important middle level function. Konosuke Matsushita, founder of Matsushita Electric Company, recognized this point when he said 'keeping the wrong man in the wrong place puts an obstacle in the way of success for any business'.[3] Other common problems are remuneration levels and lack of incentives among key employees.

These weaknesses need to be recognized and addressed, because they can cripple your team's efforts to move forward with the plan. Sometimes weaknesses can be converted into strengths with the right thinking and action. At the very least weaknesses should be isolated or neutralized. If possible, they should be reduced and eventually eliminated. Regarding people-related obstacles, there is one guiding thought: either people are with you or they are not. As Leo Tolstoy wrote: 'there are no successful games without enthusiastic participants'.[4] Performance usually flows from enthusiasm and both are bench-marks of an individual's commitment.

This simple model illustrates the relationship between strengths and weaknesses on one hand and opportunities and threats on the other.

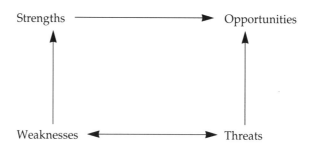

This diagram shows how opportunities should be addressed through strengths, i.e. the company should build on its strengths. Weaknesses, on the other hand, are often aligned with threats, and the ability to respond to threats, if the company is hampered by weaknesses. Weaknesses can detract from strengths and threats can attack opportunities.

Accordingly, the company needs at least to neutralize weaknesses and, hopefully, to remove them in order to deal more effectively with the external world. Remember, *you can do something positive about things inside your company because they are within your direct control.* You need to be in the best shape possible to meet things outside your control, i.e. outside the company.

Another criterion for selecting strategies, therefore, would be the number of strengths you bring to a given opportunity compared to the number of weaknesses associated with that opportunity. This criterion should be considered in addition to the basic criterion mentioned in Chapter 7.

Funds

Every opportunity will have a quantifiable financial dimension. Every business activity will have either one or both types of financial requirements: fixed and working capital.

Fixed capital requirements are the cost of tangible assets required to start or expand an activity to provide enough capacity to serve the market segment or niche. Most fixed capital commitments are made prior to the conversion of an opportunity. Consequently, there can be considerable time pressures to complete a project on schedule because profits have to be generated within a specified time to pay back the investment.

Working capital requirements determine how much money is needed to support the new activity once trading has begun. Cash flow movements try to project this financial requirement. Time pressures on working capital come from the race to reach a cash neutral position and break-even point. Once break even is reached profits can be generated to pay back the original capital investment and the team can relax in the knowledge that the leakage is over.

The total funding package for any opportunity, therefore, will be the sum of fixed and working capital requirements. The package should also include a calculation for servicing the money if borrowed and for interest lost if financed out of reserves. In addition, *prudent management teams add a contingency element to cover eventualities, i.e. if things do not go to plan* (see Risk in Chapter 9).

People

Human resources are needed for every project. People are required to run a project (direct inputs) and manage a project (indirect inputs). Moreover, the right people are needed to convert opportunities. *People* realize opportunities, not funds and technology on their own. Sometimes managers get blinded by the technology involved or the amount of funds at risk, yet managers should never forget that people are the vital ingredient and the main reason why projects either succeed or fail.

The right people for your project may exist inside the organization. If not, they have to be recruited from outside. Special training programmes for project management may be required to develop this important capability within the company. What is not always recognized is that selection of the right people for a project carries considerable risk. If the people assigned to a new activity do not perform, the activity will suffer or fail. *A prudent management team handles this risk by monitoring perform-ance against milestones and conducting periodical reviews of progress against plan* (see Chapter 11).

It is very important to think through your human requirements. You need to find the right people to ensure a successful conversion of an opportunity and create an effective monitoring system to measure pro-gress.

Technology

Technology involves change. In fact, by definition, it is always changing, but technology changes at different times in different markets and for different reasons. These changes are not limited to hardware (equipment) but also include software (processes). Your best insurance against choos-ing the wrong technology is to understand fully the marketplace in which your opportunity lives.

We noted in Chapter 7 that the dynamics of your market can also be expressed in technological trends and product life cycles. These trends and cycles will indicate the latest technological requirements. An exhaustive evaluation of equipment and process suppliers will provide an insight into the prevailing technological 'art' and likely future course of development.

Timing can be a crucial factor. For example, it can be a distinct advantage to enter a market with the latest and best technology, especially if competitors are left with old technology, low productivity and high costs. On the other hand, you could be at a disadvantage if developments are fast moving and competitors are able to leap frog over you with even newer technology.

The rate of technological change and product life cycles are critical factors in any market. Slow moving markets often present unique opportu-nities if you access and apply the right technology. Fast moving markets offer a considerable challenge which may present only a momentary window of opportunity. Fast moving markets can make extraordinary demands on innovation and marketing and certainly are not for the faint hearted. On the other hand, if you get it right, the rewards in the form of premium prices and sizeable margins can be attractive. Often the major attraction is selling the successful technology to a larger company at a substantial premium.

EXERCISE

9

HOW WILL YOU OBTAIN THESE RESOURCES?

You have identified the resources required to convert the opportunities, but how do you go about obtaining the resources? Resources can come from two places: inside or outside the company. Internal (organic) resources are accumulated over time and retained in the business. External (inorganic) resources are ones that must be obtained, usually contracted, outside the organization.

Funds

Organically, funds can be released from cash reserves or realized from asset disposals. Your company may be in the enviable position of having enough cash to finance the new opportunity. Also, the management team may wish to realize less productive assets to finance new opportunities which offer greater potential returns. Often teams do not think in terms of exchanging assets in this way. *Management teams should always consider disposing of activities that fail to perform in order to finance better opportunities.*

However, many companies do not have ready cash or realizable assets to finance new opportunities. In these circumstances the management team will usually turn to a corporate financial device. The following financial devices are most often used to fund new developments:

1. Bank credit line or overdraft facility.

2. Bank lending against assets on an instalment basis, e.g. leasing or hire purchasing.

3. Venture capital equity finance.

4. Development capital finance involving preference shares and/or debentures.

5. Private placements through investment or merchant banks and corporate finance departments in stock brokerages or directly with financial institutions such as pension funds and insurance companies.

6. Publicly quoted stock listing or offering.

Presentation of a corporate plan is often a determining factor in winning bank and investor support. A corporate plan shows that management is thinking its way to the future and provides an excellent insight into management's 'game plan'. In some countries, such as Britain, the presentation of a corporate plan from medium sized companies is such a rarity that it produces a very positive response from financial institutions.

People

People are funny. Unlike money and technology, people need to be motivated, they need to be 'turned on' to perform better and produce the best results. People are attracted by an exciting, vibrant environment which offers stimulating and challenging work combined with rewards based on results. If you want to attract and retain high quality people, you need to provide most if not all of the following:

1. Shared decision making

2. Personal growth opportunities

3. Company growth opportunities

4. Personal support and encouragement

5. Incentives and rewards

The best people are looking for participation rights in companies. A title and perks might have been sufficient for most people in the past, but this is no longer true. People want to be respected. They are demanding responsibility with authority. And they also want stroking.

From the employee's point of view, respect flows from positive leadership, performance and concern for individuals. Nowhere is this more true than in 'people' businesses where the product is individual creativity. On the other hand, all companies have become people businesses in the sense that people-handling skills and sensitivities are critical in today's businesses.

Do not shy from paying large bonuses for results which otherwise would not have been achieved. There should be room in every organization to recognize and reward outstanding achievements. Otherwise, there is not much point in continuing to produce outstanding results. Remuneration levels should be competitive. They need to be high enough to attract the best people in the first instance and then maintained at a level that will retain them. Sometimes there is a difficult problem of differentials between pay for existing employees and more attractive packages required to attract new people. Often the best way to bridge this gap is through performance-related bonuses. In any event, the age old adage certainly applies here: 'if you pay peanuts, you get monkeys'.

People issues receive varying attention from company to company. Most businesses try to do something about remuneration, differentials and incentives. Others ignore non-pecuniary issues which sometimes are more important than money. For example, shared decision making, challenging and stimulating work, personal opportunity and the buzz around the place can mean more to bright, creative and productive individuals than the size of their salaries.

Do you spend time on these 'soft' aspects of the working environment? How much thought and attention has been devoted to all members of the management team? To middle managers? To junior managers? People issues require careful consideration. Such issues should be at the top of a chief executive's agenda, beginning with the management team. People issues involve leadership and style too. All leaders need to motivate their people. In fact, the leader's most important task is managing the management team and thereby achieving the desired results. While more time will be spent on people and culture issues in Chapter 13, it is worth noting now that *people are assets* who require developing and managing. In many successful companies, people are the best asset and create a competitive advantage in their own right.

Technology

You have identified the technological requirements necessary to convert an opportunity. Now how do you acquire them?

Equipment can be sourced from suppliers. Usually, there will be a market leader for the type of technology you seek; although sometimes a technology is developed and used exclusively in-house by a competitor and consequently will be unavailable to you. If you are looking at purchasing technology to convert an opportunity, do your homework. Take a detailed look at what is being offered in the marketplace. Make a judgement about the useful technical life of existing equipment, because enabling technologies are changing capital goods radically. Also, demand user references from suppliers and find out how the equipment really performed from people who used it.

Technology, know-how and processes, can be obtained from various sources, such as technical consultants, universities, technology transfer houses, customers and suppliers. Technology also can be generated internally through research and development efforts. However, R&D can be too expensive for smaller companies and even some medium sized ones. Most companies are well advised to concentrate on applications, i.e. on the 'D' of R&D.

A major advantage that small and medium companies hold over large ones is staying close to the market. This helps to identify real market needs and meet those needs faster than larger companies. Smaller companies should not throw away this advantage by trying to compete with big R&D spends by huge companies, and they should avoid taking a high risk position by concentrating all resources on one technology.

I have never met a successful company that was technology-led and stayed that way. Rather, the best companies were ones that developed or acquired technology to meet real market needs but remained market-led or market driven. They used technology to differentiate their position in the market and gain market share. Technology became another means to the end, not an end in itself.

There is a 'technology trap'. Technology-led companies often fall in love with their technology to the exclusion of customer needs and competition. Such traps have destroyed many promising companies. Worse still some technology-led firms get caught up in missionary selling. They have to educate the customer first before he or she will buy the product.

Invariably, there often are post-sale problems, such as arguments over performance, interpretation of results, reproducibility of results or 101 issues involved with new technology. Also, technology-led companies can get the timing wrong for the use of their technology, remaining well ahead of the market's realization of the need for their technology.

Given all these negatives, it is understandable how investors shy away from new technology companies. On the other hand, new technologies are exciting. If they meet clear market needs and those needs are recognized by customers, new technology companies can flourish and prosper—not because they are technology led but because they meet a real market need.

Never become a technological missionary. We all know what happened to the early missionaries. Leave that work to universities and large corporations.

Summary

1. After identifying and prioritizing the best opportunities, resources will be required to convert them.

2. Resources invariably involve funds, people or technology or a combination thereof.

3. Resources should be allocated behind strengths and used to minimize weaknesses.

4. Funds are generated internally through retained earnings or asset disposals or externally through corporate financial devices.

5. People demand more than money and management needs to be sensitive and responsive to people-related issues.

6. Technology can be generated internally but companies are advised to focus on development in contrast to research. Companies should be market driven, not technologically led. Avoid the technology trap and missionary selling.

References

1. Arthur Bloch, *Murphy's Law and Other Reasons Why Things Go Wrong*, Methuen, London, 1979.

2. Arthur Sharplin, *Strategic Management*, McGraw-Hill, New York, 1985.

3. Richard Pascale and Anthony Athos, *The Art of Japanese Management: Applications for American Executives*, Warner, New York, 1981.

4. Sidney Bloch, *Money Talk: A Lucrative Cocktail*, Buchan & Enright, London, 1986.

Strategy Part IV—Risks and threats

*Strategy is when you keep right on firing
even though you're out of ammunition in
the hope nobody will notice.*

ANON'S LAW ON STRATEGY[1]

Introduction

You have identified and prioritized the best opportunities and know the resources required to convert them. Now you should look at threats to the strategies which might affect the outcomes. If you are prepared for eventualities, the strategies will have a much better chance of succeeding.

WHAT ARE THE CRITICAL RISKS, EXTERNAL THREATS AND RESPONSES TO YOUR STRATEGIES?

EXERCISE

10

Another important part of looking outside the company is to recognize risks and threats and then devise responses that will protect strategies. In this regard, 'threats often are defined in terms of competitors, while opportunities are usually thought of as new technologies and markets'.[2]

Change

The first external threat is change itself. As one leading business magazine described the modern commercial environment: 'Markets emerge and disappear seemingly overnight. The competition is smarter, ever quicker. Product life-cycles are shrinking. To keep up, executives demand flexibility, nimbleness, customer focus. Year by year, America's corporations centralize, decentralize, reorganize, reengineer. . . . Too often, leaders are slow to recognize the need for change . . . until it's too late.'[3]

Companies in the 1980s faced unprecedented competition in the global market from low cost producers which had been kept out previously but often were equipped by the First World companies who are now suffering. Firms also had to deal with rapid technological change which dated products and services quicker, impacting on production processes and productivity.[1]

The computer industry is an example of one industry racked by change and near turmoil. Constant technological changes and short product life cycles led to sharp reductions in profits and frantic price cutting and restructuring. But none of the responses restored sales and profits. After almost two decades in which sales grew by more than 20 per cent a year, the industry in America and most of Europe has come to a 'sudden and shuddering halt'.[4]

Competition

The threat from competition can arise from many different sources. Here are some possible areas from which competitive threats can emerge:

1. *Existing competitors in your home market as well as foreign markets.* Foreign competition is a major issue in the American domestic market and will become one in the European Economic Community after 1992 with the advent of open borders.

2. *Suppliers who choose to enter your market as an integration move.* One of your suppliers may be doing a strategic planning exercise and might identify an opportunity to take share and eventual leadership in your market. The usual restraining factor against such action is a reluctance to lose customers by becoming a competitor, but sometimes the attraction to a supplier is greater than the threat of lost business. After all, suppliers are in an excellent position to learn about your market, especially if they supply you and your competitors.

3. *Customers who choose to move backwards into your market as an integration move.* While this is less common than forward integration, there are examples of backward integration when circumstances permit and opportunities are attractive enough.

4. *New entrants might come from unexpected directions,* such as a recent acquisition which converts a minor competitor into a new force. Another surprise might come from a conglomerate moving into your market with a start-up or through the purchase of a customer base in a backward or forward integration move.

5. *Substitute products might come from unrelated industries.* This blind side move can produce real surprises, usually after aggressive pricing has made substitute products more competitive, or a major technological development might have allowed new products to enter your market. Often substitutes seem to fall from the sky because they never were regarded as threats or seemed to have little or no application in your market.

The classical barriers or defensive actions against new competitors are as follows:

1. Size

2. Cost to set up

3. Cost to acquire a competitor

4. Customer loyalty

5. Brand name strength

6. Access to customers

7. Secure distribution networks and channels

8. How long it takes to learn your business (the experience curve)

9. Technical know-how and/or patents

10. Legislative or governmental protection

How secure is your industry? Is your business or industry protected by any of these barriers to entry?

International

Some competitive threats are international. Probably the most respected competitors in the world are the Japanese. Japanese management techniques are studied in the hope of finding something useful for Western companies. How different from a few decades ago when people in the West believed that all the Japanese could do was copy products made by others! Now who is copying whom?

The Japanese influence is creeping into Western economies as Japanese firms take over Western companies or start up new operations to avoid duty barriers. For example, British Rover's former parts and accessories division, Unipart, has converted its Coventry plant to several Japanese practices. Production equipment is state-of-the-art and all 175 employees wear uniforms, enjoying the same status without special parking, canteens or washrooms. Rewards are based on knowledge and linked to quality. Supervisors are gone, replaced by team leaders in small, flexible teams.[5]

It is very human to denigrate the opposition. It certainly is easier to sneer than to take competitors seriously and do something about them. Meanwhile, the Japanese are backing more and more R&D and taking a long view of future opportunities for products and services. Japanese companies are determined to maintain a competitive edge in their markets and remain committed to increasing market share. Several observers have noted that the Japanese take a long time to make a decision, looking at an opportunity from every conceivable angle. However, once the decision is taken, they move very quickly, commit resources and stay the course.

Western car manufacturers have suffered at the hands of Japanese competition. According to Time Magazine, 'Japan's most important advantage is its management system: the way it deals with employees, suppliers, dealers and customers.' A recent study of the Japanese automobile industry at the prestigious Massachusetts Institute of Technology came to the conclusion that their advantages stemmed from just a few factors such as teamwork, resource efficiency and 'a tireless commitment to improving quality'.[6]

Threats

What about other threats? One way to look at external threats is by asking the following questions:

1. How uncertain is the environment?

2. What are the factors creating the uncertainty?

3. What are the reasons for the uncertainty?

4. After isolating each factor, how can they be dealt with?

How can you tell if a threat is really important? The best way to rank threats is by estimating their impact on your key business factors, such as market share, customer base and margins. You are looking for things that would impact severely on your fortunes. If the impact is substantial, you have a substantial threat.

Most external threats fall into the following groupings:

1. *Political changes*, such as a change in government, new or proposed legislation, taxation changes, nationalism, political crisis, threat of war, revolutions and other extreme upheavals.

2. *Economic changes*, such as growth rates, inflation, interest, unemployment, exchange rates, labour costs, raw material costs, demand and shifts in world trade.

3. *Social changes*, such as population trends, especially demographic shifts affecting the labour market, education, mobility, skill levels, life styles and working conditions.

4. *Technological changes*, such as evolutionary or gradual breakthroughs, enabling technologies like IT and biotechnology, new products, new processes, new methods and applications.

5. *Changes in your industry*, such as more or fewer competitors, larger or smaller companies, mergers, demergers, new entrants, new specifications, market segmentation, distribution patterns, new customers and new suppliers.

Argenti breaks threats into eight categories: the industry, political, economic, social, technical, local, national and world. Of these, your industry is
the most immediate concern. How is your industry changing, if at all?
What is happening with your customers? Competitors? Suppliers? What is
likely to happen to each over the next five years? Are there clear trends or
indications? After looking at all these possibilities, what is really significant? Remember, you need to respond to the important changes, not
everything that happens. You are looking for what Argenti calls the
'elephants', the really big things you cannot ignore.[7]

Ohmae flagged five environmental factors which he felt would affect all
businesses in the 1990s: growth would remain low; markets would mature
and strategies would be stalemated; resources would be distributed
unevenly; international complexities would be greater; and inflation
would not be reversed. He believes the inevitable responses would be
lower break-even points, vertical integration, restructured industries and
accelerated product life cycles.[8]

According to a survey conducted by accountants Arthur Young, now
Ernst and Young, the key issues facing American companies in the 1990s
will be hostile takeovers, strategic planning, long-term positioning, survival and management succession.[9] Charles Handy notes three broad
changes which would affect companies in the 1990s: first, a movement
from labour-intensive manufacturing; second, a movement to knowledge-
based organizations; and third, a movement towards service.[10]

Examples

A brief sampling of real external threats will illustrate this subject.

The collapse of the USSR and melt down of the Cold War are having a
profound impact on Western defence industries. Even the United Kingdom
is having its problems, as indirect and direct employment tied to defence
spending is estimated to drop from 625 000 jobs to less than 500 000 in
five years. Nor is the transition from defence to non-defence an easy
exercise for companies. It took the Dowty Group six years to reduce
military aerospace sales from 60 to 33 per cent of the company's total
revenues.[11]

An excellent example of technological change is provided by the current
race to build more powerful computers which will sell at cheaper prices. In
an industry already buffeted by an unprecedented rate of technological
change, the computer industry is about to be hit again, this time with
superscalar microprocessors able to process more than one instruction
simultaneously. People are talking about desktop supercomputers selling
for $10 000 which will have capabilities for speech and image processing
and artificial intelligence applications. These awesome price/performance
trends threaten to 'undermine' industry economics already under considerable pressure.[12]

Demographic changes can have a profound impact on industries, but sometimes the pattern is not clear cut. For example, Britain, like other European countries, will experience an ageing population, yet the impact on the way products are designed, manufactured and marketed will be more complicated than a mere shift from younger to older people. There will be at least three significant consequences for industry:

- The 1990s will end three decades of youth domination of culture and commerce.

- Consumer and related industries will need to manage a structural adjustment from youth to older markets.

- Another adjustment will be required away from mass markets with standard products to more segmented markets with individual products.[13]

Sometimes demographic changes conceal trends. For example, an ageing population together with inflation in property values is resulting in significant transfer of assets from one generation to the next through inheritances.

Changing attitudes among the working population can impact on a company's future. For the first time Japan is experiencing an upheaval in its labour market: power is shifting to employees, because there is an acute shortage of labour. A tighter labour market is forcing hours down and increasing job switching. Toyota, for example, had to cut production by 150 000 vehicles because it promised to reduce the annual hours worked by 100 to 2200 hours.

Moreover, attitudes are changing in Japan with more affluence and wider choice of jobs, raising motivation of workers as a new problem. Japan is not maintaining a stable population because the birth rate is falling 27 per cent below the number of births needed to remain level. As a consequence, school graduates will decline by 22 per cent by the year 2000. Even now there are almost twice the number of jobs available as there are people to fill them. What impact, indeed, will the erosion of lifetime employment and a change in the docile workforce have on Japan's industrial performance?[14]

It will also be interesting to see the effect of these changes on unpaid overtime which, in a recent survey, is relied on by 88 per cent of Japanese companies. Unions estimate that the actual hours worked each year average 2400 although the official estimate is 2052 and the target is 1800.[15] Concerns have been expressed in Japan about the fabled 'work ethic' and whether or not Japan has peaked in economic performance, because individualism is insidiously creeping into Japanese life and there are too many modern comforts.[16]

The Single European Market posed a very clear threat to traditional custom brokers who staged one day strikes in protest. When the frontiers fall on 1 January 1993, so do their jobs: 'no customers, no custom brokers'.[17]

A different threat motivated the American conglomerate, Tenneco: the fear of a takeover and break-up of the group to realize more shareholder value. This threat led to an exhaustive review of the company's performance. As a result, the core business, the oil division, was sold to reduce an immense debt burden and focus shifted to the rest of the business. Since implementing the new strategy in 1989, Tenneco's performance has improved markedly.[18]

What about your adopted strategy as a threat? Adopted strategies can become self-inflicted threats if they are seriously flawed. In this regard, it is well worth looking at the most common failures associated with strategy creation and implementation. McKinsey and Company noted the following potential failures:

- Mistaken focus on where, not how, to compete.

- Strategy not unique or adaptable.

- Not enough attention paid to timing.

- The wrong measures used to determine success.[19]

Another pitfall was identified by Kevan Scholes, who wrote 'that managers have grown to regard strategic change as one-off "big-bang" changes to their organisation. . . . The vast majority of strategic change occurs in an incremental way.'[20] Planning is meant to be a continual process involving monitoring and periodical reviews. When a feedback loop is made part of the plan implementation, the dangers of one-off complacency are reduced if not eliminated. Another often overlooked threat involves the bought-in, pre-packaged and off-the-shelf solutions sold as customized strategies by some large management consultancies. There is no substitute for the strategic plan you devise and own, which clearly is preferable to an outsider's solution.

On the other hand, there is an inexplicable reliance on outside 'experts' to solve a company's problems. British companies, for some reason, use far more consultants than their counterparts in France or Germany. Strategic planning should benefit with the right type of outside inputs (see Chapter 15), but the need and responsibility must rest with the management team.

In any event, the best protection against a flawed strategy is to do your homework. If you do market research correctly and regularly audit the results of your marketing effort, paying close attention to the feedback from critical sources, your strategy should not be flawed or, if there is a problem, it can be corrected. *Remember the cardinal rule: any change can be an opportunity and that applies to threats too.*

Risk

Another very common but often overlooked threat is risk *per se*, that is, the risk of things going wrong. According to Michael Lawson, 'being in business is all about taking risks but those risks must be assessed, controlled and minimised. If you don't do so you're not in business, you're merely a gambler.'[21] Sir John Harvey-Jones agrees. He said that 'the whole of business is about taking an acceptable risk. Companies that take no risk disappear. Companies that take unacceptable risk plainly also disappear.'[22]

Forward planning is important before *making commitments, not after. If risks are considered an integral part of the planning process, you will realize two important things: first, if the risks are shown to be too great, you can abort the commitment or find a way to lower the risk; and second, if things go worse than forecast, you will have a fallback plan.* Risk planning is good planning and it starts with the discipline of sensitivity analysis. Sensitivity analysis measures the impact on a project from various negatives, such as longer time to introduce a new product, lower sales than forecast and higher costs than anticipated. Identify the things that can go wrong and measure their impact on the project's future performance. If the project is too sensitive, that is, will not be viable after minimal impact from identified negatives, you should consider deferment or abandonment if no way can be found to reduce the risk.

Another way to deal with risk is to provide a financial contingency which would absorb some or all of the negative impact identified during the sensitivity analysis. An often overlooked element in risk analysis is how feasible the project is to do. If an investment project is based on familiar technology and processes, it becomes more feasible and less risky. If the project is totally new and involves new technology or a new process, the risk will increase.

One medium sized company accepted a contract worth half its existing sales, but the new contract involved an untested process. It took that company four years to optimize the process during which time it did not make a profit and diverted an excessive amount of management and financial resources to the new project. Big projects can cause big distortions and carry big risks, yet all everybody thinks about is the big benefits. Always look at the downside. There is no balanced decision making if everyone concentrates on the upside.

Much of this risk can be minimized by rigorous advanced planning before the project work begins. The Japanese have a well-deserved reputation for minute advanced planning involving endless debate and evaluation followed by very fast implementation and expected performance. Sometimes it is worth subjecting your plans to the review of outside professionals just to be on the safe side, especially if you are contemplating major engineering projects. The overriding criterion in risk analysis is never to expose the whole company to failure if one project fails. In other words, *no opportunity is worth risking the entire company for unless the company cannot survive without it.*

Another way to achieve the right balance between risk and reward is to set stringent *criteria* for returns. Payback periods and internal rates of return are two often used criteria to judge rewards against risk. If a project involves more risk, it should promise greater returns or you might be better off not doing it.

Other companies favour different discounting techniques, such as discounted cash flow (DCF) and net present value (NPV). One survey in the mid-1980s reported that 41 per cent of British companies surveyed used internal rate of return as 'their primary method of investment appraisal'.[23]

Ask yourself how the opportunity rates for reward and for risk. Before you make the commitment check that they are in balance. Are the rewards commensurate with the risks? What can go wrong? More importantly, what will you do if they do go wrong?

Threats as opportunities

One writer has noted that 'when a threat is recognized soon enough, it can often be converted to an opportunity'.[2] Like strengths and weaknesses, threats sometimes can cross over and become opportunities. For example, if your company is located in Europe, is 1993 a threat or an opportunity? Will your objectives be enhanced or hindered if European companies come into your market? How will your market change? Should you expand into the home markets of your competitors? Are you vulnerable to new competition? Or will new competitors act to expand your market, allowing greater opportunities for more players?

If British companies will have 'a more level playing field' against continental companies, it also means companies in the rest of the Community can attack British firms. Should you look at moving into continental markets? Will these potentially new markets have different requirements? Should you consider alliances or mergers with continental companies? One continental threat is that German supermarkets will be attracted by British profit margins which are three times greater. Having much slimmer mark-ups on large volumes, German supermarkets are rumoured to be preparing to take on their UK competitors head-on on price.

If you were in Hong Kong, would you view 1997 as a threat or an opportunity? How would you respond? Would it force you to make fundamental decisions about relocation which ultimately could improve your company? Or, will it mean oblivion if you stay around for the new regime? Will it be worth the risk given the strong attractions of the New Economic Zone and huge potential of China?

Sometimes threats force you to look closer at options, at the real choices for the future. These choices can radically change your direction and act as a turning point, although they might not have looked like that at the time. Take the turbulent but prosperous 1980s. Many boards became smug and created strategies based on wrong internal views, talking about imaginary strengths in production and organization. If you felt omnipotent, it was easy to move into unrelated markets and the opportunities seemed unlimited. As a result, many companies were left holding unrelated activities when the boom ended. Some of these companies were dragged down by recent acquisitions. Others struggled to survive. Why? Because companies forgot to build their business on customer needs and strategies to meet those needs.[24]

Complacency is not just a British disease. Too much success almost spoiled Compaq. Compaq grew from start-up in 1982 to $3.6 billion sales in 1990 but realized its first quarterly loss of $135 million in September 1991. The Board swiftly replaced co-founder, Rod Canion. What happened? Success had induced a 'self-satisfied view of the world' which meant reluctance to adapt to changes. And all this in only nine years.[25]

Another classic change which affected scores of companies was the rapid break-up of the USSR into the new but fragile Commonwealth of Independent States. Virtually overnight and without much warning, Russia changed from a country with a solid reputation for paying its commercial bills into almost Third World debtor status where payments were delayed, then frozen and finally cast into the unknown. What would you have done if your company faced considerable exposure? One medium sized company in the United Kingdom was looking at £4m in open credit. The company's product manager went to Moscow and camped there until the debt was squeezed to zero. Thereafter future transactions were secured by letters of credit and shipments were not made until the manager verified that hard currency was made available at the bank in the name of the company. So, a very big threat, one which might have bankrupted that company, was recovered through an innovative response and business continued on a secure basis for a limited period.

One thing is certain: when chaos and change abound, the race is usually won by people who see the dynamic and exploit it ahead of competitors occupied with hiding, reacting or moaning. As someone once said: 'Of all forces acting on man, change is the most beneficial and the most cruel.'

EXERCISE 11   HOW TO LOOK AT THREATS

By the very action of recognizing a threat and looking at it in the cold light of day, you remove a lot of the fear and panic. Thinking about the unthinkable is the first step in preparing for all eventualities. The next step in the evaluation process is to examine the problem and prepare a response. Often the hardest part is identifying a significant change and understanding how it will affect your market and your company. Again, you look for emerging key factors and trends that will impact on your business. It is almost like a search for opportunities, except you are looking for negatives instead of positives.

There are three key questions to ask in formulating a response:

1. Exactly how uncertain is your environment?

2. What are the specific reasons for this uncertainty?

3. How would you deal with the uncertainty?[26]

One company doctor takes the sting out of the unforeseen by conducting 'crisis audits' in which executives list the company's ten worst vulnerabilities in one column and match responses and capabilities in another. One team member creates the most awful crises imaginable. Teams can train for such eventualities, because there are similar incidents that happen to real companies.[27]

As long as you have thought through a realistic response to a perceived threat, where is the panic? Start this process by asking yourself what can go wrong out there? How will it impact on the company. What will happen to our profitability? What can we do about it?

This exercise increases your ability to deal with threats. It will increase your sensitivity to threats in general and build confidence in your management team for the future.

WHAT ACTIONS NEED TO BE TAKEN?

After identifying the best opportunities, quantifying the resources needed, acquiring the resources and examining risks, threats and responses, you are in a position to list the actions required to convert the strategies into reality.

EXERCISE

12

Because various actions will be required over time, we need to look at the following three time horizons:

1. Immediate actions which must be done first during the implementation phase (see Chapter 12).

2. Medium-term actions, i.e. over the next 6 to 12 months.

3. Long-term actions, from 12 to 60 months.

These timeframes may seem relatively short, but the planning process calls for annual reviews as well as progress reports at more frequent intervals. Moreover, short timeframes underscore the action orientation of the planning process. You decide what to do, then you do it.

Everything cannot be done at once for obvious reasons. Most companies do not have the human resources to do everything in a plan at one time—nor would a prudent team embark on too many strategies at one time. Some things require more time than others—time for preparation, organization and execution. Sensible time dimensions make the plans achievable and realistic. Again, *it is essential that priorities are established all the way through the strategic planning process.* Good management practice requires management by priorities against agreed objectives.

What actions?

After looking at the time dimensions associated with different opportunities, a list of actions should jump out at you. Start by reviewing what actions are required to convert the opportunities previously identified and ranked according to attractiveness. *Taking each opportunity, prioritize the actions necessary to convert it.* At this stage, you need only list the actions within each opportunity, leaving the details for operational (business) plans during the implementation phase (see Chapter 12).

You now have completed the strategy process, arriving at a ranked list of opportunities and priority actions within each opportunity. The basis has been laid to create detailed business plans to convert selected opportunities.

Summary

1. The external evaluation continues by looking at the risks, threats and responses to your strategies.

2. The important threats are change itself, competition from various sources and changes in the economic, political and social environment. Any threat is important if it will have a major impact on your company.

3. Some threats are also opportunities.

4. Threats should be listed, examined and responses considered.

5. Strategic actions over time should be listed in order of priority, which will set the stage for plan implementation.

References

1. Igor Ansoff, *Corporate Strategy*, Penguin, London, 1987.

2. Arthur Sharplin, *Strategic Management*, McGraw-Hill, New York, 1985.

3. Keith Hammonds, 'Commentary: why big companies are so tough to change', *Business Week*, 17 June 1991.

4. Alan Cane, 'A rough ride into the unknown', *Financial Times*, 5 June 1991.

5. John Griffiths, 'Japan is the catalyst for conversion', *Financial Times*, 9 March 1992.

6. S. C. Gwynne, 'Cover story: the right stuff', *Time International*, 29 October 1990.

7. John Argenti, *Corporate Strategy Workshop*, 1991.

8. Kenichi Ohmae, *The Mind of the Strategist: Business Planning for Competitive Advantage*, Penguin, London, 1983.

9. *Directors and Boards*, 'Critical emerging issues in board renewal and rewards', **13**(3), Spring 1989.

10. Charles Handy, *The Age of Unreason*, Arrow, London, 1991.

11. Michael Cassell, 'An industry looks beyond its defences', *Financial Times*, 7 March 1991.

12. Louise Kehoe, 'Faster than a speeding chip', *Financial Times*, 21 February 1992.

13. Charles Leadbetter, 'Dancing to a maturer measure', *Financial Times*, 4 January 1990.

14. Steven Butler, 'Looking west for inspiration', *Financial Times*, 24 February 1992.

15. Robert Thomson, 'Executives lament waning of Japanese work ethic', *Financial Times*, 13 May 1992.

16. Robert Thomson, 'Fall of the tireless salaryman', *Financial Times*, 27 May 1992.

17. Andrew Marshall, 'Grey clouds over brokers of Dover', *Independent*, 28 January 1992.

18. Charles Leadbetter, 'Corporate restructuring: why Tenneco sold its foundations', *Financial Times*, 5 September 1990.

19. Joel Bleeke, 'Peak strategies', *Across the Board*, February 1988.

20. Kevan Scholes, 'The way to manage strategic change', *Accountancy*, February 1991.

21. Michael Lawson, *Going for Growth: A Guide to Corporate Strategy*, Kogan Page, London, 1987.

22. John Harvey-Jones, *Making It Happen: Reflections on Leadership*, Fontana, London, 1988.

23. David Dugdale, 'Is there a "correct" method of investment appraisal?', *Management Accounting*, May 1991.

24. Peter Wilson, 'Managing for recovery: laying the ghosts of defunct strategies', *Financial Times*, 5 December 1991.

25. Louise Kehoe, 'Compaq founder fired because board had to make a choice', *Financial Times*, 28 October 1991.

26. Gerry Johnson and Kevan Scholes, *Exploring Corporate Strategy*, Prentice-Hall, London, 1989.

27. Jay Stuller, 'When the crisis doctor calls', *Across the Board*, May 1988.

Strategy Part V—Case profiles

Everyone has a scheme that will not work.

HOWE'S LAW[1]

Introduction

Case profiles are a very useful way to learn from the experience of other companies. They can be intriguing short stories about strategies which are devised in response to external and internal change. If you try to understand what happened, these commercial examples provide an important insight to the way individuals and management teams deal with the world.

I have taken several brief profiles from America and Europe which fall into four broad outcomes or positional categories:

1. Failures, where the strategy failed and the company either disappeared or was taken over against its will.

2. Troubles, where the company is in definite trouble and may not survive at all or might survive but in a markedly different form.

3. Transitions, where a company is dealing with its problems by devising strategies that appear to be working.

4. Successes, where a company has dealt with challenges and change, made positive responses and is winning.

Unfortunately, most of these examples involve large national or multi-national companies. There is a dearth of information about medium sized companies even though they will be the large companies of tomorrow. It is still rare to get an in-depth profile of these important middle ranking firms unless they get into great difficulties. While they often are mentioned in fast track compilations, follow-up stories are rare and information is patchy.

As noted previously, there are pressures on large corporations to decentralize operations, producing a whole new generation of medium sized operations as revitalized operating units or management buy-outs. While medium sized companies may change quickly, the giants can take anywhere from five to ten years to change culture and direction.

Case profiles highlight the experience of other companies and provide useful general and specific lessons. Probably *the single most important lesson is that things change and nothing can be taken for granted regardless of a company's size, market share and position.* In the longer term, management is all about recognizing this fact of commercial life and doing something about it.

C A S E

profiles

Failures

The failures itemized below occurred when a company followed the wrong strategy, made one fundamental mistake or was unable to continue an independent road to a future of its own choosing. Invariably the trouble arose from one or more factors—flawed leadership, wrong strategies and inability to respond quickly to change or make the appropriate response to new market conditions.

■ *Coloroll* was a British company that sought to become a one-stop shopping centre for all household items, including wallpaper, carpets, paints, tableware and glasses. During a meteoric rise in the 1980s, the chairman, John Ashcroft, acquired several businesses in pursuit of this strategy. Ashcroft bought at high prices hoping to keep what he wanted and sell the rest. Unfortunately the company could not sell the unwanted acquisitions. Unable to service the high level of corporate debt created to make the acquisitions, Coloroll went under.

Coloroll's failure resulted from several problems: first, the empire was built on borrowed money; second, the control and information systems were inadequate; third, the profitability of the acquired company was insufficient to finance the high purchase prices; and fourth, but not least, the public did not support management's concept of household merchandise under one brand name.[2]

Coloroll also appears to be an example of one man's dominance over a management team in pursuit of a flawed strategy. Apparently Ashcroft also went unchecked by a board and outside institutions who lent more and more against an unsound strategy in a buoyant consumer market.

■ *Parkfield Group* was another wonder company in Britain's roaring 1980s. An engineering conglomerate built on foundries, Parkfield was controlled by an accountant who successfully acquired several companies that were under-performing. The chain of successes, however, broke in 1990 when the Group succumbed with £300 million in debt. What went wrong? The company diversified into a totally unrelated field—video distribution—while highly geared in debt. It purchased £50 million worth of videos which went unsold, leaving 70 per cent of the original 10 million units purchased unsold 8 months after receivership.[2]

Parkfield is a classic example of the last diversification that did not work and brought the whole group down. It was a major move into an unfamiliar activity that proved to be its undoing. Such diversification pitfalls are discussed in Chapter 11.

■ *Davy Corporation*, another British company, went down to Davy Jones's Locker because of one disastrous contract which was taken for the best possible motives, i.e. to diversify activities. Davy was a sizeable engineering company with 12 000 employees and £1.6 billion in sales. A single contract from a small Aberdeen-based oil company, Midland Scottish Resources, led to Davy's downfall.

Davy agreed to convert an offshore oil platform, a type of work it had never before undertaken. The contract was a catalogue of disasters involving new technology but with a fixed price contract. The labour content was three times that estimated. Because the customer could not make progress payments, Davy waived the usual interim payments and funded the project from its own resources. The contract ran way over budget on costs and time. Not surprisingly, Davy came unstuck and Trafalgar House picked up the company for £114 million including an order book of £1.05 billion.[3]

Davy wanted to diversify but instead of spreading risk it created the ultimate risk. Davy appears to have paid the final price by pursuing diversification without considering carefully the risks involved with a new activity, new technology and an under-resourced customer.

■ *British Satellite Broadcasting (BSB)* was meant to be Britain's first satellite television system, having gained a licence in December 1986. It was backed by a blue chip consortium of large media companies, such as Reed International, Granada Television and Pearson, owners of *The Financial Times*. BSB vowed to 'outspend and outgun' rival, Sky Television, owned by Rupert Murdoch. It became clear that only one system would survive.

During the tight race for survival, BSB made several fatal errors. First, BSB threw away its advantage of being the market initiator. Each system had a dedicated receiver which meant the first one to lock in customers with its special equipment would hold on to subscribers. Even though BSB had an 18 month lead in licence and finance, Sky was operational 15 months before BSB. By April 1990, Sky had installed 750 000 dishes and BSB never caught up. While Sky was losing £2.2 million a week BSB was bleeding faster, losing £8 million each week.

Second, BSB was late going on the air because it concentrated on unique but untried technology which did not work and had to be redesigned. Third, after blowing its lead, BSB allowed Sky to define the market. Fourth, BSB's costs were too great. When the plan and execution are the problem, big money does not always win through. Meanwhile, BSB's Marco Polo satellites continue to orbit as lonely monuments to a major commercial failure on earth.[4]

In March 1992, soon after a merger between Sky and BSB, which really disguised a Sky takeover, the new company, BSkyB, recorded its first trading profit, an estimated £100 000, on sales of £4.8 million.[5]

BSB appears to have wasted starting advantages by not exploiting a new market ahead of its rival which eventually allowed the competition to dictate the running and terms of survival. BSB failed to implement its strategy in the time required to defeat the competition.

■ *Air Europe* grew out of entrepreneur Harry Goodman's successful International Leisure Group (ILG). Started in 1974, ILG was built on the British craze for Spanish holidays. In 1979, Goodman started his own charter airline to ferry holidaymakers. In 1981, ILG went public. But all was not well, especially with Goodman.

Associates portrayed Goodman as a 'mercurial ideas man who loved to take risks'. He appears to have had an aversion to thinking about tomorrow, preferring to deal only with today. Tomorrow finally caught up with Goodman when the recession hit the holiday boom and the high debt to finance Air Europe could not be serviced.[6]

Air Europe provides another classic tale of a company highly leveraged in a rising market which dived when demand shifted. Like many other wonder companies of the 1980s, its management probably thought the party would never end. Did the management team even look at the downside before commiting to risks? Was it prudent to expect that the growth curve would continue forever?

■ *Wang Laboratories* illustrates the rapid change of fortunes in the computer industry. Founded in 1951 by a Chinese immigrant to America, Dr An Wang, the company tied its future to proprietary systems and was slow to respond to the demand for personal computers and open systems. Wang focused on minicomputers and failed to understand the changes brought by new personal computers and software developments. Even so, in 1985, Wang still had sales of more than $3 billion and 31 500 employees. In August 1992, just seven years later, and with staff down to 13 000 people, Wang sought protection from creditors under chapter 11 in the US bankruptcy code, facing a debt of $500 million.[7]

Wang was a victim of external change in technology and markets in an industry where change is the norm. Management failed to respond to market changes and the challenges presented by competition. Wang shows the imperative need to stick close to the market, identify trends and make appropriate responses. The company needed to find a new niche for its expertise but appears to have spent more energy and resources defending an outmoded position.

Trouble

It is a sobering lesson that even huge corporations can get into trouble following the wrong strategy. Miscalculations can be punishing, resulting in radical transformation or even bankruptcy. Remember that over 35 per cent of *Fortune's* top 500 companies disappeared during the turbulent 1980s.

The following companies are in some form of trouble and it is not clear how they will get out of their difficulties. However, it is unlikely they will ever be the same.

- *Philips*, Europe's largest electronics manufacturer, is fighting for its future. Troubles have arisen on many different fronts. First, it grew into a 'complacent big bureaucracy' while insulated from fierce Asian competition. Second, although Philips is a very innovative company, it has been unsuccessful at marketing. Third, costs spun out of control and profits turned into enormous losses.

    Philips has responded by closing factories, cutting payrolls and reorganizing but it 'may still be too little and too late'. Yet, it still employs 344 000 people and operates 271 factories. Rather than decentralizing, like General Electric and Sony, Philips went the other way, concentrating management in four divisions: lighting, consumer electronics, professional products and systems and components.[8]

    After losing a record £1.3 billion in 1990, Philips finally took decisive steps to get out of loss-making ventures. It sold the information systems division and interests in white goods and withdrew from a joint venture in telecommunications. Philips is making determined efforts to change from a technology-driven innovator to a market driven company in consumer electronics which represents almost half its sales. Emphasis is shifting to software but the company still needs a large payoff from at least one heavily backed technology: digital cassettes, wide screen television or compact disc interactive. The next two to three years will be critical.[9]

Philips demonstrates how even a huge company can suffer by leading with technology without effective marketing strategies. Philips should have decided where it could best compete and focused resources on activities where it had a definable advantage. It may yet emerge triumphant with one of three key technologies but it can never return to the days of trying to be everything to everyone without focus and controls.

- *Laura Ashley* was a success story in British design, expanding from its UK base to stores in North America, Australia and Japan. Manufacturing got the company into trouble, creating a large interest burden on new textile machinery. While sales continued to rise, overheads dragged profits down. Moreover, the City view was that management was too committed to company roots (Sir Bernard Ashley controls the family foundation's 70 per cent shareholding) to be tough about cutting costs. One commentator noted that Laura Ashley's 'added value is in the name and style' and there was no need to be in manufacturing, especially when other specialists could do it better and cheaper.[10]

  Under new leadership of American Jim Maxmin, the company reported a significant improvement for the year ending in January 1992. A profit of £2.7 million before tax was recorded and debt fell from £103 million in March 1990 to £4.4 million at year end with a £45 million injection from the Aeon Group in Japan. Overheads were cut by £9 million and stocks were almost halved in two years with more to follow.[11]

  Laura Ashley illustrates the need for niche players to concentrate on what they do well, that is, focus on core competencies. Maxmin is looking at what an average Laura Ashley buyer wants to purchase in the company's shops, concentrating on the name and retail drawing power. Laura Ashley also highlights the dangers of integration from retailing to manufacturing, which is discussed in Chapter 11.

- *L.A. Gear*, the running shoes company, rose like a rocket in the sky, booming sales from $11 million in 1985 to $902 million in 1990. But this runaway marketing success placed an enormous strain on the company and internal controls failed. L.A. Gear was becoming another Hollywood tragedy, 'too much, too soon'. A major restructuring is now taking place around discounts and margins under pressure. If the restructuring does not work, L.A. Gear might become 'L.A. Disappear', according to a local wag.[12]

  L.A. Gear is a good example of a fashion-led business that enjoyed immense success in a very short time period. Unfortunately, the success was so great and happened so fast that control slipped from the hands of management. At the same time, market conditions were changing and competition was tougher. Did the management realize what was happening or did it feel the ride was going to last forever?

■ *Daimler-Benz*, Germany's premier luxury car maker, was a battleground between traditionalists who wanted to stay in vehicles and new management which sought rapid diversification. The new management won and the company became a huge conglomerate. But new activities in aerospace, electricals and financial services failed to produce results, leaving 90 per cent of profits still tied to Mercedes cars. Management has not turned around AEG which was acquired in 1985, nor have things improved at aircraft maker MBB. Meanwhile, employees involved in car production resent their profits being lost at the other companies.[13]

Daimler-Benz is another candidate for the practice of core competency and a strong case against diversification for the sake of prestige and growth. You need to be very clear about how you can change performance at an acquisition before committing resources. (Chapter 11 discusses the risks involved in making acquisitions.)

■ *IBM* may seem an unlikely candidate for trouble, but trouble there is. As chairman John Akers expressed it: 'Everyone is too damn comfortable. We have too many people standing round the water cooler waiting to be told what to do.'[14] Trouble? What trouble? IBM's stock is at a nine year low, profits at a six year low and sales are declining, staff is being cut for the first time in 45 years and morale is at an all time low. At least these circumstances have persuaded the bureaucracy that changes proposed three years ago really have to be implemented. IBM needs to be decentralized, slimmed down and, somehow, become entrepreneurial. But is management up to these stiff challenges? There are a lot of downside risks: open systems continue to break the grip of 'Big Blue', the company might degenerate into a cluster of 'middling' competitors strung across many markets and there may be conflicts between being a software and system integrator and a hardware manufacturer.[15]

Chairman Akers is trying to break the central hold by creating distinct business units. Each new business will control its own costs, devise its own strategies and have its own board of directors. But can it be done? More important, will it work? Market conditions have changed in the computer industry and continue to change at an alarming rate. Meanwhile, IBM's overall share of the key personal computer market fell from around 40 per cent in 1982 to about 12 per cent in 1992.[16] Today, 60 per cent of sales come from personal computers compared to only 2 per cent in 1981.[7]

Like Philips, IBM is trying to be market led instead of technology driven. Having dominated a marketplace for so long, IBM grew quite comfortable and insulated. Ironically, the market IBM developed spawned new technology companies that compete effectively in niche markets and core competencies.

■ *General Motors* is the world's largest manufacturing company and, like IBM, is an American icon. GM was dubbed by *Automobile News* as 'uncreative, complacement, arrogant, fat, sluggish, devious, greedy and simultaneously stingy and overly generous'. Making matters worse, GM set another record, it lost $4.5 billion in 1991. One newspaper observed that 'GM seems to blame everyone but itself for its problems [It] is like a blazing supertanker; the fire goes on and on, but it takes an age to sink.'[17]

GM's vehicle manufacturing operations in North America lost a staggering $10 billion, or $3000 on every car and truck made in 1991, and the company made 3.5 million vehicles! What could have gone wrong on such a gigantic scale? Several factors were responsible. First, GM's management could not accept that the Japanese found a better way to make cars. In fact, the last two decades were a sad testament to General Motors' entrenched management and resistance to real change. At first, GM believed that Americans would never give up their big cars even though they clearly were 'gas-guzzlers'. Japanese competition put a partial end to that thinking.

Second, then chairman Roger Smith tried to leapfrog over the Japanese by spending $90 billion on technology, but critics claimed much of the money was wasted. A lot was spent on unproven technology which just did not work.[18]

Third, like many large corporations GM is run by a bureaucracy which is slow-moving and set in its ways. Accordingly, the company did not react with sufficient speed or 'vigour' to inroads by Japanese competitors. GM continued to produce a confusing range of products, serving overlapping markets with seven brands of mixed designs and reputations, and volume depended heavily on large fleet customers who discounted heavily.

Having watched market share slide from more than 50 per cent in the 1970s to 35 per cent in 1992, the Board finally changed top management and took steps to accelerate the pace of change. The Board pushed through Jack Smith as the new president over chairman Robert Stempel's objections, hoping Smith would reproduce the success he had in turning around GM's European operations.[19]

The company returned to its first profit in 18 months, recording a net $179 million on quarterly sales of $32 billion. Management now is pursuing five strategies for increased profits, including rationalizing the product sub-structures and components, use of more 'lean' manufacturing techniques established by Japanese companies and sourcing cheaper materials worldwide (70 per cent of GM's components are produced internally).[20]

GM is a classic example of not responding to changes in the market, failing to recognize a shift in customer needs and failing to respond to competitive challenges. When GM finally came out of its self-imposed isolation, the chairman pursued the wrong strategy, because management had not identified and faced the real problem. It will be a long road back and the world's largest industrial company will never be the same again.

■ *Sears Roebuck* started commercial life as a mail order house and became a household name for 106 years. Sears was once America's largest retailer until it was overtaken by an aggressive discount chain established only 42 years ago, Wal-Mart. Now it is struggling to reduce costs and improve operations in the face of overstaffing and inefficiency. The fundamental problem is a familiar one. Enjoying great success after the Second World War, Sears did not recognize that 'the world passed it by' during the 1970s. Since recording peak profits after tax of $1.63 billion in 1987, Sears has been sliding every year and made less money in 1991 than it did in 1983.

Employing more people than any other corporation except General Motors, Sears tried to remain all things to all people despite the rapid rise of speciality and discount retailers. While there were several basic changes occurring in the retail sector, Sears started to slip against the competition. For example, costs at Sears ran to 30 per cent of sales compared to 23 per cent at Kmart and only 16 per cent at Wal-Mart. Moreover, Sears was handicapped by a merchandising bureaucracy slow to respond to changes in tastes and buying patterns. Now there is talk of breaking up the company by spinning out its financial services companies, Allstate Insurance Group and Dean Witter Stockbrokers.[21]

There will be a lot of work ahead and stiff competition to revive the core business of merchandising. Like GM, Sears did not stay close to markets and failed to respond to changes in customer needs and behaviour and tougher, specialized competition. Will the Sears' management have the will and energy and, more important, will they find the right strategies in time?

■ *Honda*, a legendary Japanese car maker, believe it or not, may be in trouble. Once envied for doing everything right, Honda broke into the American market but failed to produce fast selling models. Moreover, quality is suffering and reputations are falling. Honda faces even greater pressures on margins from price wars, ageing factories and even more intense competition.[22]

With the recent death of founder Shoichiro Honda, the company may have undertaken more than it could handle in the hugely competitive American market. Honda's management will face serious challenges and needs to turn around the company's performance. Could Honda become the first major international company from Japan to come unstuck in America?

Transition

Companies in transition have recognized their problems and devised strategies to deal with them. These companies are on course to a future of their choosing.

- *Laura Ashley* under the helm of Jim Maxmin may be moving from 'trouble' to 'transition'.

- *Courtaulds*, the specialist textile manufacturer, notched pre-tax profits of £201.4 million on sales of £1.94 billion in the year ending 31 March 1992. Much has changed since the textile operations were demerged two years ago and the future looks bright. Chief executive Sipko Huismans took the group from a disadvantaged textile company in old factories to a modern company seeking its own destiny. Progress was achieved through tight financial controls and well-managed high margin businesses. Staff levels were reduced and cost savings were realized. Future success depends on two strategies: exploiting a new material called Tencel and reproducing the UK success on a global scale. Huismans feels that there is always room for more efficiencies. Admitting to several mistakes, he feels that '*all of them were because the group failed to understand the market or underestimated the reaction of the competition*' [italics added].[23]

- *United Technologies*, the American conglomerate, makes Otis elevators, Carrier air conditioners, Sikorsky helicopters and Pratt & Whitney jet engines. With carefully selected acquisitions, United has reduced its dependency on defence contracts, down to 24 per cent of sales and 10 per cent of profits in 1989. It seeks 'Japanese standards of excellence' while allowing decentralized control and promoting foreign partnerships—both new departures in corporate strategies.[24]
  Chairman Robert Daniell announced plans for radical consolidation, shedding 14 000 jobs (7 per cent of the total) and rationalizing 100 facilities around the world. More cost cutting is expected with improvements in manufacturing techniques and

control of inventories. He is also pushing cultural change by devolving responsibility to smaller groups which focus on customer needs. Radical change was needed at Pratt & Whitney which was losing customers to General Electric because of poor service.[25]

- *Siemens* of Germany is Europe's biggest electrical company. Since the 1980s, it has made numerous takeovers, bids and joint ventures to become more focused, competitive and market sensitive. Siemens believes in the benefits of convergent technologies and being a one-stop shopping centre for electronics. Yet, it will have to change shape and size before it realizes the full benefits.

  Siemens has come a long way from the parochial German-speaking base in the mid-1970s. Since then, new products less than five years old have risen from 45 to 55 per cent out of a total of 200 000. About half of its 200 companies are profitable, the rest split between borderline and loss-makers. Estimates are that it will take five years for changes to have any effect. Unlike Philips, however, the company is still profitable. It remains such a vast empire that observers wonder if many benefits go unrealized 'if only Siemens knew what Siemens knows'.[26]

- *Neste*, Finland's largest company, is an excellent example of adaptation to change. When national oil consumption fell by almost 30 per cent in the early 1980s, Neste shifted away from oil refining into chemicals. Now Neste is Europe's second largest producer of polyolefins, which account for half of all plastics. Neste's strategy is geographical: to expand in North America, the world's largest market, and in South-East Asia, the world's fastest growing. Neste moved its headquarters to Brussels. Last reported profits were $500 million on sales of $8.5 billion.[27]

- *Corning* is another example of clever footwork, exiting from mature and slow growth industries into young, fast-growing ones and doing both with exquisite timing: Corning moved out of light-bulbs when sales and profits slowed in the 1970s. Thus, went other 'cherished' products like ceramic bricks and passive electrical components. This willingness to let go of products and move to better opportunities enabled management to nearly double the company's return on equity to 15 per cent between 1983 to 1990. Greater benefits are likely from 17 years of investment in optical fibres, which are cheap enough to compete with copper, and joint technology ventures which accounted for almost half of the profit in 1990.[28]

- *Apple Computer Inc.* might be the most written about computer company in the world. Apple pioneered the personal computer, growing from start-up in 1976 to $5 billion sales and 12 000 employees in 1990. Record growth has slowed recently and Apple has seen its share of the $42.3 billion American personal computer market slide from 15 per cent in 1987 to 9 per cent in 1990. In 1988, Apple reorganized and destroyed two separate kingdoms along with its 'arrogant not-invented-here syndrome'. New chief executive, Michael Spindler, is pledging teamwork and 'no more prima donnas at Apple'. Chairman John Sculley admits that 'the organization was confused about where we were going'. Sculley and Spindler are changing things, bringing in much tighter controls and making planning a discipline. Meanwhile, Sculley has taken charge of development, aiming to get products into the marketplace in half the usual time. Something has to work because overheads remain almost twice the industry average.[29]

Perhaps Apple has to find a radically different strategy to survive in an ever-changing industry with heavy competition. Apple recently formed an alliance with hard pressed IBM and is launching a new generation electronic notebook and computer interface, the Newton. There is still a lot of life yet in the *enfant terrible* of the computer world.

Successes

Some companies survived the excessive 1980s in good shape and continue to enjoy success. These winners followed strategies that are continuing to yield results. Many of the success profiles below came from sticking to fundamentals and making continual improvements in performance.

- *Hanson* is the global conglomerate that broke the rules on both sides of the Atlantic. When most conglomerates were breaking up and falling out of favour, Hanson was pursuing its proven formula: investing in basic companies that produce essential products with continuing demand, avoiding high technology and capital intensive, centralized businesses. Hanson's philosophy, like all good ones, is deceptively simple: decentralize decision making but keep strict financial control. Subsidiaries run themselves but must account for all capital investment, cash flow and profit to working capital ratios.

    Hanson has made an art of buying businesses that are under-managed or become over-extended. Clever moves can reap huge rewards. For example, Hanson recovered 92 per cent of Imperials' purchase price by selling off Courage, Golden Wonder and smaller units. In fact, Hanson recovered 55 per cent of the £8.7 billion worth of acquisitions between 1984 and 1990 by selling off unwanted parts, realizing a net profit of just over £1 billion in the process.[30]

■ *General Electric* has been transformed under the leadership of chairman Jack Welch. Sales grew from $26.8 billion in 1980 to $58.4 billion in 1990 and profits from $1.5 billion to $4.3 billion, posting, respectively, annual growth rates of 8 per cent and 11 per cent. The return on equity averaged almost 19 per cent per annum. Welch's strategy was only to retain businesses that were either first or second in their market. If they did not measure up to this criterion, he sold them. In fact, Welch sold $10 billion worth of businesses, but he bought £25 billion more.

Now Welch wants to transform the company's culture, making GE into a 'boundary-less' organization. His goals are to blur internal divisions, make everybody work as a team, bring suppliers and customers in as partners and eliminate the lines between domestic and foreign operations.

Welch dismantled GE's bureaucratic core, because he believes that people 'closest to the work really know it better'. GE also believes in studying good practice in other companies. Welch uses 'bench-marking' to improve his company's performance, taking the best parts to apply throughout the company. For example, Ford provided ideas on new product development and worker participation, Hewlett-Packard on supplier partnerships and improving quality and Digital Equipment on asset management.[31]

What has GE done? It has devolved its strategic planning from the centre to line management. GE constantly reviews and tests its strategies to reflect changes in the marketplace and incorporates market experiences. Strategies are also communicated and shared throughout the company.

■ *Singapore Airlines* might strike you as an unusual choice for a successful profile, but it is the most consistently profitable airline in the world. In 1991, Singapore Airlines made profits of $513 million on sales of around $2.7 billion. Moreover, its balance sheet revealed long-term debt of less than $250 million and cash of more than $1 billion. This is hardly the financial profile we expect from most airlines let alone the world's fifteenth largest one.

How did this happen? One factor is the airline's 'relentless investment' policy, which has left it with the youngest fleet of any airline in the world—46 aircraft with an average age less than 5 years. It has 40 new aircraft on order and another 25 under option, all of which use 35 per cent less fuel. Another factor in its success is continual expansion regardless of the business cycle, but clearly the most important factor is service to customers. As chairman Joseph

Pillay said: 'our mission remains inviolable: offer the customer the best service that we are capable of providing'.[32]

How could an airline from such a small city-state grow into such a prominent international carrier? What accounts for its incredible success? Here are some of the success factors:

1. Singapore International Airlines (SIA) used skilful marketing to exploit traffic rights throughout the world.

2. SIA made a commitment to support high service standards with the latest technology, which resulted in 'a youthful fleet with the lowest operating costs'.

3. SIA undertook from the start to provide superior service in order to get established and maintained it to differentiate itself from other carriers.

4. SIA gives high priority to staff development and training and delegates authority to the 'lowest level consistent with accountability and efficiency'.[33]

■ *Simon Access*, a division of Simon Engineering in England, is a classic medium sized niche business that knows what it is doing and does it very well. Since 1974, Simon Access grew from virtually no business to £150 million sales a year with profits in 1990 just under £12 million. John Barker built it into the largest producer of powered access equipment in the world, using database marketing to keep tabs on 350 competitors and markets by territory and product sector.

The company's market is fragmented and challenges Barker to find synergies in design, engineering and manufacturing, but he is determined to build a global market by acquiring companies, hopefully local market leaders, to fill the gaps. Barker's next two targets are Germany and Japan.[34]

■ *Levi Strauss* in San Francisco is led by chairman Bob Haas, a descendant of Levi Strauss, who sold canvas trousers to the miners in the 1849 gold rush. The Haas family owns 95 per cent of Levi, which makes it a rather large family business. When Haas took over in 1984, Levi had lost its way, diversifying into a confusing range of businesses including skiwear, men's suits and hats and its most profitable product, corduroy, went out of fashion virtually overnight.

In 1985, Haas borrowed $1.65 billion from banks and took the company back into private ownership and back to the core business, denim. The rest is history. Sales now top $4 billion with operating margins around 15 per cent. Levi has prospered with greater sales abroad, which account for half of annual profits, and a new range of casual clothes at home. Haas also attributed success to his vision in making the company 'empowered', creating a company that looks to the long term and is run by its employees. Probably the greatest compliment is that Levi is often compared to the feel and texture of a Japanese company.[35]

Levi's is the only American clothing company that is really a worldwide business. Foreign sales are driving Levi's growth. The company cleverly established manufacturing and distributing units around the world, opting to open subsidiaries rather than license local companies. Levi's is now casting an eye eastwards to Europe and the CIS.

- *Toyota* is Japan's largest vehicle manufacturer and is driven by *kaizen*, 'continuous improvement'. One outsider labelled Toyota's strategy 'rapid inch-up', that is, take enough tiny steps and soon you outrun the competition—and outdistance it has. Here are just a few recent accomplishments: Toyota introduced six new models in 14 months, took 43 per cent of the car market in Japan and sold more than 1 million vehicles in America for the first time in 1990.

How did Toyota achieve these milestones? According to *Fortune* Magazine, 'the company simply is tops in quality, productivity, and efficiency. In short, Toyota is the best car maker in the world. And it keeps getting better.' Toyota has the highest operating margin in the global automobile industry, spends $2.2 billion on R&D and sits on $22 billion in cash which could buy Ford and Chrysler. It also operates just-in-time as a fine art. Toyota manufactures only 'what is needed, when it is needed, and in the quantity needed'.

A customer will get his or her built-to-order car in 7 to 10 days. It only takes 13 man-hours to build a car at the best Toyota plant compared to between 19 and 22 hours at Honda, Nissan and Ford. Toyota's labour force is a mere 91 790 compared to GM's 766 000.[36]

- *Medeva* was created in 1990 but now is the world's fifth largest manufacturer of vaccines. It also is Britain's largest generic pharmaceuticals manufacturer. Managing director Ian Gowrie-Smith put together a top-notch management team of former big company pharmaceutical executives. Results in 1991 were sales of £82 million and net profits of £17 million. In early 1992, the market value of this company which was floated four years ago was £550 million.

Why is it successful? Medeva is unique, because it is becoming a force in pharmaceuticals without a traditional (and expensive) R&D activity. Rather, Medeva buys drug portfolios or divisions from larger companies. It acquired Evans Medical in 1990, adding Welcome's vaccine portfolio, MD Pharmaceuticals and Adams Laboratories in 1991.[37]

- *Dell Computers* in Austin, Texas seems an unlikely success story, but it demonstrates how spotting a market opportunity and converting it quickly and innovatively can produce handsome results. Oh no, not another computer company, you might say. But this one is different, because it approaches the market in a totally different way.

  Led by 27-year-old wonderkid, Michael Dell, the company assembles personal computers at plants in Texas and Ireland and sells them direct to customers over the telephone, eliminating retail outlets and high distribution costs. It also has no finished product inventory. This unique market approach allows Dell to undercut larger competitors. In the last year for which figures are available, Dell recorded profits up 87 per cent at $50.9 million on sales up 63 per cent at $889.9 million. Since starting in 1984, sales have grown by 67 per cent a year. And Michael Dell says proudly 'we are not slowing down'.

  Dell has been successful because computers have become commodities. Customers no longer wish to pay premium prices demanded by the major computer companies. As computers have become so reliable, people are willing to order machines by telephone. Dell forges close relationships with customers by offering some of the best support services in the industry, which builds brand loyalty.

  As Dell is constantly in contact with users, it can respond quickly to customer needs and get fast feedback on good and bad points. The company continually designs new products to meet needs—its oldest product is only 11 months old—and sells them down the database. Dell's database contains 750 000 names which is a powerful marketing asset. Can Dell keep up this blistering pace? Michael Dell says yes, if the company remembers that customer service never can be taken for granted and always needs to be improved.[38]

- *Direct Line* Insurance Company, a subsidiary of the Royal Bank of Scotland, is another pioneer of direct marketing. Established by Peter Wood in 1985, Direct Line sells car and house insurance over the telephone following carefully targeted media campaigns. Using customized software, telephone operators are able to provide instant quotations based on answers to a few simple questions. Details are confirmed by post. Savings in overheads are passed on to customers who enjoy premium savings of 20 per cent or more. Payment is accepted by credit card or direct debit. Premium income for 1991 was £213 million with profits of £15.1 million after paying founder Wood a £6 million bonus, up from the £9.1 million recorded in 1990. As you might expect, this success has attracted competition from such companies as Churchill, a Swiss subsidiary, Royal Insurance, General Accident and Eagle Star.[39]

While this exercise could attract better examples in each category, that is not the point. The purpose of case profiles is to look at what happens in other companies, understand their experience and, if appropriate, apply it to your company.

There are two ways of learning: the first and most important is through your own direct experience and the other is indirect through the experience of others. Hopefully, this chapter will enable you to start looking at the experience of other companies through different eyes.

References

1. Arthur Bloch, *The Complete Murphy's Law: A Definitive Collection*, Price, Stern, Sloan, Los Angeles, 1991.

2. *Investors Chronicle*, 'The offspring of corporate collapses', 15 March 1991.

3. Alan Pukiss, 'The demise of Davy', *Accounting*, November 1991.

4. *Economist*, 'Management focus: how BSB was KOed', 10 November 1990.

5. Raymond Snoddy, 'BSkyB claims trading profit for first time', *Financial Times*, 10 March 1992.

6. Mark Marement, 'Transportation: how Harry Goodman crashed and burned', *International Business Week*, 15 April 1991.

7. Susan Ellicott, 'Software revolution fells computer stars', *Sunday Times*, 23 August 1992.

8. *Economist*, 'Philips fights the flab', 7 April 1990.

9. Michiyo Nakamoto and Ronald Van De Krol, 'Philips faces its moment of truth', *Financial Times*, 25 February 1992.

10. Bill Robinson, 'Double whammy for Laura Ashley', *Investors Chronicle*, 27 April 1990.

11. Maggie Urry, 'Laura Ashley recovery under way', *Financial Times*, 7 April 1992.

12. Kathleen Kerwin, 'LA Gear calls in a cobbler', *International Business Week*, 16 September 1991.

13. *Economist*, 'The flawed vision of Edzard Reuter', 27 April 1991.

14. Alan Cane, 'A rough ride into the unknown', *Financial Times*, 5 June 1991.

15. *Economist*, 'Scenting extinction', 14 December 1991.

16. Michiyo Nakamoto and Alan Cane, 'IBM dons a different suit of clothes', *Financial Times*, 10 June 1992.

17. Edward Lucas, 'The rusting giant of the west', *Independent*, 24 January 1992.

18. Philip Robinson and Andrew Lorenz, 'American tragedy', *Sunday Times*, 1 March 1992.

19. Martin Dickson, 'Impatient GM board flexes its muscles', *Financial Times*, 8 April 1992.

20. Martin Dickson, 'GM tunes up its recovery', *Financial Times*, 30 April 1992.

21. Nikki Tait and Barbara Durr, 'US retailer all over the shop', *Financial Times*, 12 May 1992.

22. *Economist*, 'Japan's car makers: Honda loses its way', 14 September 1991.

23. Paul Abrahams, 'A future based on a dual-track strategy', *Financial Times*, 21 May 1992; 'Courtaulds improves 8% to £201.4m', *Financial Times*, 21 May 1992.

24. *Economist*, 'United technologies: like Japan, but different', 3 November 1990.

25. Martin Dickson, 'Second stab at the cost-cutting exercise', *Financial Times*, 23 January 1992.

26. David Goodharty, 'Corporate restructure: radicals and conservatives in a cultural revolution', *Financial Times*, 3 March 1989.

27. *Economist*, 'Neste's corporate strategy: Finnish first', 2 June 1990.

28. *Economist*, 'Corning's strategy: time to get out of the kitchen', 5 January 1991.

29. Barbara Buell, 'Cover story: Apple loses its way', *International Business Week*, 15 October 1990.

30. *Economist*, 'How Hanson holds the reins', 25 May 1991.

31. *Economist*, 'Management focus: Jack Welch reinvents General Electric—again', 30 March 1991.

32. *Economist*, 'Singapore Airlines: flying beauty', 14 December 1991.

33. Bernard Taylor and John Harrison, *The Manager's Casebook of Business Strategy*, Heinemann, Oxford, 1990.

34. Andrew Baxter, 'A business with its sights set on gaining new heights', *Financial Times*, 7 February 1992.

35. *Economist*, 'A competitive fit', 22 June 1991.

36. Alex Taylor III, 'Managing/cover story: Why Toyota keeps getting better and better and better', *Fortune International*, 19 November 1990.

37. Richard Gourlay, 'Building a dream on drug marketing', *Financial Times*, 5 March 1992.

38. Paul Taylor, 'Profile: Michael Dell, "I'm having a great time"', *Financial Times*, 7 April 1992.

39. Richard Lapper, 'Bank that underwrote a recipe for success', *Financial Times*, 2 September 1991.

Strategy Part VI—Other models and views

*If all you have is a hammer, everything
looks like a nail.*

BARUCH'S OBSERVATION[1]

Management teams have choices. There is a wide choice of strategic options and models. Rather than ask you to commit to my approach, the comments below provide an insight to other models. You may find some ideas and concepts useful on their own or in combination with my framework and process.

Strategic options

Johnson and Scholes list the following strategic options open to companies:

1. No action, i.e. do nothing.
2. Withdraw from an activity.
3. Consolidate a position in a market.
4. Increase market share and penetration.
5. Develop a product or service.
6. Develop the market.
7. Integrate the activity backwards.
8. Integrate the activity horizontally.
9. Integrate the activity forward.
10. Diversify into a new activity.[2]

Growth strategies

Many companies paid management consultants to devise growth strategies. Some have been fashionable, taking the corporate world by storm at one time or another, while others have faded into management archives. It is still worth while to take a brief look at some of these concepts because they contain elements that remain important for medium sized companies today.

The commonplace model

Conventional wisdom and experience have produced the following commonplace strategies used by companies to grow by 'looking first in their own backyard':

1. Stimulate sales by reducing prices based on lower costs.

2. Increase prices across the board or selectively to improve profitability.

3. Promotion, especially through advertisements. For example, the Hollywood producer Joseph E. Levene said: 'You can fool all the people all the time if the advertising is right and the budget is big enough.' On the other hand, Eric Blair (better known as George Orwell) called 'advertising . . . the rattling of a stick inside a swill bucket'.[3]

4. Increase sales activity.

5. Product development.

6. Integration, backward or forward.

7. Technology acquisition.

8. Attack competitors.

9. Buy competitors.

10. Geographical expansion.

11. Saturate a market.

Core competencies

A popular strategy for companies is the core competency strategy. Companies should concentrate on their core competencies, that is, what they do exceptionally well. Everything else should be contracted out to specialist suppliers. For example, a company might concentrate on product development, design and engineering and subcontract manufacturing and distributing. Some companies subcontract manufacturing but assemble and test products in-house.

A recent example was provided by Laura Ashley which has agreed that Federal Express should assume the functions of supply, delivery and storage on a worldwide basis. It is expected this move will save £1.8 million and free resources to concentrate on a mail order business. Moreover, Federal Express will handle better a complex distribution system which involves 540 shops in 28 countries and between 10 and 15 suppliers.[4]

The Hanan model

Mack Hanan suggested a different approach for the 1980s, focusing on two critical questions for the fast track company: How can it grow? How can it manage growth? He believes that growth is found in markets, not in fighting competition.

Markets have been undergoing dramatic changes, becoming smaller, more specialized and demanding tailored benefits. Hanan suggests there are two ways to grow such markets: select customers who can grow you by reducing their costs and find customers and help them realize sales opportunities. As there is a limit to growth by reducing somebody's costs, the real opportunities are finding ways to increase your customers' sales and getting premium prices in the process. Hanan remarks that the growth process 'begins with management's vision of a market that can be grown, of the values that will grow it, and a definition of a mission that will add the growth value to the market'.

Fast growth businesses that form growth partnerships are transient monopolies because they become the industry standard and demand premium pricing. Hanan notes that 'a user's problem is a grower's profit'.[5]

Pareto Principle

Hanan uses it. Other people talk about it. If you do not use it, maybe you should. The *Pareto Principle* simply says that the top 20 per cent of any grouping will account for 80 per cent of its value. For example, your top 20 per cent of customers will generate 80 per cent of your profits. A variation states that 80 per cent of a task gets done with 20 per cent of the available effort but the remaining 20 per cent of the task will require 80 per cent of the effort.[6]

Another variation is the Pareto Corollary, that is, the 80 per cent of customers accounting for 20 per cent of revenue will account for a disproportionate amount of the costs.[5] With this corollary you get the worst of both worlds: low revenues and large costs.

If Pareto applies to your business, it can focus your efforts for maximum impact. The principle is more of a mechanism than a model, but it can be very important in getting you to focus on key customers and suppliers in your business. If you use the 20/80 principle, your actions may become much more focused and effective.

Diversification as a growth strategy

My experience with small and medium sized companies indicates that there are two major reasons why they fail: either they over-trade, that is, run out of cash, or they diversify. A common reason for diversification failure is the management team's over-confidence and misplaced view that it is able to take on *any* business challenge. As Robert Heller has said: 'the second myth of management is that success equals skill'.[3] Because your team has been successful in one type of business, it does not automatically follow that you will succeed in another. As Argenti has stated: 'Diversification is the wrong strategy for most companies'.[7] In fact most diversifications end in tears of failure (see Acquisition below). Alfred Chandler, Emeritus Professor of Business History at Harvard Business School, believes that companies would do much better if they concentrated resources on 're-inventing' their existing businesses, like the chemicals industry did in the 1980s by shifting away from commodity products to pharmaceuticals and biotechnology.[8]

On the other hand, diversification may be justified if a one product company faces problems, if the existing market cannot provide enough growth or the existing market cycle is unattractive. Even under these circumstances, however, companies should not diversify if there is something basically wrong with the existing business, if the required expertise is not available or if the risk cannot be minimized.[9]

Bombardier, the Canadian manufacturer of transportation equipment, has followed a unique form of diversification. Since 1985, it has paid bargain basement prices for several companies in trouble. After a takeover, Bombardier helps companies to recover by 'encouraging managers to try different restorative treatments', not drastic cuts and dismissals. With 1990 sales expected at $2.6 billion, it bought Learjet (USA) for $75 million, Short Brothers (Northern Ireland aircrafts), Canadair (business jets), ANF-Industrie (French railcars) and BN (Belgium railway equipment).[10] Short Brothers has been a success story and a near model turnaround. After two years, sales had doubled, a £47 million loss was turned into a £26 million profit and an additional 1000 people were employed. Bombardier had revolutionized a run-down business with a £200 million four year investment programme which forged new attitudes among a 'dispirited' workforce.[11]

While there are successful diversifications, few people would expect an 'outsider' to come into their industry and perform better than existing companies. On the other hand, is it not odd to believe that you could move your company into a strange industry or acquire and manage a new company in an unfamiliar industry and expect to do better than you have done in your own industry where you had vast experience? Yet most diversification moves through acquisitions are done by management teams with that belief.[12]

My view is simply that *you diversify in order to spread risk, not to increase it. Diversification is a high risk strategy fraught with uncertainties and should be considered only if you have exhausted the potential of existing activities.*

Michael Porter devised three test criteria that should ring positive before any diversification attempt is made. First, the industry must be 'structurally attractive'. Second, the entry cost must not 'consume all the future profits'. Third, the buyer needs to add or provide 'some significant competitive advantage'.[12] For example, Philip Morris paid four times book value for 7-UP. Profits had to increase four times to justify such an enormous acquisition price and increases of this magnitude were impossible in the mature soft drinks industry. The result was that Philip Morris sold its acquisition at a loss.[13]

My rules for diversification are as follows:

1. Do not fall victim to an exaggerated sense of your own ability. Do not believe your own lies that you and your team can overcome any challenge.

2. Assess your team and identify realistic strengths and weaknesses. What additional managerial skills are required for the diversification? Can you acquire them?

3. Look at related products in adjacent markets which provide some comfort and familiarity.

4. Build on your basic strengths, such as industry knowledge, customer base and technological skills.

5. Minimize risk by market research and careful planning.

6. Establish a cut-off point, that is, a time to leave if preselected milestones are not achieved.

Again, *you diversify to spread risk, not create it.*

Acquisition as a growth strategy

Diversification moves involve starting a new activity or getting into another activity by acquiring another company. Most diversification occurs through acquisition because it appears easier to measure and value an existing company. It also appears less risky but that is not always the case.

Many of the large successful conglomerates sustained growth by buying the profits and cash flow of other companies. They were able to do this because the value of their shares increased enough to finance more takeovers. With this strategy, however, more and more companies have to be acquired in order to maintain growth unless the acquired companies dramatically improve performance or have assets for disposal which will offset the acquisition cost. Furthermore, this process depends on favourable economic conditions and a buoyant stock market. Conglomerate building is not easily done during a downturn in the cycle unless the conglomerate has a lot of cash available.

Organized hunts for acquisitions on this scale are familiar to everyone who reads the papers. They have been going on since the end of the Second World War, although the 1980s was exceptional in the number and size of deals and the leveraged buy-outs with 'junk' bonds. There is nothing new about the rise and fall of conglomerates or the fashion of takeover fever followed by an inevitable return to core activities or 'back to your knitting'. What receives less attention is the acquisitive nature of medium sized companies which are busy building larger shares in core niche markets or creating mini conglomerates in various niches. William Holdings and Simon Access are good examples in the United Kingdom.

During the 1980s several mini conglomerates rose to considerable heights in the hothouse atmosphere of entrepreneurial Britain. In fact, in the mid-1980s Britain, albeit briefly, had the fastest growing economy in Europe. However, many high flyers, such as the Parkfield Group, stopped flying and crashed ignominiously. An often quoted cause of failure was excessive borrowing and the inevitable crippling high interest burden, but the most prevalent reason was diversification through acquisitions that went wrong.

In exhaustive research, Michael Porter found that the average post-acquisition divestment rate exceeded 60 per cent. In other words, only two out of every five acquisitions lasted. The corporate divestment rate was exceeding the personal divorce rate of California! This is hardly surprising when you consider Alfred Chandler's finding that during the mid-1970s half of acquired assets were in unrelated industries.[14]

An American study was completed on acquisitions by large corporations between 1950 and 1980. If the acquisition was made in an unrelated area, that is, in an activity outside the acquirer's existing business, three out of four such acquisitions were later divested. In other words, *unrelated acquisitions had only a one-in-four chance of survival.*[7]

British companies have a large appetite for growth through acquisitions. In America, for example, British companies have been greater buyers in recent years than companies from any other country. Often they spend more on acquiring companies than on their existing businesses. While Hanson has an excellent track record, other British companies have failed miserably. Here are four recent acquisitional disasters:

1. Midland Bank bought Crocker Bank in California for $820 million in 1980, made another investment of $375 million in 1984 and was left holding an estimated loss of $450 million, which substantially weakened Midland and forced it to find a partner.

2. British & Commonwealth bought Atlantic Computers for £416 million in 1988 which led to a £550 million write-off and eventual collapse of B&C.

3. Ferranti bought International Signal and Control in 1987 for £630 million which led to a loss of about £250 million, countless lawsuits and the restructure of Ferranti.

4. Imperial bought Howard Johnson in 1980 for $630 million which it sold for $400 million in 1985 after five years of trading losses.[15]

AT&T was under severe criticism for trying to acquire National Cash Register (NCR). AT&T had already invested $2 billion in its computer division which was still losing $200 million a year. Why buy more manufacturing capacity? Robert Allen, AT&T's Chairman, believed that telecommunications and computers were converging industries. But this assumption was wrong because computers comprised a manufacturing activity and telecommunications involved services and there was no 'real' fit. If AT&T had acquired NCR at the enormous price of $7.5 billion, computers would still represent less than 20 per cent of total sales.[16]

Johnson and Scholes cite three major reasons why so many acquisitions fail:

1. Poor assessment of the prey's strengths and weaknesses.

2. Over-assessment of the attractiveness of the industry in which the prey lives.

3. Failure to consider whether the takeover price can be recovered from future earnings.[2]

The cardinal rule for any acquisition is whether or not you can add clear value to the acquisition and realize the potential which attracted you in the first place.

If you are considering an acquisition, you should at least ask the following fundamental questions: What are you really buying? Why are you buying it? What will you do with it if you are successful?

Other questions worth asking are as follows:

1. Is there a clear 'fit' between your company and the target?

2. Will the combination of your company and the acquisition be significantly greater than you on your own?

3. Does the enhanced market position justify the price?

4. Can your management team absorb the new business?

5. Will your existing business suffer during the acquisition process?

The most important part of any acquisition move is whether or not you have done your homework. Do you really know the target in depth? Are you familiar with its true market position? Have you talked to the target's customers and competitors? How realistic are your views of the company, market and potential? Is the target's management team critical to the deal? Will you retain its services?

You should not ignore the soft factors in an acquisition: the people and the culture. Many mergers and acquisitions fail because too much importance and time is spent on financials. Time is not spent on planning the transition, especially on dealing with 'people' issues. Changes in corporate ownership are stressful, because of the ambiguity and uncertainty while negotiations are taking place. Sometimes the culture of one company floods the other and people leave. Many times poor planning results in lower output, greater staff turnover, higher absenteeism, more accidents and strikes.[17]

Other observers believe that human factors are the principal cause of failures. In particular, two key elements are cited: 'the cultural compatibility of the combining organizations and the way in which the merger/acquisition is managed'. If the cultures 'fit' between organizations, the chances of success are much greater.[18]

How should 'the human factor' be managed? Experts suggest that the way an announcement is handled is important and should include official information on future jobs and the new culture to be adopted. Announcements should be concerned with 'paving' the way for change and 'allay' fears, as well as provide a positive introduction to the new owner. Most announcements, however, provide minimal information, are badly timed and insensitively handled. It is best to make announcements face-to-face, rather than rely on cold written communications.

Brian McGowan, Chief Executive of Williams Holdings, a successful conglomerate in the United Kingdom, believes the acquirer has to 'stamp his mark' on the new company quickly, usually in 'less than a week'. Williams Holdings make a presentation lasting 45 minutes, covering its company and its culture for all employees in a newly acquired company. If you are making a presentation, provide a brief history, structure, objectives and values of your company, which will convey something of your culture. Then you should continue with 'high visibility' to maintain the momentum of change.[19]

After discussing the downside and pitfalls in acquisitions, I have devised the following acquisition evaluation format which may be useful if you still wish to consider an acquisition:

Part One: Pre-acquisition questions

1.0   What is the detailed information on the target for the following items?

   1.1   Quality of the existing business (sales, margins and continuity)?

   1.2   Quality of the future potential business?

   1.3   What will be immediate impact on our profits?

   1.4   What will be the impact on profits over five years?

   1.5   Management team quality (depth, functional cover, balance, autonomy, who is retainable)?

   1.6   Site and equipment (condition, capacity, capability, complementary, capex requirement, health and safety)?

   1.7   Are there any pending or hidden liabilities on or off the balance sheet?

2.0   What are the target's realistic strengths and weaknesses?

   2.1   Will its strengths increase ours?

   2.2   Will its strengths reduce our weaknesses?

   2.3   Will its weaknesses increase ours?

3.0   What is the real 'fit'?

   3.1   What do we think is there?

   3.2   Why do we want it?

   3.3   What is the commercial imperative for the acquisition?

   3.4   What and where is the specific gain (market share, complementary products or service, greater competitiveness, management, productivity, etc.)?

   3.5   How will the combined business be greater than our own?

   3.6   Can we specify how and where it will be greater?

4.0   How are we going to add clear value to the acquisition?

   4.1   Can we specify where and what value will be added?

5.0   What impact will the acquisition have on us?

   5.1   Are there any risks or threats which could seriously affect the deal?

5.2   What sensitivities exist that could affect the deal?

5.3   If the target's performance went wrong, would it put us at risk?

6.0 What does the target's management want to do with the company?

6.1   Where do they want to go and how would they get there?

6.2   Are their vision and strategies compatible with ours?

6.3   Is their culture compatible with ours?

7.0 Why has nobody bought the target before?

7.1   Why is the target for sale now?

7.2   Has the target's uncertainty affected customers?

8.0 What are the financial parameters?

8.1   How much is the purchase price?

8.2   How much can it be purchased for?

8.3   Are there other buyers?

8.4   Will other buyers force the price up?

8.5   Are we sure the takeover price can be recovered from future earnings?

8.6   How long will it take to recover the purchase price?

8.7   Will there be real overhead savings?

8.8   Can we specify the savings at the target company?

8.9   Can we specify the savings at our company?

8.10 What is the target company's working capital requirement?

8.11 What is our combined working capital requirement?

8.12 Will both companies be stronger financially after the takeover?

9.0 What is the funding requirement?

9.1   How will we fund the purchase?

9.2   How will we provide working capital for both companies?

Part Two: Post-acquisition questions

10.0 How are we going to manage both companies?

10.1   What would be the new management structure?

10.2   Who would do what by each management function?

10.3   Who would report to whom?

10.4   What would be the new financial controls?

11.0 How are we going to lead and motivate the acquisition's management?

11.1   How will we avoid the 'us' and 'them' syndrome?

12.0 Do we have a clear vision where both companies will go?

13.0 Do we have strategies for how we will get there?

13.1   How will we realize the combined potential?

14.0 Will our existing business suffer during the transition process?

14.1   If so, how can we prevent or minimize disruption?

15.0 Do we have a detailed takeover and integration plan?

15.1   Does it recognize the human factors, especially the uncertainty among middle managers?

15.2   Does it recognize the cultural differences between companies?

15.3   Does it call for swift action and positive leadership?

15.4   Does it allow the target's management participation in the future?

One of the most effective ways to evaluate a target's existing management and company potential is to conduct a strategic planning exercise with them along the lines outlined in Chapter 15. If it is a friendly acquisition, the strategic planning exercise will provide you with a better, more rounded and clearer understanding of the entire business and the management team's ability to grow it.

If you acquire a company, you are advised immediately to conduct a strategic planning exercise. This exercise should involve the management in deciding their future and show positive leadership to the rest of the employees.

The case for the start-up

Michael Porter makes a strong case for creating a new business rather than buying an existing one. If a company has the internal strength and resources to start up an activity, it might be 'safer and less costly' to start a company from scratch than depend entirely on an acquisition and deal with takeover problems. When you start a venture, everything is within your direct control and you are not taking over somebody else's problems. Japanese companies often diversify using start-ups.[13]

Other growth strategies

Other less used strategies including the following:

1. Licence or royalty deals, either selling or buying which will generate returns. One way to exploit overseas markets, either minor or difficult to access, is through the use of licences, especially if you sell products as part of an arrangement. Conversely, licensing-in technology or product can enhance your market offering and generate direct sales.

2. Corporate venturing, taking minority stakes in smaller companies, is quite an accepted practice in the United States but less so in Europe and Japan. Minority stakes can create windows on new technology and markets which might directly impact on existing or future activities. Moreover, corporate venturing can be an innovative way to generate enormous returns for small investments.

   For example, one medium sized company has created two corporate ventures with outsiders for minimal outlay: one that annually generates more than £2 million sales with net returns of 25 per cent and the other which attracted £2.2 million in venture capital. Like acquisitions, however, you need to add clear value through structuring, marketing, resourcing and managing the venture to be supported. Passive investments make little sense, because the corporate sponsor adds nothing but money and most ventures need at least managerial and marketing assistance. Corporate venturing, however, requires the larger partner to commit management time and resources.

3. Joint ventures are another way to penetrate a market and achieve growth while minimizing risk. Unfortunately, joint ventures take considerable time to create and manage. They are usually not attractive unless one party has clear control, which may make it less acceptable for the minority player.

Business portfolio model

This model begins by deciding what business you really are in, where the 'golden heart' lies, that is, what activity makes most of the profits, assesses opportunities, threats and strengths and allocates key staff and resources based on strengths and market attractiveness. In this way, the model allows a large company to develop a balanced portfolio of businesses. While the BPM has been disparaged recently, it still contains a lot of common sense. Looking at its constituent parts, the following points are worth noting:

1. Identify your 'golden heart', that is, what activity really is making the money.

2. Assess opportunities against threats and strengths.

3. Allocate resources based on those strengths and the attractiveness of markets.

World competitive model

This model looks at the company as a portfolio of investments in different businesses. Accordingly, the following steps are taken:

1. Assess the position of each business in world markets.

2. Identify certain target market segments.

3. Move into more sophisticated products with higher value added.

4. Invest in technological innovation.

5. Work to achieve scale of economies and standardized products.

6. Expand into new markets.

Porter's choices

Michael Porter at Harvard Business School concluded that there are only two acceptable routes to best performance: 'you either become the lowest-cost producer in your industry, or you differentiate your products/ service' in ways to obtain premium prices.[12]

Market niche model

This model calls for the creation of a distinctive image in the minds of customers for a company's products based on actual performance factors or intangibles. Success results from focus and concentration on 'a specific type of customer, product or geographic locale'.[13]

Global niche market

The latest and most fashionable model is to focus your business on an international niche market and then to dominate that global niche.

The magnificent sevens

Based on their earlier work at McKinsey & Company Management Consultants and published in their landmark book, *In Search of Excellence*, Thomas Peters and Robert Waterman suggested that companies should be viewed by seven factors which all begin with the letter 'S'. Accordingly, the seven 'S' factors are as follows:

1. Structure

2. Strategy

3. Systems

4. Staff

5. Skills

6. Style

7. Shared values[20]

Most of these are 'soft' factors which contrast markedly with traditional 'hard' items like capital, plant and money. The motivation to look at these new factors was just that—'motivation'—that is, unlocking the motivation of human resources to create a new competitive edge. A gain in competitive advantage might result from a gigantic leap in productivity. Many large companies are focusing on 'cultures' and new methods to tap this potential.

In other words, are there new ways for companies to 'turn on' their employees and realize a quantum jump in performance? Fragmentary indications suggest that significant improvements can be realized by giving employees the fundamental freedoms we often talk about but rarely implement within organizations—democratic participation, responsibility and control over their workplace. In short, devolve power from the centre to the line.

The revolution that started in the 1980s is set to continue in the 1990s. Approaches and techniques may differ from company to company but structures, management and work are changing along with everything else in the marketplace.

Boston matrix

The Boston Consulting Group created its renowned cash cow and rising star matrix (also known as the 'Boston Box') to indicate which businesses a company should back and which it should divest. This model assumes that market share is the prime determinant in strength and the market's rate of growth shows opportunity.

Businesses with high market share and high growth rate are called 'stars', and ones with low market share and low growth are named 'dogs'. If a business has high market share in a low growth market, it should be earning a lot of profit and generating a lot of cash, which the model denotes as 'cash cows'. These cash cows should fund the stars, but beware of the 'question marks', which eat up large amounts of cash because they are low market share businesses in high growth markets.

The Boston Box became popular in the 1970s when managers were looking for a strategic approach and 'a way of communicating strategies simply and effectively'.[21]

Ohmae five step model

Kenichi Ohmae created a model with the following five step process:

1. Define clearly the business domain.

2. Analyse the basic forces at work in the business environment, extrapolate into the future and express the most logical and succinct scenario.

3. Choose only a few strategic options and deploy resources boldly and aggressively.

4. Regulate the strategy according to available resources.

5. Stay with the strategy unless basic assumptions change.[22]

Alliances

Alliances are fashionable, especially when sharing trade information on technology and markets. Such alliances may become more important among larger corporations as new projects and developments become more and more expensive. However, it is possible for medium sized companies to form alliances for mutual advantage, especially when entering new markets.

Bench-marking

Bench-marking is a method of identifying admirable practices in another company and asking to study the practice with a view to adopting it in your company. Jack Welch, chairman of General Electric, is an admirer of this approach and has used it extensively in developing his company.

Charles Handy suggests you think of organizations that you know and admire. Ask them if you can study their methods. After studying what they do well, apply the lessons to your business.[23] That is the process of bench-marking. Find the practice worth examining, observe it and use it. Bench-marking, however, implies that you wish to look outside your business for inspiration. It means you are not complacent, but are eager and willing to learn from others.

Bench-marking involves different stages. You need to work out where your company needs improving. Then you have to find out who is a leading performer in that area. You next make contact and ask to visit and observe. Usually, there is a *quid pro quo* in the process, that is, offer to share some expertise of yours. In this way, companies exchange consultancy services based on actual work practices.[24]

The success of bench-marking lies in the learning process. If you cannot learn from direct experience, the next best thing is to learn from the experience of others. In order for this to work, however, you need humility and willingness to learn from others and determination to understand the value of other practices. Bench-marking can improve performance by learning how to do things better. Having come of age in the 1980s, it may become an important tool for enhancing competition in the 1990s.

Total quality management (TQM)

TQM qualifies as a model because it encompasses so many current practices. Coined by Armand Feigenbaum, who was in charge of General Electric's quality, TQM is an embracing term for best practices in manufacturing, including just-in-time inventory, customer services (internal and external) and different work practices such as teamwork, training and empowerment.

The objective of TQM is clear: reorientate production to deliver products/services to meet customer requirements on time and at consistent quality. Advocates of TQM also emphasize that it involves constant measurement and continuous improvement. The managing director of Rank Xerox (UK) likens TQM to satisfying the customer in 'a race without a finish'.[25]

Models *et al.*

These brief models illustrate different approaches to corporate futures. Many models contain elements that are common to one another including my approach. After all, you can look at the world only so many ways.

The synergy between models is more important than each model on its own. Models offer different ways to look at the same problem and may spark some thoughts and insights. If so, they will have served a purpose. On the other hand, you may wish to take one or more aspects and integrate them with my approach or vice versa. The important thing is that you find an approach that works for you and your team and produces results for your company. You may have to experiment but be sure to measure results. If you find something that works, you may refine the application and enhance performance. In any event, think things through before you start applying. And give your approach enough time to make an impact. A note of warning: *keep the model as simple as possible and make sure it is complete, that is, covers the agenda, strategies and implementation.*

Other views

Tom Peters, who has been in the forefront of reporting new management practices, noted the following fundamental changes in marketplaces:

1. There are no old products, only new ones.

2. The economics of manufacturing scale are disappearing.

3. Every market is fragmenting, i.e. becoming 'thinner, slimmer and more narrow'.

4. The real value is information and databases to exploit the new markets which demand product customization and rapid response.

Peters quotes Rapp and Collins who said: 'The 1960s was the era of mass marketing, the 1970s the era of segmentation and line extensions, the 1980s the era of niches and the 1990s will be the era of one-to-one marketing which is what database marketing is all about.'

According to Peters, management's top priorities will become in order of importance: time, quality and profit. He urges companies to take all eight of the following actions:

1. Pioneer the use of information technology inside and outside the company.

2. Turn the organizational structure upside down and involve key outsiders like suppliers, customers, distributors and franchisees.

3. Empower everyone in the organization which means destroying middle management.

4. Reorient away from adversarial to partner type relations.

5. Radical decentralization.

6. Redesign administrative blocks to match technology.

7. Measure everything based on time.

8. Eliminate all job descriptions.[26]

In 1987, Peters wrote *Thriving on Chaos* which argued that companies would survive only by adopting fast change in strategies, products/ services, organization and managing people. Along with Bob Waterman's *The Renewal Factor* and Richard Pascale's *Managing on the Edge*, Peters and company feel that excellence must be all encompassing even though it constantly changes. You stay on top through continual self-questioning about what you are doing, the way you do it and what is happening in the world.[27]

Peters argues that all markets are interconnected and that global issues are roughly the same whether you are in New York, London or Frankfurt. Although implementation of strategies will be different in each of these places, he believes the key issue is whether or not your management 'believes in the primacy of the work force or not'. Peters suggests we may be in the midst of the most profound change in the last 2000 years in the way we organize things. As evidence, he points to a whole new range of organizational shapes that are emerging. 'New companies just do not look like old ones', he says.[28]

Andersen Consultants call for an integrated strategy of technology, operations and people through the following actions:

1. Create a flexible strategy to match fast change, use uncertainty as an advantage.

2. Organize the company for fast response through broad control spans, short command channels and planned change projects.

3. Set clear criteria to measure success or failure with cut-off points to abandon or change plans not working.

4. Appoint dedicated change leaders to manage impact.

5. Stick to knitting by eliminating all non-essentials to core business.

6. Subject white collar paper factory to same engineering discipline as on the factory field.

7. Stay current with changes in information technology (IT).

8. Fight restrictive thinking among managers.

9. Do not treat organizational change as a spectator sport.

10. Simplify before automating.

11. Cut organizational layers and shorten the chain of command, improve information flow to keep top management responsive to what is happening and allow junior managers to input change in policy.[29]

Peter Senge, a professor at America's Massachusetts Institute of Technology, points out the only 'sustainable advantage' will be to learn faster than competitors and to 'anticipate changes' in the market, because quality and technology are becoming widely available at comparatively low cost. The way forward is to become a learning organization which encourages learning and generation of knowledge at all levels, moves knowledge around the organization and translates knowledge quickly into change. In these ways, the organization expands the 'capacity to create its future'.[30]

There is talk of a new 'paradigm', a pattern. The new pattern puts people, customers and employees first, replacing the rigid structures of the industrial age with networks. Old bureaucracies are just too slow and the key factor today is speed. Productivity is the driving force and it is 'in the minds and hearts of people'.[31]

What ever is going on out there?

Summary

What is going on out there is a revolution. The revolution is taking place among huge multinationals in America and may soon spread to other international giants in Europe. It is a concerted attempt to respond to the amazing levels of productivity and quality set by the Japanese. In fact, however belated, it is beginning to look like the Western response.

Unable to re-create the unique conditions of Japan, American supernationals are trying their own versions of Jack Welch's 'work out' at General Electric. Briefly, they are pushing power further down the line, to the line, where self-managed teams are empowered to do their own managing. Power is being delegated from the centre down the line, because that is where people have the information to make the decisions and are closest to the customers. It is the power of information technology that makes all this possible.

In progressive companies teams hire and fire, manage and even invest. To what ends? Jumps in productivity of 40 per cent or more have been recorded by self-managed teams. Quality has improved remarkably too. When workers have been asked for the first time to participate directly in managing their own destinies, the results have been nothing short of amazing.

Consider the benefits:

- The Western corporation reaps higher productivity and better quality because the workers are 'turned on'.

- The problems of motivation and incentive disappear with empowerment.

- Overheads drop because you do not need so many middle managers, whose primary function, according to numerous studies, is to spend two-thirds of their time passing paper up the line.

- Another major consideration is improved quality, which can dramatically reduce costs by up to one-third.

Higher output, lower manufacturing costs and reduced overheads are an unbeatable combination and the possible response to Japanese competition. *That is what is happening out there.*

An excellent example of all these practices was provided by the resurgence of Harley Davidson Motorcycles of York, Pennsylvania. At one point in the 1980s, Harley was on the verge of bankruptcy. The last place the company could go was to its workforce. A vice-president for manufacturing, according to Tom Peters, supported a woman worker who took the executive at his word about complaining if product was not up to quality. This sparked off a revolution in attitudes which resulted in huge jumps in productivity and quality. Formation of semi-autonomous teams transformed 25 year veterans on the factory floor into quality controllers and statisticians. Harley went from 27 production controllers where no product went out on time to one controller and all products out on time. Quite a story.

Peters also cites Wal-Mart Stores Inc. from Bentonville, Arkansas which generates more sales than Sears Roebuck & Company and any other retailer in the world, even though Wal-Mart was established less than 45 years ago in a backwater town in a small southern state. Wal-Mart has 3 layers of bureaucracy and Sears has 15.[28] The number of management layers is also important to the chairman of Glaxo, a huge British pharmaceutical company, who believes there should never be more than two people between him and an operating manager.[32] *Middle management is under threat.*

After several decades of continual expansion, middle managers evolved to the point where two-thirds of their time was devoted to administration, passing information back and forth, and only one-third involved decision making. Companies now can replace the information function with computers and decision making is being devolved to teams.

Where does this leave the middle manager? The middle manager needs to find a new role, perhaps as a 'mentor' or 'coach' to the teams. But this will require an enormous change of attitude for managers used to instrumental relationships and power over workers. Middle managers can easily be perceived as excess overheads when self-managing teams are formed and empowered. So it is not surprising that many of the recent layoffs involve large numbers of middle managers for the first time. It is understandable why middle managers feel threatened about these changes and trends.

Strategic planning, of course, can facilitate such changes. In fact, strategic management is a vehicle for managing change. The creation of self-managed teams fits neatly in the implementation phase. But these teams, like all employees in a company, still need direction which is provided by the company's vision, objectives and goals and strategies which can be set from above and devolved down to operating units. *Corporate life is getting very interesting.*

Now that we have set the company's agenda and devised strategies to achieve the objectives, we can look at how you can make the plan work inside the company.

References

1. Arthur Bloch, *The Complete Murphy's Law: A Definitive Collection*, Price, Stern, Sloan, Los Angeles, 1991.

2. Gerry Johnson and Kevan Scholes, *Exploring Corporate Strategy*, Prentice-Hall, London, 1989.

3. Jonathon Green, *The Cynic's Lexicon: A Dictionary of Amoral Advice*, Sphere, London, 1986.

4. Mary Fagan, 'Laura Ashley opts to go Express', *Independent*, 20 March 1992.

5. Mack Hanan, *Fast-Growth Strategies: How to Maximize Profits from Start-up Through Maturity*, McGraw-Hill, New York, 1987.

6. Robin Hirsch, 'Getting the ratios right', *Management Today*, April 1990.

7. John Argenti, *Practical Corporate Planning*, Unwin Hyman, London, 1989.

8. *Economist*, 'Corporate structure: why big might remain beautiful', 24 March 1990.

9. Michael Lawson, *Going for Growth: A Guide to Corporate Strategy*, Kogan Page, London, 1987.

10. *Economist*, 'Bombardier: That gentle Canadian touch', 14 July 1990.

11. Harvey Elliott, 'Short takes off after decades in the hanger', *Times*, 15 August 1992.

12. Cliff Bowman, *The Essence of Strategic Management*, Prentice-Hall, London, 1990.

13. Danny Miller, 'Configurations of strategy and structures: towards a synthesis', in David Asch and Cliff Bowman (eds), *Readings in Strategic Management*, Macmillan, London, 1989.

14. *Economist*, 'Surviving the deluge', 13 October 1990.

15. Jason Nisse, 'The ten greatest merger disasters', *Independent*, 22 December 1991.

16. *Economist*, 'American Telephone and Telegraph: the wrong choice?', 27 April 1991.

17. Diane Summers, 'Stress blamed for failed mergers', *Financial Times*, 8 January 1992.

18. Philip Sadler, 'Books: mergers and acquisitions, the human factor', *Director*, January 1992.

19. Sue Cartwright and Cary Cooper, 'The forgotten factor', *Director*, December 1991.

20. Jan Szydlowski, 'A plan for Europe', *Director*, November 1988.

21. *The Journal on General Management*, 'Manager update', 3(1), Autumn 1991.

22. Kenichi Ohmae, *The Mind of the Strategist: Business Planning for Competitive Advantage*, Penguin, London, 1983.

23. Charles Handy, 'Is there time to raise our standards?', *Director*, July 1991.

24. *Economist*, 'Management focus: first find your bench', 11 May 1991.

25. Simon Holberton, 'An idea whose time has not only come but will prevail', *Financial Times*, 20 March 1991.

26. Tom Peters, 'Towards the entrepreneurial and empowering organisation', The Royal Lancaster Hotel, London, 13 February 1990 (A summary provided by 3i plc).

27. Christopher Lorenz, 'Followers of fashion: "Excellence": How not to singe your wings', *Financial Times*, 25 January 1991.

28. *Business Matters*, BBC Television Channel 2, 1 March 1992.

29. Andersen Consulting (UK), *View 90*.

30. Christopher Lorenz, 'Bending minds to a new learning circle', *Financial Times*, 17 February 1992.

31. Frank Rose, 'A new age for business?', *Fortune International*, 8 October 1990.

32. *Risk Business*, BBC Television Channel 2, 1 September 1992.

Implementation Part I— How can we make it happen?

An idea is only as good as its execution.

ANON

Introduction

You make the corporate plan happen in your company through the implementation process. Many companies fall down in this critical area because they fail to pay sufficient attention to human resources, business plans and monitoring. There is another hidden danger at this stage in the planning cycle: your team may believe the hard work has already been done. You may have set the company's agenda and devised strategies to achieve the objectives but you still have to translate everything into reality, and a well-executed plan is just as essential as the plan itself. Perhaps this metaphor illustrates the point: the archer concentrates on pulling back the string on the bow but still needs to devote equal concentration before letting the arrow fly. Pull, release. The implementation process is the archer's release, demanding the same attention as the pull which is the agenda and strategies.

There is no point in going through all the effort to create a vision, establish objectives, set goals and devise strategies if you fail to implement the corporate plan inside your company. If the plan is not successfully implemented, most of the preparatory work will have been wasted. PA Consultants have estimated that 'over 95 per cent of all strategies designed in the late 1970s and early 1980s were never fully or effectively implemented'.[1]

Nature of change

The implementation process is not an easy one because it deals with change. By the very process of making plans, you are planning to change the organization and the way it performs. Change may involve handling problems which have accumulated over time, like clearing out that spare room or attic at home that you have been avoiding. Plans mean change and most people do not like change.

Writing in *The Prince* in 1513, Machiavelli said:

'And one should bear in mind that there is nothing more difficult to execute, nor more dubious of success, nor more dangerous to administer than to introduce a new order of things; for he who introduces it has all those who profit from the old order as his enemies, and he has only lukewarm allies in all those who might profit from the new.'[2]

There also is a saying in Nuro Linguistic Planning (NLP) that goes something like this: 'as long as you do what you've always done you'll always get what you always got'. If this is true for individuals, it applies equally to organizations.

There may be no forward progress and no real improvement without change. And change will meet resistance and resistance may be encountered at each step in the implementation process. How much resistance is met and how easily it is overcome rests largely with the management team, especially with the chief executive. Charles Handy comments on resistance as follows: 'Some people do not want to keep moving. Change for them means sacrificing the familiar, even if it is unpleasant, for the unknown, even when it might be better. Better the hole they know rather than the one not yet dug.'[3]

Resistance can occur at senior levels in management. Some executives may refuse to participate in the planning process or, if involved, only respond half-heartedly. Others may seek to undermine the process once the management team ends the session. Often an executive has difficulty dealing with the uncertainty and perceives the process as a personal threat to his or her position.

You deal with resistance by recognizing it up front. Real change will meet direct and indirect resistance and you have to find a way to deal with that resistance. The following chapters suggest several ways to capture the 'hearts and minds' of your people, getting them to 'own' the plan and become a part of the future you hope to achieve. For example, one of the most effective ways to overcome resistance is by educating people before the change occurs. Hence, 'communication of ideas helps people see the need for and logic of a change [and] *participation leads to commitment, not merely compliance*' [italics added]. A word of warning: if the communication process is not managed properly, it can be very time consuming.[4]

Management has no option. Being in business means dealing with change. There are no safe harbours any more, even in the public sector. As Harvey-Jones says,'*management is about maintaining the highest rate of change that the organisation and the people within it can stand*' [italics added].[5]

Managing change

Several points should be made about change:

- First, as a manager, you need to recognize that creation of a corporate plan will start an internal change process by providing clear direction for the future. In fact, *corporate planning is the most effective vehicle for creating and managing positive change.*

- Second, you need to believe that the change process can be managed and managed effectively to produce positive results.

- Third, communications are vital to managing change.

- Fourth, leadership is the fountain-head in the change process.

- Fifth, effective implementation and positive change will rest on pushing responsibility and accountability down into the organization, raising the critical issue of balance between consent and compliance and between central power and line authority.

- Sixth, do not underestimate the difficulties in managing change or regard it to be a one-off event but rather look at it as a continuous process of improvement akin to TQM.

- Seventh, growth puts demands and creates strains on structure and reporting channels. So, you need periodically to rethink structure and reporting relationships.

- Eighth, during the leadership process, senior managers should remember that their behaviour acts as a powerful role-model.[6]

The very process of growth forces change on companies. For example, several problems arise when sales and employees increase, such as need to coordinate, communicate widely, handle new functions and develop more management hierarchies. Growth periods can become crisis periods in which companies fail because they cannot change to new practices and are unable to abandon old ones.[4]

As *Business Week* noted, 'we often want change but not if it hurts'. And it takes time. Some observers reckon it can take up to ten years for fundamental change in big companies. While it takes time, change requires a vision, 'something more than the desire for profit' and solid business plans to back up the vision.[7] On the other hand, medium sized companies have the ability to change in much shorter time because the management team is closer to the employees.

A study of high and low performing British companies over twenty years revealed five key factors needed for effective change management:

1 Leadership by the management team.

2 Constant evaluation of the changing commercial environment.

3 Handling people as assets, not costs.

4 Conversion of strategic change into operational actions.

5 Constant all-embracing 'coherence', which means a sustained sense of purpose.

High-performing companies in the study were Peugeot-Talbot in automobiles, Kleinwort Benson in merchant banking, and Longman in publishing. Their low-performing counterparts were Jaguar, Hill Samuel, and Associated Book Publishers.[8]

Relations with a union, if you have one, can be another trouble spot in managing change. Some trade unions see new human resource initiatives as an attempt to side-step officials and deal with workers directly. Such attempts can meet resistance because they are perceived as weakening the strength of unions standing between workers and management. On the other hand, management does not want to restrict communications through union channels, because planning requires continual communication to all employees.[9]

Real test of implementation

The real test of implementation is whether or not the management team and middle managers actually make decisions based on the corporate plan.

If you fail to act within the framework established by the corporate plan, you will undermine the exercise. Actions taken outside the plan's agreed parameters will be counterproductive, causing confusion and detracting from the company's focus. The plan exists to shape decisions for the future of your choosing. If managers do not make decisions that move the company towards agreed ends, they will be choosing to go in a different direction.

What is implementation?

Implementation is the process to convert strategies into realities. It is said to be the sternest test of management's ability to lead and manage.

Implementation involves the following important elements:

1 Leadership

2 Communication

3 Action plans

4 Budgets

5 Timetables

6 Milestones

7 Reviews

Key elements

Leadership

The first and most important element is *visible leadership*. What does visible leadership mean? First, the chief executive demonstrates his or her full commitment to the plan. Second, it means that every senior manager on the management team takes ownership of and makes a public commitment to the plan and the forward direction for the company. Third, the chief executive and each team member provide inspirational leadership, that is, they communicate their excitement about the future to employees and periodically report progress against plan. As Napoleon said, 'a leader is a dealer in hope.'[10] Fourth, leadership is leading by example, setting the model for the type of behaviour and performance you want from your people.

John Harvey-Jones said 'the task of leadership, after all, is to obtain extraordinary results from ordinary people'.[11] His view was echoed by Konosuke Matsushita's fundamental tenet 'to develop extraordinary qualities in ordinary men'.[12] According to Sharplin, there is common agreement that an able leader 'should be active rather than passive, consistent rather than inconsistent, principled rather than unprincipled, powerful as opposed to impotent and communicative instead of taciturn'. He also indicates that the good leader is humane, farsighted, inspired and confident.[13] Another factor in a successful leader is obsessive single-mindedness.[12] Writing almost 2500 years ago, Sun Tzu said 'leadership is intelligence, credibility, humanity, courage, and discipline'. He also pointed out there were five flaws 'common to leaders'; recklessness, excessive caution, a short temper, fastidiousness and deep personal attachments.[14]

Observers have noted that leadership styles may vary with different situations, but effective leaders create a 'climate' for change and increase a company's energy level. Moreover, visitors can detect energy levels the minute they walk through an organization's front door.[15] In any event, change itself means the need for more leadership, not less.

Charles Handy points to one common agreement in all the studies of leadership, that 'a leader shapes and shares a vision which gives point to the work of others'.[3] And vision appears as a key element in Warren Bennis's statement on leadership. He discovered that all strong leaders had a believable and compelling vision of where they wanted the company to go, but translating a vision into practice is a long-term exercise. Meanwhile, the market determines the short term and strategies 'bridge the gap' between the short and long term.[16]

Max de Pree feels that a leader must first define reality, becoming in the process both servant and debtor. Leaders have to bear pain, not inflict it. They need to provide and sustain momentum based on a clear idea of what the company should be. Leadership depends on carefully 'conceived and communicated' plans in which everyone must be able to participate and be held accountable in achieving the company's goals.[17] Most of the outstanding leaders that MIT's Peter Senge knows do not stand out in a crowd. They often appear as mediocre public speakers unable to sway audiences with eloquence or brilliance. What makes them stand out is the clarity and power of their ideas, deep commitment to their companies and continual willingness to learn.[18]

By leadership, I mean the collective leadership of the management team as well as leadership of individual members. Clearly, the chief executive is the most visible leader and needs to take a positive and confident lead. On the other hand, too many times the outside world just pays attention to a company's leader and forgets that every successful company must have a good team. In truth, management is a team effort and an effective leader ensures the whole team owns the plan and takes that pride of ownership to everyone throughout the company, not leaving it to the chief executive to do alone. In this regard, each team member is obliged to successfully implement the plan in the areas of their own involvement.

On the negative side, a chief executive can be *the* principal obstacle to integrating strategic planning into the management process. For this reason, the *chief executive has to lead* the planning process and its implementation. *If the chief executive opposes the planning exercise, it will be doomed.* Management teams, under these circumstances, would be advised to find a new leader rather than try to introduce strategic planning against a hostile chief executive.

While the chief executive can block the whole planning process, he or she cannot realize the plan without a management team. The management team has to be committed to the process for the plan to be successful. In this way, both chief executive and team have to be equally committed to making the plan work. *The leader and team need each other and need to take joint ownership of the plan if it is to be realized.*

An example of poor leadership was provided by John Ashcroft, the determined former chief executive at Britain's Coloroll. Comments about Ashcroft from those who worked for him demonstrate how bad leadership can eventually result in disaster:

- 'Cash management to John Ashcroft meant squeezing creditors.'

- 'Managers were expected to hit targets that had not been set in the real world.'

- 'As Coloroll acquired companies it replaced the management with its own people far too quickly [and] they were arrogant.'

- 'He made it clear that he regarded us as "operational management" and that we were therefore considered inferior to management at corporate level.'

- 'There was no doubt that Ashcroft dominated the board and was too powerful.'

- 'Ashcroft didn't welcome outsiders and wouldn't allow consultants into the group.'[19]

Other key elements

While every company will have its own house style, there are other universal elements for successful implementation.

Internal marketing

Internal marketing involves communicating the vision, objectives and goals to everyone in the company. The internal communication exercise needs to be done well and often. Like the planning process itself, communicating is not a one-off exercise. *You need to communicate effectively to get everyone mobilized behind the plan*, and you need to keep right on communicating to keep them mobilized, retaining their enthusiasm and maintaining their morale. *If the management team does not find the time to communicate, who else will?*

The guiding principle behind communicating is simple: *clear communication of ideas helps people to see the need and logic for change.* Understanding about the future also allows people to worry less about specific changes and helps them to think how they can contribute to the plan, not fight it.

It may sound foolish but people like to know where they are going. People do not like uncertainty. More importantly, people respond positively to firm leadership. The message, therefore, should be loud and clear: communicate, communicate and communicate. If you want your people to support your plan, you need first to let them know what it is and how, as individuals, they will be involved (see below). *The first cardinal rule in implementation is COMMUNICATE.*

How much should you communicate? Some companies find it useful to present each employee with a one page summary of the plan, explaining the company's agenda. Detailed information on strategies and their implementation appears later in business plans and can be discussed with individual teams. Other companies find that their employees get overwhelmed with a lot of information and do not want to share bad news. You are the best judge of how your people will respond and how much information and involvement you feel is appropriate. As always, you need to seek a balance in the communication process to get positive responses.

When you communicate, are you aware of the importance of non-verbal communication? Research revealed some surprising results about the process of communication. The communication's content or message represents only 7 per cent of the total perception. Voice accounts for 38 per cent and body language for even more, 55 per cent. It is worth paying close attention to what you do physically when communicating rather than relying only on the message you are sending.[20] Thus, it is not just what you say but, more importantly, how you say it that counts.

Problem solving appointments

Appoint teams to solve problems and implement the strategies. Every implementation team should have an identifiable leader. The importance of action teams cannot be ignored. The most effective way to get anything done in an organization is to create a highly motivated team, provide a clear but tight brief, give the team authority and then monitor progress. *Creation of special implementation teams will achieve greater and faster results than any other single act during the implementation process.* That is why *the second cardinal rule is to form action teams to implement the plan.*

The third cardinal rule in the implementation process goes like this: PARTICIPATION LEADS TO COMMITMENT, *not merely compliance.* If you believe in shared decision making, industrial democracy and, above all, delegation, you will create commitment to the plan through participation.

Clear accountability

Once the plan is communicated to your people and implementation teams are formed, individual team leaders need to be made accountable for their assignments. Accountability is the cornerstone of management delegation and performance measurement. It has a vital role in the implementation process.

Cardinal rule number four is never split an assignment between two leaders, that is, always make one manager clearly responsible for the assignment. Do not, of course, forget to give the responsible manager clear authority and power over that for which he or she is responsible. Responsibility without authority is one of the worst forms of management torture and a nightmarish source of confusion and frustration among managers.

Entrepreneurial managers

If your strategy calls for entrepreneurial flair, find the entrepreneurs within your company and appoint them as leaders. If you do not have any latent entrepreneurs within the company, appoint them from outside. Entrepreneurial leaders need to be made directly responsible for profits and growth, reporting back through the appropriate channels in the management structure. If you want fast results, find fast people and monitor them closely.

Incentives

We have talked about loading the new team leaders with additional work and responsibilities, but what about rewards? *Implementation assignments require a link between results and rewards.* Also, you will want to provide adequate incentives which will foster teamwork. If teamwork is to be promoted, incentives need to be shared among the entire team, not hogged by team leaders or individual members of the management team.

W. Edwards Deming believes that performance-related pay is divisive and works against cooperation. As teams are the cornerstone for effective plan implementation, the team needs to be rewarded, not the individual. While many companies look at incentive schemes for the whole workforce, the most effective reward is one linked directly to team performance. Also, *do not be afraid to award cash bonuses for results not otherwise expected. Cardinal rule number five is that team rewards encourage further performance and cement commitment.*

The next best thing to cash rewards is recognition. Your best performing people should be recognized formally by the management team and, if appropriate, throughout the entire company.

Management information

Above everything else, make sure that you have an excellent management information system which can measure progress accurately. As Michael Lawson stated: 'Without a competent information system you will be unable to monitor progress.'[21] Your management information system is the cornerstone for monitoring performance against plan and budget and determining if additional resources need to be committed or should be diverted elsewhere. Because continued communication and rewards will depend on reporting progress against plan, it is essential that you are able to measure accurately and quickly.

While you will want to know the progress of each team, it is equally important to know the contribution of each product or service to profit. As a necessary concomitant, you should be able to allocate realistic costs against each product or service. *The sixth cardinal rule is that the management information system needs clearly to reflect progress of each strategy selected for implementation.* It is not helpful if managers and leaders need to hunt and pick at information to find out what is going on. Information should be presented in a format that mirrors what is happening by priority.

Controls

Along with a first rate management information system, it is vital to have a top class control system. The information system needs to present the progress of each project to allow the monitoring and controlling of revenues and expenditures. It makes no sense to complete the planning process by creating project teams and then fail to monitor and control their progress. Monitoring and controlling are among the most important on-going functions of the management team, but you need accurate and timely information to do the job correctly. Yet, some companies rush into growth without proper information systems and controls in place; other companies embark on radical change without working systems. As a result, such companies often come unstuck and do not realize what is happening until it is too late to do anything about it. *Cardinal rule number seven is to control your projects by monitoring management information and measuring progress against milestones.* By milestones we mean specific key actions to be accomplished at predetermined points in time.

In summary, find the best performers in your company, give them direction through an agreed plan in which they take ownership, delegate responsibility with authority and monitor by using clear channels of reporting and controls tied to your management information system. By now you can see that the use of information technology will be very important during the implementation process.

Again, national and cultural factors can affect change management. Richard Scase, Professor of Organizational Behaviour at the University of Kent, England, commented on many implementation points when comparing British companies to the latest developments among a handful of American high-technology companies like IBM, 3M and Hewlett-Packard. He criticized management thinkers in their belief that all new cultural changes, such as flat structures, removing hierarchies and decentralization and devolution of responsibilities, are applicable to every company in every Western country. Scase observed that the new thinking assumes a 'high trust' culture where managers inspire leadership, promote teamwork and cooperation and goal setting and achievement and let their people get on with the job. But, Britain is a 'low trust' society. A history of poor industrial relations and an infamous class structure promoted division and suspicion. The system moulds people to expect 'security, routine and stability' in their jobs, not constant change and upheaval. British managers will not be equipped to handle and manage change.[22]

Are any of these comments applicable to your company? If so, the implementation process will be shaped as much from resistance as action, which gives rise to *cardinal rule number eight: you need to shape the implementation programme to your company.* You will be able to change some things for the better, but not others. On the other hand, not everything needs to be changed to get results, nor is change worth while for its own sake. *Cardinal rule number nine calls for change only when necessary to achieve an important objective*. Remember that all progress is the result of change but all change is not necessarily progress.

When considering change, the prayer of acceptance, adapted here as the 'corporate cultural prayer', seems worth recalling: 'Oh Lord grant me the strength to change things that need changing, the courage to accept things that cannot be changed, and the wisdom to know the difference.'

As we have seen, two companies will not have the same strategy even though they operate in the same industry. The same is true about strategic management. There is no single, optimum formula for the way a company should be managed. If there were, everyone would use it and business schools would become redundant. There are, however, universal principles that have worked in strategic planning.

Mechanics: short cut

Larry Alexander advocates a four step approach for the implementation phase. His model is as follows:

1. Start with a good concept or idea.

2. Obtain employee commitment and involvement.

3. Provide sufficient resources, i.e. money, manpower and time.

4. Develop an implementation plan for who does what and when.[23]

Like all good short cuts, Alexander's approach is crisp and simple but, unfortunately, there is more to it than these few steps imply.

Mechanics: longer version

The mechanics for successful implementation can be broken down into the following six steps:

1. Select only a small number of projects. It is both sensible and practical to set a few top priorities and focus limited resources on converting them. Do not get carried away with the process and stretch yourself too thinly. As the old sage warned: Rome clearly was not made in a day and nor will your corporate plan be.

2. Assign one manager to each project. Form action teams each under the leadership of one individual who has responsibility with authority. Do not share assignments.

3. Write detailed business plans which include the following elements:
   (a) market plan and strategy;
   (b) targets;

      (c) budgets with all details including assumptions;
      (d) timetable with identifiable milestones (important actions to be accomplished by certain dates).

4. Make sure a member of the management team assumes accountability for each project, including the obligation to report progress to the team.

5. Measure progress at regular intervals.

6. Review formally the entire corporate plan at least once a year.

Budgets

A special word about budgets. Budgets, the old tried and true workhorse of the management system, still play a key role in strategic planning. However, rather than existing as the only annual exercise, budgets are relegated to the implementation stage, because other things must be decided first. You need to know where you are going and what you have to do to get there before you set about allocating expected revenues and expenditures. Arthur Sharplin comments that 'budgets are necessary to translate strategic plans into concrete activities'.[13] They were necessary before strategic management was invented and they remain as necessary today, but after you have completed the company's agenda and strategies.

Milestones

Milestones are very effective in establishing defined points to measure progress and hold team managers accountable. However, you need to take care in establishing milestones. Problems can arise if milestones are not 'concrete' and, therefore, cannot be measured. Each milestone must be defined clearly and be achievable. Milestones need to be tied to strategies to have meaning. And they have to be clearly communicated and accepted by the teams who are to reach them.[12]

Resource allocation

One of the most important aspects of strategic planning is the resource allocation process. *The planning process allows you to allocate resources behind the best opportunities and in the most efficient way.* Planning promotes effective allocation for the following reasons: first, the best opportunities are identified during the strategic evaluation process; second, they are ranked in order of priority based on criteria including the risk/reward ratio; third, resources are allocated on the basis of these priorities; and fourth, once allocated, projects are monitored closely against plan before additional resources are allocated or diverted.

When management allocates and measures results according to established guidelines, it eliminates the capricious use of limited resources according to whim or hunch. This is important, because resource allocation is arguably the most critical management task after identifying, evaluating and prioritizing opportunities for resourcing. *Resources are allocated effectively by defining a small number of major projects and assigning each to an individual with progress measured by milestones over predetermined periods.*

Resources need to follow the opportunities identified, evaluated and prioritized during the strategic planning phase. Risk and rewards should be considered carefully, striking a balance before commitments are made. Risk is handled by setting *defined criteria* for payback and rate of return. If the risk is higher, the rate of return should be higher and the payback period quicker.

A good management structure also helps achieve balanced resource allocation, because the management team makes recommendations which are reviewed and decided by the board of directors. Gluck has identified three classic dilemmas involved in resource allocation:

1. Which criteria to use in determining the allocation.

2. How to match resource needs with resource availability.

3. How to schedule resource commitments over time.[13]

But, the most important thing to remember in resource allocation (*cardinal rule number ten*) is to make sure that every resource allocated is tied to an approved business plan. No business plan, no resource. No one in the company should be spending money or buying technology or hiring people without a detailed plan that has been approved by the management team and the board. In this way, you kill the proverbial two birds with one missile: first, no project is started in the company without an approved business plan; second, all projects will conform to the strategic plan. Thus, we all row in the same direction with the best oars available.

Management structure

A company's management structure plays a vital role in the implementation of a strategic plan. The reason why the management structure is important in the strategic planning process is because it can promote *balanced decision making* and provide necessary *checks and balances* in reporting and controlling, which are essential to management in general and to plan implementation in particular.

Structures should exist to make management work better and be more effective. It is an irony that many structures actually do the opposite: they create bureaucracy, unnecessary paperwork and slow response times.

The basic management structure discussed below will promote effective planning and benefit the whole company's management. The structure is kept to a minimum in order to facilitate the best communications and fastest response time to market conditions. Any management structure, therefore, that promotes fast response and balanced decision making is good for the strategic planning process. Balanced decision making begins with industrial democracy, that is, sharing of decisions between the chief executive and management team and, in turn, between individual members of the management team and their implementation teams, and so on. We are talking about participation in decision making at all levels of the company.

There is little point in having a strategic planning activity in a company dominated by an autocratic chief executive. The chemistry in successful strategic planning depends on participation and shared decision making which lead to ownership and commitment. Autocrats will not suffer such democracy, because it represents a source of potential challenge to their authority. Invariably, autocrats will not accept or keep an independent board of directors for the same reason. Nor would the autocrat have much use for a management committee or any other participatory element in the structure. An autocrat is threatened by democracy but the best managers demand participation and shared decisions to have some control over their own destinies. As a consequence, autocrats are usually unable to build management teams and, therefore, the best people leave such companies.

A company's management structure usually reveals how much democracy is practised inside the organization. It can send a clear message to any new high quality people you may wish to attract. From this point on the discussion assumes that you practise a form of participatory democracy.

Current thinking

Recent attention has been focused on management structure, because the structure itself has become an issue in company development and culture. The general trend is towards flat structures with fewer layers of bureaucracy, that is, management.

Peters admits it was a mistake to play down structures in his book, *In Search of Excellence*: 'Good intentions and brilliant proposals will be dead-ended, delayed, sabotaged, massaged to death, or revised beyond recognition or usefulness by the overlaid structures at most large and all too many small firms.'[24]

The trend to evolutionary new structures is most evident in the creation of teams which virtually manage themselves. When self-managed teams are formed, middle managers and hence management layers will be eliminated. For example, Peters cites the change at Harley Davidson Motorcycles where 27 production controllers were reduced to one. Such radical restructuring leads to flatter organizational structures and more direct communication between senior management and the factory or office floor.

Structural elements

If you look at a properly structured company, three elements are readily apparent:

1. *Board of directors.* Ideally, the board guides the company in the present through policy making and in the future by allocating resources within an agreed corporate plan. While boards play other roles and perform additional functions, policy making and resource allocation *within the context of the strategic plan* are their most important contributions.

2. *Management committee.* The management or executive committee concentrates on the day-to-day running of the business, solving operational problems and exchanging information among managers.

   If the structure has devolved management to product group managers, each product group may have its own management committee. In this case, however, there still should be an overall management committee for the company which would include managers of key central functions and each product group manager.

3. *Other special committees.* Companies often find it useful to have functional committees, such as sales, production, research, new product development, etc. However, specialized committees deal with business problems in a narrowly defined function compared to the management committee and board which deal with problems affecting the entire company.

H. Ross Perot, founder of Electronic Data Systems, was quoted as saying: 'If you see a snake, just kill it—don't appoint a committee on snakes.'[10] Other pithy comments on meetings and committees include the following:

- 'A meeting is an event at which minutes are kept and the hours are lost' (Gourd's axiom).

- 'A committee is twelve people doing the work of one' (Kennedy's comment on committees).[25]

- 'If an hour has been spent amending a sentence, someone will move to delete the paragraph' (Kim's rule of committees).

- 'Those who are unable to learn from past meetings are condemned to repeat them' (McKernan's maxim).[26]

And everyone knows that a camel was a horse designed by a committee.

Yet, for all these pot shots at committees, there is no better way to gather people, share information, discuss issues and reach consensus. I am afraid committees will be with us for a long time yet. On the other hand, a lot of difference can be made by running meetings in an orderly and efficient manner, which is a function of the chair. A properly balanced and managed agenda conducted against time limits will go a long way towards making committees more effective. *Minuting actions assigned and raising them at the next meeting will ensure accountability through the chair and peer group pressure.*

The board

Much has been written about the role of the board and governance of a company. What should be abundantly clear is that the board plays a much different role than the various executive committees. The board is responsible for the forward development of the business, making policies that will advance the strategic plan. While the board monitors the performance of the company, it must also keep an eye on the future.

Management structures are critical to the operation of any organization, especially commercial ones that live in an ever changing world. Structures should promote *balanced decision making*, that is, *the most appropriate response to changing conditions based on different views within the organization.*

Sir Lewis Robertson, a renowned British company doctor, noted that 'delinquent' boards did some or all of the following things:

1. They fail to balance internal (executive) with external (non-executive) experience.

2. They accept weak financial information usually from an inadequate finance executive.

3. They do not challenge the case for acquisitions.

4. They do not question management in depth on market changes and development of products.

5. They allow painful decisions to be deferred.

6. They allow the position of chairman and chief executive to be combined.[27]

A board and management committee promote balanced decisions by sharing information, exchanging opposing views and reaching decisions democratically. The balance comes from different places: first, the board and management committee play separate but complementary roles; second, the composition of both should create opposing views based on different experiences, roles and disciplines.

Non-executives on the board

Let us explore this further. Objectivity on the board should be provided by non-executive (often called independent or part-time) directors who are detached from the business and are free to act solely in the company's best interests. While non-executives are supposed to have wide business experience and knowledge, their most important qualifications are a strong sense of independence and ability to concentrate on the key business issues. In this regard, it is pointless to have non-executives who are beholden to the chairman for their appointment or who need their fee to survive.

It is worth taking a moment to look at the specific role of a non-executive director. Non-executives contribute to balanced decision making in the following areas:

1. Look at major business issues with objectivity and detachment.

2. Act in the best interests of the company and represent specific interests of minority shareholders.

3. Be devil's advocates in forcing the executives to justify their actions.

4. State opposing views, looking at the downside to offset management's inevitable upbeat outlook.

5. Act as guardians of the corporate plan, pressing for effective implementation to achieve objectives.

6. Deal with senior personnel matters such as appointments, remuneration and dismissals.

Non-executives add two elements that do not exist in an all-executive board: objectivity and independence. Appointments in larger companies are usually meant to monitor performance and assist governance, while non-executives at smaller companies help widen the board's 'horizons'.

With the recent demise of some very public figures and major corporations in the United Kingdom, attention has focused on corporate governance. The Committee on Financial Aspects of Corporate Governance, called the Cadbury Committee after its Chairman, Sir Adrian Cadbury, made several recommendations to increase board accountability. The Committee suggested that the offices of chairman and chief executive should be split, boards should have audit and remuneration committees dominated by non-executives and the audit committee should meet at least annually with the external auditors but without executives in attendance. The Committee also felt non-executives should be able to seek outside independent financial advice, even at the company's cost.[28]

According to one journalist, the Cadbury Committee is a typical British fudge, 'well-meaning, reasonable, intelligent and worthless. It is based on the age-old British myth that capitalists are mild-mannered animals capable of learning good behaviour if only they go to the right schools.' But, in fact, 'capitalists are predators who render their benefits to society through a process that is both creative and destructive'. As a result, they need to be put in a strict legal system to prevent abuse of power and wealth.[29]

Will Cadbury's largely voluntary recommendations stave off restrictive legislation? A lot may depend on the behaviour of large company boards and whether they allow powerful chief executives or chairmen to dominate to the detriment of their shareholders.

Regardless of the size of the company, there is no point having a board without independent directors. If there are no non-executives, there will be only executives who might just as well meet as an executive committee. *There can be no balance on a board unless you have outsiders.* Sir Lewis Robertson made this point as follows: 'If a board is entirely executive, what use is it? The result will be simply management talking to itself, with no fresh thinking, and nobody daring to disagree or to put up alternatives, because the man at the top has power over their jobs.'[27]

Non-executives should monitor and challenge executive performance, but their greatest long-term contribution is to help shape the future development of the company through a strategic plan. In this way, non-executives become the *guardians* of the future. Yet, they are often poorly treated and given the mushroom treatment: kept in the dark with heaps of manure. A survey of 149 chairman of top British companies showed that 60 per cent appointed non-executives 'without defining their role and many do not provide them with sufficient information to make a significant contribution'.[30]

Another survey of 340 non-executives at 250 companies found that 67 per cent felt briefings by executives were 'inaccurate, poorly focused and badly presented'. And 59 per cent were frustrated because executives failed to listen to their advice.[31]

Many times appointments are made for the wrong reasons. A common practice is for chairmen to appoint friends or at least people who will be friendly, rather than true independents who will contribute objectively in the best interests of the company. For example, Charles Batchelor comments that too many companies still appoint the firm's solicitor or banker to the board or reward retiring executive directors with non-executive posts, but these people are most unlikely to provide an independent view.[32]

Because executives control the information flow to non-executives, there must be a strong sense of trust and sharing. If they wish to, executives can easily mislead non-executives through manipulating the quantity and quality of information. Such action would be short-sighted, because it denies the benefits of 'sharing the pain' and collective responsibility.

Balance at management committees starts with keeping all managers informed of developments within the company. You cannot rely on word of mouth getting to everyone or getting the correct message across. Formal committee meetings with fixed agendas ensure that everyone knows about key developments and all are able to deal with the impact on their own area. Balance is also achieved by pooling the collective experience of managers and talking through problems. *Remember, participation in decision making leads to ownership and commitment.*

A necessary adjunct to all this is effective communication. In order to communicate it is necessary for people to talk directly. People also need to talk openly and honestly which means creating an atmosphere in which frank conversation can occur. This is the direct responsibility of the chief executive and will be influenced considerably by his or her style and behaviour as a role model.

One major danger in communication is that people will personalize issues which can block or frustrate problem resolution. The way to deal with this is always to bring people back to the business issue, asking what can be done to solve the business problem and what is the best decision for the company. In short, concentrate on the business issue until it is solved. *The guiding rule is to seek solutions that are in the company's best interests. If you continually ask what is in the company's best interest (shareholders and employees and customers), everyone will focus on the business issue and the most positive solution for that problem.*

Executives often say that they do not need to meet because they talk all the time. Yes, they may talk all the time, but are they talking about all the key business issues and are they really talking, listening and responding? If you do not maintain the discipline of formal meetings at regular intervals you cannot be sure that your managers are communicating or solving problems in any integrated or coherent fashion.

Management committees

Management committees are important mechanisms in the management structure because they permit formal and widespread communication on key business issues. They also allow the chief executive to deal with and manage his or her team in one place at one time, allowing team building and bonding and promoting balanced decisions which are owned by the team.

One way to look at a healthy management structure is to examine the management or executive committee: who sits on it, what it discusses and how often it meets. A key operational factor is the accountability mechanism by which people are given assignments and are subsequently held to account. *The best way to achieve a simple accountability mechanism is to minute assigned actions and open the next meeting with these minuted actions as matters arising.*

A well-structured company, therefore, has an independent board providing overall direction for management to manage and a management committee implementing board policies and solving problems at an operational level. Both are responsible to each other and need to respect one another's different role and contribution. In short, the board governs and the management committee manages.

Roles and reporting

For management structures to work successfully they need another vital element: clear definition of managerial roles. Much confusion and conflict can result if roles are not clearly defined and roles often become blurred when a company experiences rapid growth. One way to define roles is through a job specification, but specifications can be limiting, especially if people work only to their job definition. Also, job specifications tend to be written in a limited way, making them static. 'Fixed' job definitions can become an obstacle to change and fast growth.

No, roles should be defined in a broader functional sense, including what the manager is supposed to do, with whom he or she works, to whom he or she reports and in what specified reporting format. After roles have been defined clearly, time-related targets can be set.

Controls

Another important aspect of roles is controls. All managers should have clearly defined controls that are linked to the reporting system. Controls are there to protect the company from making wrong decisions and from the inevitable consequences that follow wrong decisions. Controls also have a positive side for managers, they offer protection against foolish commitments. Financial approvals, for example, force consultation at defined commitment levels, which means there is a second opinion before the company is committed.

All management structures need reporting and controlling mechanisms to be effective. Reporting and controlling systems need to be formally reviewed from time to time, especially during and after rapid growth. *You need to ask the management team if it is getting the right information it wants on time and in the desired format.* You also need to review with your financial manager whether or not controls are working and remain adequate. A key question is: does the financial manager feel he or she is in control and know what is happening? If the financial manager does not feel comfortable, you may have a serious problem with dire implications for management information and cash management.

The management plan

I find it useful to record formally the management structure in a document called the *management plan*. This plan lists the composition of the board and all management committees. It details the functions of each organizational entity, along with the mechanics about when it meets, what it discusses (standing agenda) and who attends. The management plan also lists the name, job title and role description for each senior manager. It should also list who reports to whom and what information and control systems the company operates. The plan should include an organization and management chart which ought to be combined where possible in one diagram. A written plan enables the board and management team to review the organization and management structures when change requires modifications. The plan also serves as a useful guide to how the company works for any new people who join the company.

Individual performance

A basic building block in the implementation process is individual performance. Managers have wrestled with the subject of individual performance since the start of industrialization and the issue remains very much alive today. However, today the issue is becoming more and more about how an individual performs inside a team or leading a team. As self-managed teams evolve, possibly to become the norm, individual performance is subjected to peer pressure from within the team and is less a matter between a manager and an employee.

The process of dealing with performance starts with a clear definition of an individual's role. Performance is best measured against agreed results. In this way, management focuses on outcomes upon which performance should be judged. Individual and team targets can be set and progress monitored.

Many companies use a formal appraisal system, because it forces communication between workers and managers in a two-way process. Everyone gets appraised in the company, including the executive directors who can be evaluated by non-executives. In this way, the appraisal system is applied equally throughout the organization. However, appraisal systems are time and resource consuming and may not yield clear results. *It is much easier and more effective to focus on targets and performance against those targets which is tangible and can be measured.*

At regular intervals (quarterly, semi-annually or annually) the manager should sit down with each individual in his or her team or with the whole team and formally review performances against previously agreed targets. At this point, rewards can be linked to performance on an individual or team basis.

People like to know where they stand. Individuals and teams want to know if they are performing to an acceptable level even if the discussion is uncomfortable. If you use targets and reviews, they will be quite aware of progress. Individuals and teams also want recognition for work well done and regular review sessions provide an excellent opportunity to recognize good performance. If you want the best from your people, you need to tell them if they are doing well or if they are doing poorly. If individual performance is poor, an employee needs to know that sooner than later. *The quicker below standard performance is identified and discussed, the sooner performance can improve or the person can leave.*

Performance can be changed through training programmes focused on needs and weaknesses identified during the appraisal process or review sessions. In this way, you can prevent people from becoming obstacles. People do not like to be left in an informational and feedback void where only their fears can multiply. As the American writer William S. Burroughs once said: 'a paranoid is a man who knows a little of what's going on'.[33]

Changing an individual

A common obstacle in organizations is a long-serving employee holding down an important position who is not performing well enough or who might be resisting change. There usually are four ways to deal with such people:

1. *Training.* You can sit down with the person and, through the appraisal and review process, analyse strengths and weaknesses and training needs. You can arrange internal, external or combined training inputs and insist the person takes the training. You can measure post-training performance to determine if improvement occurs and progress is being made towards agreed targets.

2. *Counselling.* If the person resists training or changing behaviour, you can arrange to counsel the person inside or outside the organization.

3. *Compensating.* If the person does not change with training or counselling, you can push him or her sideways out of the management loop where little harm can be done. Compensating

indicates your unwillingness to remove the person for some reason, such as recognition that the person might still contribute something worthwhile or cannot be dismissed for a historical, financial or other reason.

4. *Removing.* If training and counselling fail and compensating is not applicable, the last step is to dismiss the person. You should not feel all bad about taking such action because you are not doing the person any favours by carrying him or her. The individual in question would be far better pursuing a different activity elsewhere which provides more satisfaction and better results. In fact, under these circumstances you are acting in the company's and the individual's best interests.

Summary

1. There is no point in planning if you fail to implement the plan successfully.

2. People do not like change and they resist it.

3. Management can manage change by implementing the plan.

4. The real test of implementation is whether or not managers make decisions with reference to the plan.

5. The most important factors in implementation are leadership and communication followed by action plans, budgets, timetables, milestones and reviews.

6. Key elements in implementation are leadership, internal marketing, problem-solving appointments, clear accountability, entrepreneurial managers, incentives, management information and controls.

7. Resources are allocated over a small number of major projects under separate managers and tied to approved business plans.

8. The management structure will impact on the strategic planning process. Balanced decision making is important and is promoted through an independent board including non-executive directors and a management committee.

9. Individual roles need to be defined and performance targets agreed for individuals and/or teams.

10. Individual performance can improve with training and counselling. Otherwise, non-performing people should be removed before they become obstacles.

References

1. *PA Consultants Fast Track Seminar*, 'The reality of implementation', 1991.

2. Niccolo Machiavelli, *The Prince*, Oxford University, Oxford, 1984.

3. Charles Handy, *The Age of Unreason*, Arrow, London, 1991

4. Larry Greiner, 'Evolution and revolution as organizations grow', in David Asch and Cliff Bowman (eds), *Readings in Strategic Management*, Macmillan, London, 1989.

5. John Harvey-Jones, *Making It Happen: Reflections on Leadership*, Fontana, London, 1988.

6. Kevan Scholes, 'The way to manage strategic change', *Accountancy*, February 1991.

7. Keith Hammonds, 'Commentary: why big companies are so tough to change', *International Business Week*, 17 June 1991.

8. Christopher Lorenz, 'Management study stresses teamwork', *Financial Times*, 12 November 1991.

9. John Gapper, 'Planning a response to a perceived challenge', *Financial Times*, 11 February 1991.

10. *Forbes Executive Calender*, 1992.

11. Igor Ansoff, *Corporate Strategy*, Penguin, London, 1987.

12. Richard Pascale and Anthony Athos, *The Art of Japanese Management: Applications for American Executives*, Warner, New York, 1981.

13. Arthur Sharplin, *Strategic Management*, McGraw-Hill, New York, 1985.

14. R.L. Wing, *The Art of Strategy: A New Translation of Sun Tzu's Classic The Art of War*, Aquarian, London, 1989.

15. Christopher Lorenz, 'Corporate renewal: Juggling lots of balls in the air', *Financial Times*, 9 January 1991.

16. *Director*, 'Doing the right thing', October 1988.

17. Max de Pree, 'Leadership is an art', *Success*, April 1990.

18. Christopher Lorenz, 'Bending minds to a new learning circle', *Financial Times*, 17 February 1992.

19. Tom Nash, 'When Coloroll's rainbow faded', *Director*, February 1991.

20. John Seymour Associates Newsletter, Bristol, England, 1987.

21. Michael Lawson, *Going for Growth: A Guide to Corporate Strategy*, Kogan Page, London, 1987.

22. Richard Scase, 'Dinosaurs in the new organisation', *Financial Times*, 25 November 1991.

23. Larry Alexander, 'Successfully implementing strategic decisions', in David Asch and Cliff Bowman (eds), *Readings in Strategic Management*, Macmillan, London, 1989.

24. Leslie Hannah, 'Books, designing organisations: the foundation for excellence', *Director*, August 1991.

25. Arthur Bloch, *Murphy's Law Book Two: More Reasons Why Things Go Wrong*, Price, Stern, Sloan, Los Angeles, 1980.

26. Arthur Bloch, *The Complete Murphy's Law: A Definitive Collection*, Price, Stern, Sloan, Los Angeles, 1991.

27. Sir Lewis Robertson, 'Good sense goes by board', *Sunday Times*, 22 March 1992.

28. Norma Cohen, Michael Cassell and Alison Smith, 'Cadbury panel calls for board reforms', *Financial Times*, 28 May 1992.

29. John Cassidy, 'No way to police predators', *Sunday Times*, 31 May 1992.

30. George Bickerstaffe, 'Appointments: on the corporate beat', *Times*, 9 May 1991.

31. *Financial Times*, 'Directors unhappy at limited roles', 19 April 1991.

32. Charles Batchelor, 'Value for money from an outsider's view', *Financial Times*, 20 March 1990.

33. Jonathon Green, *The Cynic's Lexicon: A Dictionary of Amoral Advice*, Sphere, London, 1986.

Implementation Part II— Corporate culture

Where there's a will, there's a won't.

GUALTIERI'S LAW OF INERTIA[1]

Introduction

We have looked at the role of the individual and what can be done to change his or her behaviour. Now let us look at what happens when a whole lot of individuals get together and create a company culture.

What is it?

Allan Kennedy believes 'it costs a fortune and takes forever'. Stanley Davis at Boston University likens it to 'putting your hand in a cloud'.[2] What is it? It is corporate culture. Williams, Dobson and Walters say that 'definitions of culture tend to deal primarily either with the way we act or the way we think'.[3] Culture encompasses thinking, feeling and reacting. Cultures are like personalities, 'once formed [they] are difficult to change'. It is very difficult to forge common values and they require 'constant renewal and fresh impetus' to keep going. Good cultures develop loyalty from employees and customers and create a reinforcing cycle. Good cultures determine the success of change management and support strategic planning. The key to good cultures is 'good communication'.[4] *I believe the best and most functional way to view culture is just to regard it as 'the way people do things around here'.*[5]

Managers became preoccupied with corporate culture throughout the 1980s, because they realized that culture could become a useful tool of strategy. In fact, a pressing strategic question was how management could 'transform corporate cultures to meet competitive standards in productivity, quality and customer service'.[6] Williams, Dobson and Walters also noted that culture 'is a source of motivation and demotivation, of satisfaction and dissatisfaction'.[3]

Why change?

Cultural minders have concluded that culture is a major factor in strategy, acting either to promote or to constrain strategies. If you wanted to change the way people behaved, it became necessary to change 'people's beliefs and attitudes'.[3] While managers came to understand how a negative culture impeded business, they were slower to recognize that a positive culture could become a competitive factor. In fact, it is still being discovered that positive culture can transform moribund organizations into 'extraordinary' performers. The movement to empowered, self-managed work teams is the greatest manifestation to date of cultural positivism. The prerequisite for this change is the recognition that *people are an asset and an investment, not a cost.*

One company found that it could not change direction until employees changed their knowledge, skills and thinking. The management team's vision and commitment were essential, but it still took a long time for the culture to change. Senior management had to send consistent signals over time. A leading consultant observed that management had to 'prevent [corporate cultures] from hindering the development of new approaches'.[7]

People have to feel they are really involved in order to be emotionally committed. But here is a rub: disempowered people welcome power but those already in power feel threatened. While change has to begin with managers, managers may resist change because it appears as a threat to their position. It is human nature to resist a disruption to comfortable patterns.[4] This is why cultural change requires leadership.

Even successful companies require change. Minoru Makihara, the new President at Mitsubishi Corporation is set on changing his company, but he faces strong opposition. Traditional consensus building, *nemawashi*, acts as a brake against fast change. People become set in their ways and resist change. Mitsubishi also is like 'an aircraft carrier' and it will be difficult to change direction but Makihara thinks 'change is necessary'.[8]

You can understand management's concern over cultures when considering the costs of a negative one: alienation, dissatisfaction, little or no commitment, reduced effort, high staff turnover, absenteeism and jurisdictional disputes. Also, there are related costs for close supervision, formalized rules and procedures and inflexibility.

On the other hand, there are clear positive benefits from a good culture, such as organizational commitment, extra effort, self-reinforced behaviour, cooperation, initiative and creativity without 'prescribed rules, supervision and external rewards'.[3]

Kennedy noted five possible reasons why you would want to impose rapid cultural change in a company:

1. If your company has strong values that do not fit in a changing environment.

2. If the industry is very competitive and moves with lightning speed.

3. If your company is mediocre or worse.

4. If your company is about to join the ranks of a very large company.

5. If your company is smaller but growing rapidly.[2]

Sometimes very successful companies get choked by the very culture that produced the success in the first place. Take Apple Computers for example. Chairman John Sculley felt the need to tackle Apple's 'self-indulgent, almost unmanageable culture' head-on. Once that culture was a major driving force and considered an important asset. Apple people believed they would change the world and they worked hard to achieve that 'lofty goal'. Now Sculley seeks pragmatism. In the meantime, a survey revealed that morale had slipped because employees felt the company had lost its vision. Senior management responded by discussing the company's strategy and technological priorities at an annual gathering of 300 top managers, letting the message filter down to the other 12 000 employees.[9]

Culture is also critical in service businesses because so much depends on the direct experience customers have when receiving the 'service'. Services are usually delivered instantly at the point of purchase, which makes service personal because it involves the interaction of people. It is 'the quality of this interaction that either spells success or failure for the marketing effort of a service organization'.[10]

How to change culture

If your culture is holding you back or if it will become an obstacle to achieving your objectives, you need to change the culture. Strategy-led companies may have to change their culture to move forward with their strategic plan. Change means just that. *If management wants to change the culture, it needs first to understand what it is. In defining your company's culture, you are forced to look objectively 'at the way things are done' around your organization. Next, management needs to identify what is worth retaining and what needs changing. Once the change areas are clearly identified, management needs to lead the change.*

Cultural change is a critical factor in increasing organizational effectiveness. When executives look for cultural change, they want people to change their behaviour, to do things differently. But, it can be a long, hard and time-consuming process. As cultures are built socially, they can be re-built socially. If your people can learn assumptions and values, they also can re-learn them.[11] In this regard, Allan Williams and his colleagues listed *six ways to change culture.*

1. Changing the *people* in the organization.

2. Changing the *positions* of people within the organization.

3. Changing directly *beliefs, attitudes and values*.

4. Changing behaviour *by example* or otherwise.

5. Changing the *systems and structures*.

6. Changing the *corporate image*.[3]

Another way to change the culture is to alter the physical layout at work by reorganizing, relocating work areas or moving whole departments. Professors at Harvard Business School observed that the most powerful method to change behaviour was by giving people 'new roles, responsibilities and relationships' in new organizations, which forced new behaviour on to people and changed attitudes.[12]

Generally, culture watchers observed that companies which focused on the outside world were more able to change their culture than companies which were 'internally focused'.[3] During the process to change culture, the following range of personnel practices could be used:

- 'recruitment and selection

- induction

- training and development

- communication

- payment and reward

- appraisal

- employee relations

- terms and conditions of employment

- organization structure

- counselling and redundancy

- social activities'[3]

After studying companies over many years, Professor Gerry Johnson at Britain's Cranfield School of Management complained that culture change needed to be translated into mundane and detailed tasks, not just left to mission statements and improved communications. He believes cultural change will not work until the daily behaviour of everyone in an organization is affected.[13]

Another observation was that too many companies failed to express the need for change in terms that people on the line could understand, such as better customer service. It was not clear that change could be decided at the top of a company and made to flow down through the organization.[14]

Change may come from anywhere in an organization. If it is not initiated by management, management needs to respond and facilitate it. Some change programmes start at the edge of companies led by general managers in specific plants and divisions. Senior management, therefore, should concentrate on creating a climate for change and spreading successes from the grassroots throughout the organization.[12]

A major discovery about cultural change was made by accident in 1924. Managers in Western Electric's Hawthorne plant in Chicago (later the birthplace of statistical process control and the start of the modern quality movement) began experimenting with different lighting strengths to boost output. When they increased the light for one group of workers and left it unchanged for another, both groups produced more. The same response occurred whatever changes were made to lighting. Output increased even when light was dimmed and workers could barely see. The company asked Professor Elton Mayo from the Harvard Business School to investigate and studies continued through 1932. His main finding was that production was influenced by social interactions between workers, not only by individual abilities. This observation became the basis for production cells which eventually lead to self-managed teams. Yet Mayo is still remembered for the 'Hawthorne effect' that workers respond if they are the focus of attention.[15]

While training plays a key part in improving performances of individuals and teams, it still remains the poor stepchild in many companies. For example, a recent estimate showed that less than 2 per cent of British firms provide training, which accounts for less that 1 per cent of total spending.[16] Training is needed before benefits from new management practices like TQM can be realized. Too many companies seem to play at change, looking for quick hits and immediate benefits. If they are not forthcoming, management loses interest. If you want things to change in your company, you have to spend time and resources to make it happen. *The underlying theme through all change programmes is the imperative need for management to make a commitment to the new programmes and back that commitment with resources over time. Once again, change becomes a leadership issue.*

Training might well start with management itself. According to a recent survey of 120 managers in large companies, British managers displayed an appalling grasp of financial skills. Around 68 per cent of managers believed a company would not encounter cash flow problems if sales jumped by 50 per cent in one year. Managers failed to understand the purpose of profit and loss statements, with 33 per cent of managers and 42 per cent of senior managers confusing it with a balance sheet. A large number of managers did not know what made up working capital: 48 per cent believed reserves were working capital, 38 per cent pointed to sales and 27 per cent indicated overheads.[17]

A common factor in successful cultural change is devolving power and responsibility down the line. If top management wants this to happen, it has to behave differently and constantly reinforce the change. For example, chairman David Simon at British Petroleum discourages managers from passing decisions upwards. He tries to change by asking people below 'why are you asking me that question?'[18]

Setting an example is critical for cultural change. But senior managers sometimes have personal difficulties changing the behaviour that enabled them to reach the top—their interventionist and control mode. It takes considerable patience and faith to step back and let the people underneath develop and do things their way. If you want continuous improvement, you cannot get defensive. You might get some heat if your people hold very strong views on management's ability to manage. If you expect your people to change, you need to be prepared to change too. Remember Old Pogo the Possum who left the swamp with his friend Albert the Alligator to find the enemy, only to return disillusioned having found out 'the enemy was us'. Or, as Tom Peters said pointing to 150 British managers in one of his seminars: 'There is an attitude problem and the problem is you.'[19] It can take time. Best estimates of the time required for new values to be internalized and taken for granted range from three to five years. Some larger, more bureaucratic companies could take even longer, up to ten years. But, if you don't start now, when will you?

Cultural change will not happen without clear leadership and commitment to change from the top. Line managers can become models and facilitators of change. But if you expect line managers to be good examples, you have to train them and deal with their fear of insecurity. Training starts by winning them over to the plan and getting them committed through participation. If you need to promote change, line managers can be effective agents of change in your organization, especially if you get them integrated into self-managed teams as mentors or coaches. Even though it takes time, trouble and expense, a bad culture must be dealt with sooner or later. Remember the downside of not changing: alienation, dissatisfaction, lack of commitment, minimal effort, high turnover, poor customer relations, bad service, absenteeism and union problems. If you have a negative culture and do not change it, the culture will frustrate and eventually defeat the strategic plan.

Keys to cultural change

There are three keys to a positive culture:

1. *Recognition.* Before culture can be changed, management must recognize and understand it and decide what needs to be done differently.

2. *Take ownership.* Cultural change and implementation are

successful when people take ownership of the problem and its solution by becoming involved at an early stage in decision making. Remember, participation leads to commitment.

3. *Critical mass.* Cultural change will occur if you get a critical mass of people involved and enough people want change.

The old suggestion box

The tried and true, old reliable suggestion scheme is making a come-back in the new age of human resource management. Joan Balcombe, coordinator of Britain's Industrial Society, estimates there are between 400 and 500 schemes in operation within the United Kingdom. Moreover, there is an Association of Suggestion Schemes which was founded in 1987 and has over 100 members. In 1988, 103 schemes were surveyed and 73 400 suggestions were received or 5 for every 100 people. Just over 16 000 or 22 per cent were adopted.

Suggestion schemes originated to save manufacturing costs. Now they are being used to make improvements in customer care and quality where savings are difficult to measure. Suggestion schemes also lift morale by allowing individuals to make valuable contributions to the company. Successful schemes should meet the following key criteria: first, they need careful planning backed with resources and management commitment; second, they need to be promoted continually; third, they should be enjoyable; fourth, they need to respond quickly to suggestions; fifth, they should reward suggestions that are adopted. For example, the surveyed schemes paid out an average of 18 per cent of any savings made.[20] While there is a noticeable drift towards teams, there is still a clear role for a mechanism that allows individuals to make direct contributions.

The cutting edge: self-managed teams

The most talked about innovation in cultural change is the creation of self-managed teams. Self-managed teams also have a dramatic impact on productivity, quality and lower costs. The principle behind these teams is 'empowerment', which means allowing employees to make their own decisions. The push for teams came from three pressure areas: to make companies more responsive to markets; to make companies more cost effective; and to create teamwork between disciplines which communicate horizontally. In teams, the role of manager shifts from controller to coach or disappears and the span of management moves from 5 to 15 people to 20 people or more.

There are three stages of empowerment. First, employees are asked to contribute ideas and recommendations. Second, employees have their jobs re-designed as individuals or in teams and they decide how to do the work with supervisors offering support. Third, employees decide how they will work and solve problems and they run the unit as a business.[18]

Tom Peters extols the virtues of self-managed teams in transforming companies like Harley Davidson. But what is the experience at other companies?

At Xerox in America teams constantly form and disband depending on the task involved or the problem to be solved. Xerox uses action teams to break through cross-functional lines and generate results. Teams are used to communicate across the organization, breaking strangleholds and restrictive horizontal and vertical flows. Xerox gets people from different functions to work together by focusing on a common objective they can share, such as 'satisfy the customer'.[21]

Jack Welch at General Electric has assaulted the old bureaucracy, eliminating layers of management. Divisions have been converted into 350 strategic units. A tremendous effort is being made to remove vertical and horizontal barriers, allowing the exchange of ideas and information. Welch is pursuing a 'boundaryless company' where all the lines are blurred between functions, labour and management and customers and company. These changes are meant to increase productivity by demanding more from employees who are given greater responsibility and from managers who must lead and be flexible but be open to criticism.[22]

General Electric has 298 000 people. According to Len Schlesinger from Harvard Business School, Jack Welch's plans are 'one of the biggest planned efforts to alter people's behaviour since the Cultural Revolution'. The key to this change is GE's programme of Best Practices. GE people went to other companies and asked them 'what is the secret to your success?' The answers were strikingly similar. *'Almost every company emphasized managing processes, not functions; that is, they focused less on the performance of individual departments than on how they work together as products move from one to another'* [italics added]. They beat competition in introducing new products and treating suppliers as partners. They tied up less working capital in inventories. It dawned on GE that they were measuring and managing the wrong things. Business development manager George Zippel says 'we should have focused more on how things got done than what got done'. One of the critical lessons taught as management discipline now at GE is 'that processes need owners – people whose responsibility and authority reach through the walls between departments'.[23]

The old Fort Dunlop tyre factory has changed since Sumitomo Rubber took over in 1985. Production has been broken into self-managing cells, just-in-time is a common practice and labour relations have improved out of recognition. The benefits are there too: production up 50 per cent with one-third fewer workers, waste and warranty costs down by 50 per cent and an annual loss of £20 million has been turned into a profit of £3.7 million.

While Sumitomo invested £10 million in the site, a large investment was made in qualitative practices, including communication and management. There are monthly team briefings with information flowing from the board to the factory floor and thrice yearly meetings between board members and groups of floor workers. Multi-disciplinary teams deal with production problems. A major push was made on quality and more than 1000 people were trained in SPC. When everyone realized that 85 per cent of the quality problems were not on the factory floor, multi-disciplinary teams were formed and led by senior managers.[24]

According to Jerry Junkins, CEO at Texas Instruments, 'no matter what your business, these teams are the wave of the future'. Jamie Houghton, Corning's CEO, agrees wholeheartedly, remarking that 'if you really believe in quality, it's empowering your people, and it's empowering your people that leads to teams'. Corning operates 3000 teams.

If 'superteams' work correctly, they run themselves and no boss is needed. The superteam may be composed of between 3 and 30 workers, sometimes a mix of blue and white collar employees. It sets schedules, targets and orders materials and equipment. The superteam also may hire and fire and look after and improve quality and 'stroke' customers.

How big is the movement? While nearly 50 per cent of the *Fortune* 1000 companies responded to a 1990 survey, only 7 per cent used self-managed teams but 50 per cent of respondents felt they would be used much more significantly in the future.

General Mills is so pleased with the concept that it is forming self-managed teams in all its factories. Why? Demonstration teams increased productivity by up to 40 per cent, and often set higher goals than management. In order to work, however, teams have to be given the real authority to make decisions, they have to have power.[25]

ICI uses teams at its Macclesfield pharmaceuticals plant. Managers have been given more active roles to get individuals to work in teams. During the 1980s, ICI spent £100 million upgrading plant and equipment and on computer systems but not much money was devoted to people. As a result, ICI had a 'task orientated culture' and lacked skills to build teams and manage people. Teams were formed in 1986 and results were soon realized: in the next three years, products delivered on time increased from 60 to 98 per cent, quality increased by 5 per cent, lead times fell by 30 per cent and accidents plummeted by 86 per cent.[26]

The 1990s look to become a watershed in the organization of work. Teamworking is expected to develop from a widespread experiment to the norm, as human resource managers try to find ways to involve workers by giving them more control over their working environments. Experience indicates that it is easiest to form teams with less than a dozen people who work closely together physically and interact frequently.

Trebor, a medium sized British confectioner recently acquired by Cadbury Schweppes, formed teams at its Colchester factory. The labour force of 280 people were consulted about changing the organizational structure and the factory floor responded by asking for more complicated jobs and welcomed the elimination of foremen. Thirteen work groups were formed with between 5 and 12 people. These groups organize work methods including job rotation, break times and quality control. They also help select new workers and are involved in training. Production and personnel issues are raised at regular meetings with management. Decision making has been pushed down the line to the lowest point where information is available to make decisions. While it is early days, results so far show improved industrial relations and much lower absenteeism. Meanwhile management is kept close to the factory floor, because there is no longer an inter-layer of foremen.[27]

Teams figure prominently in service companies too. For example, a London-based design group, Imagination, forms teams around every assignment which expand as projects develop. Peer pressures play a big part in team performance because team members do not want to let their colleagues down. This team-based structure allowed Imagination to produce 50 per cent increases in sales each year during the late 1980s.[28]

Charles Handy has observed that a lot of organizations are 'unbundling' into self-contained units, such as profit centres, strategic units and even separate companies. The push for decentralization tries to get decision making closer to the markets where companies have to respond to changes. Decentralization also cuts the cost of maintaining large central operations. But not everyone welcomes the new responsibilities and accountability which go with ownership and control. On the other hand, 'the young and the clever relish the freedom'.[29]

While a lot of attention has been devoted to the creation of teams on the factory floor, the most important single team to be formed is the management team. The creation of a well-bonded, highly motivated senior management team again depends on the lead of a visionary chief executive, who shows people a clear direction and gets them to follow. *The first real team to be formed, therefore, must be the management team. This team needs to act as one in pursuit of the strategic plan with each member serving as a role model to other employees.*

In this regard, four specific conditions help the management team to function effectively. First, the management team needs to formulate strategy. Second, the team must have the time to 'think and learn about its strategic role'. Third, the team needs to delegate problem solving to people in operations. Fourth, the team should recognize that learning is continuous at all levels in the organization.[30]

Following the formation of the management team, many organizations need to promote cross-functional or departmental communications. A survey of 700 manufacturing companies in Britain revealed that managers in manufacturing, finance and marketing do not talk to one another about their needs and what can and cannot be done for each other. If they do not talk about objectives, how can they work together to achieve the same ones?[31] The management committee can become an excellent mechanism to facilitate cross-functional dialogue. Another proven device is the formation of action teams composed of people from different functions to solve a specific problem or achieve a clear objective.

On the other hand, the management team needs to be careful about empowering people. Sometimes it is not appropriate and attempts can prove counterproductive or even backfire. Many people do not want to take responsibility over their work life. Some do not welcome the pressure or relish the challenge. Managers at various levels in the company may not like the change in their roles either. If the management team is not sure of its ground, it might find line workers and middle managers digging in collective heels to resist any change. Accordingly, any move towards empowerment should be considered and planned carefully. Moreover, it should be started in a small way where it will stand the best chance of success. A demonstration of the benefits and responsibilities can act as a useful example to other potential teams in your company. In this way, if it proves effective in your company, the empowerment movement can develop and extend into other areas.

Cultural case profile

In 1962, IBM's most illustrious leader, Tom Watson, stated in a lecture at Columbia University: 'I believe that if an organization is to meet the challenges of a changing world, it must be prepared to change everything about itself.'[32] Watson's creed did not become practice at IBM.

IBM's basic cultural tenets remain intact: respect for the individual, promotion by merit and job security. Employees cannot be transferred against their will and everyone has the right to appeal to the chairman. The company spends $1.2 billion a year on training and education.[33]

So, what's the fuss all about? IBM has lost its way. Sales and profits have deteriorated. IBM had its worst year in history in 1991 when sales slipped by 6 per cent to $64.8 billion and a loss of $2.83 billion was recorded.[34] Technological change and new market realities were taking their toll, even on the 'Big Blue One'. Pressure was coming from three directions:

1. A previously traditional and homogeneous computer market was fragmenting into several niche markets with different individual market leaders. IBM was not leading in notebook computers, workstations, UNIX servers and parallel supercomputers.

2. Japanese competitors were eating into the mainframe business and threatening IBM's leadership role. Japanese companies are now in third, fourth and sixth places in the world league.

3. The customer changed from dedicated processing personnel who depended on IBM to direct users who shopped around; and equipment decisions were being taken by non-technical boards concerned with IT as an issue of competitive advantage.[33]

Leading executives at IBM asked their customers what the company was doing wrong. The answers were unsettling: products were lagging behind competitors, customer needs were being ignored, products were being pushed instead of solving customer problems and the bureaucracy was stifling 'creativity, enterprise and responsiveness'. As one IBM manager said 'there were more tree-huggers than maze-runners'. In other words, IBM's culture insulated the company from market needs and changes, creating a comfortable, secure inner world where employees did not take risks. Meanwhile, other things were happening in IBM's markets.

IBM's management team took two and a half years to figure out what went wrong, followed by a year to restructure and re-position the company. Now IBM is looking at a four to five year implementation plan.[34] The strategy is to transform the company into a federation of business units which will become the best in their niche and be accountable for their financial performance. In this way, IBM plans to fight back against several successful competitors who focused on individual niches.[35] For the first time, managers of these new units will have remuneration tied directly to performance. Each unit will be measured against tough financial criteria. If a unit fails to perform, investment will suffer. But, can IBM's managers respond to these new challenges? The culture has reinforced uniformity, not enterprise.[36] Chairman John Akers avowed in late 1991 that 'we are going to push the pace as fast as we can'.[37]

By any standards, it is a bold experiment in cultural transformation, expecially in the face of all the changes already racking the computer industry. In any event, IBM remains a classic example of the impact of corporate culture on performance and change.

It can be argued that the absence of competition and change fosters complacency, insularity and an anti-customer atmosphere. Consider the number of public departments or agencies that exist to serve the needs of their employees, not the customers. Sometimes the organization itself can become the biggest obstacle. For example, if a company is not led positively by a determined chief executive, management teams can break into power camps and vacuums can form. One camp wars against the other. The wrong people can move into the void. Each manager may paddle his or her own canoe, without much regard for the company's interest, and if the management team is divided, what sort of message is sent to other employees?

Summary

1. Corporate culture is 'the way people do things around here'.

2. Culture can be a positive tool for competitive advantage or a barrier to change.

3. There are six recognized ways to change culture but change takes a lot of time, resources and management commitment.

4. Self-managed teams are the latest vehicle for change, delivering higher productivity and quality and eliminating middle managers as overheads. While empowerment can be a powerful tool for change, it should be considered carefully before implementing and may not be appropriate for all companies.

5. IBM is a case study of the impact of culture on change.

References

1. Arthur Bloch, *Murphy's Law Book Three: Wrong Reasons Why Things Go More*, Price, Stern, Sloan, Los Angeles, 1982.

2. Arthur Sharplin, *Strategic Management*, McGraw-Hill, New York, 1985.

3. Allan Williams, Paul Dobson and Mike Walters, *Changing Culture: New Organizational Approaches*, Institute of Personnel Management, London, 1989.

4. Tom Attwood, 'Corporate culture: For or against you?', *Management Accounting*, January 1990.

5. Gerry Johnson and Kevan Scholes, *Exploring Corporate Strategy*, Prentice-Hall, London, 1989. The expression 'the way we do things around here' as a description of culture was coined by Deal and Kennedy in their book, *Corporate Cultures: The Rites and Rituals of Corporate Life*.

6. Bernard Taylor and John Harrison, *The Manager's Casebook of Business Strategy*, Heinemann, Oxford, 1990.

7. Marion Devine, 'Appointments: how to set new corporate targets', *Sunday Times*, 30 October 1988.

8. Robert Thomson, 'Monday interview: Shrimps to global strategies', *Financial Times*, 16 March 1992.

9. Brenton Schlender, 'Corporate performance: yet another strategy for Apple', *Fortune International*, 22 October 1990.

10. Herbert Holtje, *Theory and Problems of Marketing*, McGraw-Hill, New York, 1981.

11. John Hassard and Sudi Sharifi, 'Corporate culture and strategic change', *Journal of General Management*, 15(2), Winter 1989.

12. Christopher Lorenz, 'The steps needed to create change', *Financial Times*, 11 January 1991.

13. Christopher Lorenz, 'Why it is the little things that matter so much', *Financial Times*, 22 May 1992.

14. Christopher Lorenze, 'The great top-down fallacy', *Financial Times*, 1 June 1992.

15. Michael Dixon, 'Motivation: power of the limelight', *Financial Times*, 17 November 1989.

16. Charles Batchelor, 'Planning: thinking of tomorrow instead of just today', *Financial Times*, 6 March 1990.

17. Paul Taylor, 'Managers lack financial skills says survey', *Financial Times*, 24 February 1992.

18. Christopher Lorenz, 'Changing corporate cultures: power to the people', *Financial Times*, 30 March 1992.

19. *Business Matters*, BBC Television Channel 1, 23 February 1992.

20. Charles Batchelor, 'Staff suggestion schemes: putting a premium on employees' best ideas', *Financial Times*, 3 September 1991.

21. Brian Dumaine, 'Managing/cover story: the bureaucracy busters,' *Fortune International*, 17 June 1991.

22. Martin Dickson, 'Transforming corporate culture: why GE encourages lese majeste', *Financial Times*, 5 October 1990.

23. Thomas Stewart, 'GE keeps those ideas coming', *Fortune International*, 12 August 1991.

24. Charles Leadbetter, 'Corporate culture: a shop floor transformed', *Financial Times*, 5 January 1990.

25. Brian Dumaine, 'Managing/cover story: who needs a boss?' *Fortune International*, 7 May 1990.

26. Michael Smith, 'Managing to create the right team chemistry', *Financial Times*, 15 January 1990.

27. John Grapper, 'At the end of the honeymoon . . .', *Financial Times*, 10 January 1990.

28. Christina Lamb, 'Corporate structure: stimulating creativity', *Financial Times*, 20 March 1990.

29. Charles Handy, 'The parable of a fallen city', *Director*, February 1991.

30. Bob Garratt, 'The short-sighted rhinoceros', *Director*, April 1990.

31. Ian Hamilton Fazey, 'Confused?—they certainly are', *Financial Times*, 8 March 1991.

32. Richard Pascale and Anthony Athos, *The Art of Japanese Management: Applications for American Executives*, Warner, New York, 1981.

33. Alan Cane, Roderick Oram, Louise Kehoe and Ian Rodger, 'Small earthquake: IBM slightly hurt', *Financial Times*, 24 April 1990.

34. Roderick Oram, Alan Cane, Louise Kehoe and Ian Rodger, 'Why the teacher has started taking lessons from its pupils', *Financial Times*, 25 April 1990.

35. Louise Kehoe, 'IBM plans to compete directly with "clones"', *Financial Times*, 4 March 1992.

36. Louise Kehoe, 'IBM creates three subsidiaries as restructuring commences', *Financial Times*, 6 December 1991.

37. Louise Kehoe, 'Off into the Big Blue yonder', *Financial Times*, 18 December 1991.

Implementation Part III— Reviews and problems

Last year's was always better.

LAW OF REGRESSIVE ACHIEVEMENT[1]

Plan review

The strategic planning process is an on-going activity which requires periodical reviews. As things change, the plan needs to reflect those changes to stay current and be realistic. Also, the review provides a good opportunity to evaluate progress towards the objectives and goals. Moreover, *the strategic planning process benefits greatly from successive iterations. As events unfold, the plans get more focused and gain in quality when experience is absorbed and integrated.*

It is essential that the corporate plan becomes a living document which is formally reviewed once a year. A review should be similar to the first planning meeting. You follow the format and see what has changed and what your experience has been. Your strategies will be validated in the marketplace and you need to listen carefully to what the market is saying. Your plan needs to be modified by your market experience.

You may find it useful to involve an outside facilitator in the initial planning and review sessions. Each session requires a different approach and an outsider will produce a better result. (For a more detailed discussion of an outsider's role, see Chapter 15.)

The review process should be off-site, well away from the office, and take no more than two days. *During the review, you will be looking primarily to see how your strategies have fared and how well you have implemented the plan inside the company.*

Some companies find it useful to review the plan on a monitoring basis every quarter or every six months. At these interim review sessions experience is evaluated and changes made if appropriate. However, a formal annual review is mandatory to determine if substantive modifications are required in objectives, goals and strategies, as well as implementation.

Thompson and Strickland suggest the following six step approach during the annual review:

1. Review why the present strategy was selected.

2. Identify new external and internal factors which may call for altering the strategy.

3. Reappraise external opportunities and threats.

4. Reassess internal strengths, weaknesses and resource constraints.

5. Consider risk/reward trade-offs and timing aspects.

6. Judge how to modify strategy in light of present and future conditions.

Seymour Tilles proposes another six questions to be considered:

1. Are the mission (vision), objectives and plans internally consistent?

2. Do the strategies fit the current environment?

3. Are the strategies consistent with internal resources that are available?

4. Is the amount of risk appropriate?

5. Is the time horizon an appropriate one?

6. Is the total integrated strategy workable?

Argenti raises the following review issues: how effectively have strategies reduced weaknesses, avoided or diminished threats and exploited important opportunities?[2]

Who should attend the review process? Certainly the original people involved in creating the plan should attend, also those who make key decisions and who are responsible for achieving objectives should participate. Moreover, they should be encouraged to speak their minds in an open atmosphere created and maintained by the chief executive.

What do you review? *You set an agenda to deal with the key business issues by priority as they impact on the plan's vision and objectives.* For example, one chairman made sure that every review included detailed and careful discussion about market trends, the competition, sales and market shares and 'real' financial performance. After this discussion, the team looked at progress against previously set goals.[3]

Feedback loop

The feedback loop, that is, channelling external reactions and responses to the company through the management team, is important at several stages in the planning process and the review stage is no exception. In this context, it would be extremely helpful if each team member regularly visited half a dozen key customers and/or suppliers to ask for feedback on the company's performance. It is also useful to find out what are the leading business issues among your customers and suppliers because that provides insight into their priorities and future requirements.

The direct experience of your customers and suppliers helps the review process by validating internal perceptions of performance and keeping the team close to the marketplace. If you have lost sales, it is particularly important to know why in order to prevent further lost revenues in the future.

If you build in this feedback loop, be sure to find customers and suppliers who will be critical. It does little good to rely on the company's supporters and friends for honest comments. Do not place faith on questionnaires and surveys. In depth, face-to-face conversations will be much more rewarding and, as a by-product, they can generate useful public relations.

While critical comments should be regarded as opportunities to improve performance, praise can lead to complacency and inflated egos. In order to gather a balanced view of external opinion, change the mix of suppliers and customers from time to time. It will be interesting to see if results vary with the sample and to discover why there is a variation.

Implementation problems

Implementation is the place in the planning process in which many companies fall down. Failures can be traced to a variety of problems. Research has shown that the ten most frequently encountered problems in implementation *in order of importance* are as follows:

1. Implementation took more time than originally allocated.

2. Major problems surfaced which were not identified beforehand.

3. Coordination of actitivies was not effective enough.

4. Competing activities and crises distracted attention.

5. Employee capabilities were insufficient.

6. Inadequate training and instruction for employees.

7. Uncontrollable external factors.

8. Inadequate leadership and direction by department managers.

9. Key tasks and activities were not defined in enough detail.

10. Inadequate information systems for monitoring.[4]

Michael Lawson cites three main reasons for strategic planning failures: the company failed to set objectives correctly; the company failed to modify objectives in light of changing experience; and the company failed to execute the necessary actions.[5]

Daniel Gray surveyed 300 American companies that used strategic planning. Almost 60 per cent expressed 'discontent' over the difficulties in implementing the plan and nearly 70 per cent of these attributed their problems to the following six factors:

1. Line managers were poorly prepared.

2. Business units were not clearly defined.

3. Goals were vague.

4. Information was not adequate enough for action planning.

5. Business unit plans were reviewed and handled badly.

6. Strategic plans were poorly linked with control systems.[6]

Summary

1. Things change, therefore the plan must change to reflect reality.

2. Corporate plans improve over time with successive iterations as experience is absorbed and integrated.

3. New questions are raised at formal reviews.

4. It is useful to obtain feedback from customers and suppliers to use in reviews.

5. There are ten frequently encountered problems in implementation which should serve as warnings.

References

1. Arthur Bloch, *The Complete Murphy's Law: A Definitive Collection*, Price, Stern, Sloan, Los Angeles, 1991.
2. Arthur Sharplin, *Strategic Management*, McGraw-Hill, New York, 1985.
3. Charles Batchelor, 'Strategy: the value of planning ahead', *Financial Times*, 13 June 1989.
4. Larry Alexander, 'Successfully implementing strategic decisions', in David Asch and Cliff Bowman (eds), *Readings in Strategic Management*, Macmillan, London, 1989.
5. Michael Lawson, *Going for Growth: A Guide to Corporate Strategy*, Kogan Page, London, 1987.
6. Daniel Gray, 'Uses and misuses of strategic planning', *Harvard Business Review*, **64**(1), January/February 1986.

Step-by-step guide to strategic planning

You can't tell how deep a puddle is until
you step in it.

MILLER'S LAW[1]

Introduction

Now that you have been through my approach to strategic planning, it is time to look at how you and your management team can start the planning process.

Who should participate?

Key members of your management team should participate in the planning session. Invitations should be issued by the chief executive to his or her marketing, sales, financial, production and technical executives and any other senior personnel who could make an important contribution to the future direction of your company.

The number of participants is an important consideration for the planning session. I find that the optimum number of participants is five and that it gets awkward to work with more than eight people. If you have more people who need to participate, you can consider a two tier approach: first, the actual planning session with no more than eight people; and second, a review session with the next tier who can contribute to the draft plan before it is presented to the board. You also may wish to invite one or more non-executive directors to attend the planning session. It is useful to have balanced views during the planning exercise, which can be provided by your independent board members. In any event, you have to present the plan for discussion and debate at board level and it helps to have a supporting voice when it is discussed there.

Where should it be held?

Strategic planning sessions must be held away from the office. If you attempt to plan at the office or factory premises, one or more participants will be called on urgent business to the telephone or out of the meeting room to deal with a 'crisis'. Also, the executives might have difficulty focusing on planning if one ear is cast for sounds of trouble. Either way, these disruptions will play havoc with the planning process and continuity of thought and debate.

You should find a comfortable hotel more than a few miles away. Participants are best to arrive the night before, enjoy a dinner together and get started early the next morning. I suggest that the participants work through the first day into the early evening, establishing the company's agenda and taking the first crack at strategies. Work should stop in time for a leisurely dinner. Work the next day should also start early, finishing the strategies and looking at how the plan will be implemented. You should aim to complete the exercise before 6.00 pm on the second day. In all, then, the planning session should take no more than two full days. If you attempt to work beyond that time, you will find that people's energy, creativity and concentration wane and the exercise will start to unravel and become counterproductive. The chairman, usually the chief executive, should ask one participant to take notes and draw up a draft plan according to the format below. The draft should be circulated to all participants for comment before being finalized and presented to the board.

When should it be held?

I prefer planning sessions to be held on weekends, because it marks a different occasion and makes it more relaxed. If a planning session is held during the week, you will find individuals with diary problems and it might be difficult to get everyone together at the desired time. Also, the weekend gives people the opportunity to dress casually and comfortably. Some companies like to combine a Friday and Saturday but a Saturday and Sunday are preferable. A different place, casual dress and a weekend all help to mark the planning exercise from other types of work. This difference helps to set the stage for dealing with fundamentals and key issues affecting the whole organization.

As to when on the annual company calendar a planning session should be held, it should precede your year end by at least two months. If your financial year is the calendar year, therefore, your planning or review session should be held in October. If the year end is 31 March, the planning session should be during January. Two months lead time is required to set the framework for the annual budget cycle. It also allows enough time for the board to approve the plan and then review the budget in light of the strategic decisions taken in the plan.

What should be on the agenda?

The agenda will be dictated by the framework and process already discussed. However, special issues might be important to the company. In fact, any subject that requires urgent attention should be listed prominently on the agenda. *The rule is that subjects of strategic import that require to be dealt with urgently should be listed in order of priority and placed in the planning format at the appropriate point.* Priorities can alter during the planning session, but everyone should emerge from the weekend with a sense of relief that the important issues have been discussed and positions taken.

A word of caution: *it is difficult to deal with more than three or four urgent key issues during the planning session.* You have to be ruthless in deciding what are the really important issues and set priorities accordingly. Fringe or side issues should be tabled for discussion elsewhere as the planning team needs to focus on the big items that will affect the company's future.

What period should the plan cover?

The plan should look forward three to five years. Goals should be set to cover this period, serving as bench-marks to measure progress. As the plan will be reviewed formally each year, it really becomes a rolling three to five years. It is important to look forward for a time beyond the normal budget exercise of six to twelve months. If you look forward beyond that period, it forces you and your team to consider actions and implications over time and allows the plan to evolve from year to year.

What about preparation?

It is very useful if participants can prepare their thoughts, key information and projections in one or two page position papers and circulate them prior to the planning session. Such papers considerably enhance discussion during the planning session, because they allow people to think about issues before discussing them. Probably the most important single paper will be on markets. The discipline of limiting position papers to no more than two pages promotes clarity of expression and ease of understanding and avoids getting bogged down in details.

Sometimes, however, position papers are not appropriate for an inaugural planning session because collective and free discussion is needed to establish the first company agenda. Thereafter, position papers based on experience are excellent contributions to future review sessions and should be encouraged if not requested by the chief executive. As corporate plans go through successive iterations, they get better. And the use of position papers improves the quality of the plan.

Should we use an outside facilitator?

Some planning teams will benefit from the participation of a strategic planner. The role of an outside planner is as follows:

1. Help guide the team through the planning process within the prescribed timeframe.

2. Lead the exercise or assist the chair in leading.

3. Add objectivity to discussions, raising the awkward questions and encouraging honest debate on difficult points.

4. Summarize the debate and reach consensus on key points.

5. Get the team through the complete process.

6. Help the chair deal with any personality issues that might emerge and which are better handled by an outsider.

7. Write up the draft plan for circulation to the other participants.

When I lead a planning session with companies, it takes a lot of pressure off other participants, especially the chief executive. If someone else leads the discussions, the chief executive can participate freely like any other member of the planning group. Also, the participant who would have taken notes is able to participate fully as well. It is easier for an outsider to act as a disciplinarian, curtailing discussions that wander or become counterproductive. It sometimes takes a firm hand to drag everyone back to the point and remain there until the issue is resolved and a consensus emerges.

The most valuable contribution of the outside facilitator, however, may appear intangible but clearly emerges after the planning session. This contribution involves the dynamic interaction between the team and the facilitator with the outsider probing and challenging the team to find the best and most appropriate answers to the critical questions. In this regard, the outsider becomes part catalyst, part devil's advocate, pushing the team to strive towards the true potential of their company. For those people with group experience, the 'group dynamic' also plays an important role in strategic planning and it often depends on the talents and chemistry of the facilitator.

A well-run planning session contains rigorous debate, intellectual challenge and, all in all, is pretty exhausting work. In the end, the final product, the plan, is much better for all the work and it will get even better over time. The most important thing, however, in favour of using a competent outsider is to make sure that the planning process is executed professionally and that a solid result emerges.

How will we know the session was good?

Everyone should know if the planning exercise was worth while. It can be measured in the quality of the decisions taken which is confirmed when the draft is circulated to participants. The team should be more cohesive after the exercise, reflecting the open discussion and consensus building. This 'bonding' is an extra benefit from the planning process. I have yet not to see a 'high' generated from planning sessions when the team gets excited and ready to take on the world by making its plan work. Of course, this enthusiasm is critical during the implementation phase. If you cannot 'turn on' the people inside your company, who will? Your excitement should become their excitement.

You should emerge with a complete plan, unless there is additional information required before the plan can be finalized. If this occurs, it will most likely involve the need for more data on the market and might require the commissioning of market research. However, you should leave with an outline of a complete plan, even if some detail needs to be added later. Do not make the mistake of this executive vice-president of an American health care holding company: 'The way to get into a planning bind is to go at everything piecemeal. First the organization chart—that's done. Then the plan—that's done. Then the budget—that's done. The bonus system—that's done. All that hard work and then nothing fits.'[2]

Sir John Harvey-Jones provides some helpful background on planning sessions in his book, *Making it Happen*. And Barrie Pearson relates useful suggestions in his book, *Common-sense Business Strategy* (see the Bibliography for publication details).

Step-by-step guide

1. How did we get here?
   Each participant should record the points he or she feels accounted for the success of the company to date. All points should be discussed and agreement reached on which are the most important.

2. Where do we want to go?
   Each participant should write two visions—the one that got the company to this point and the one needed in the future. Each vision should be limited to no more than three sentences. The visions

should be discussed and one agreed for the future. The vision should be contained in one sentence, if possible.

3. Is the vision real?
Are there any conflicts between personal ambitions and the vision? Are there any differences still remaining about the future direction? Is the vision compatible with the kind of people you are? Does the vision build on the things you really do well? These questions need to be answered before the vision can be adopted.

4. What are the company's strengths and weaknesses?
Each participant should list the strengths and weaknesses of the company in order of importance, including ones for each major product and service line. The strengths and weaknesses should be the most important ones and should be limited to no more than a dozen each. After discussion, the list should be limited to six key strengths and six weaknesses.

   Also ask: Do the strengths support the vision? Will the weaknesses prevent realization of the vision? Is the vision realistic given these strengths and weaknesses?

5. What are the objectives?
Each participant in open discussion should suggest the specific objectives needed to realize the vision. Each should be discussed and a list agreed. Objectives should be limited to no more than eight items. These objectives should be achievable in light of the strengths and weaknesses identified above.

6. What are the goals?
Each participant in open discussion should suggest goals to be achieved. How do they compare to the industry average? To that achieved by the market leader? To the fastest growing company in the industry? Are figures logically built up and defensible? Are there other goals to be set for quality, customer care, innovation or any other important aspect of your company? Goals should be agreed for the most important indicators.

7. What and where are the best business opportunities?
Using criteria of the highest return, least risky and most feasible, what does the market offer? You may have to break the session here for collection of market data and commissioning of market research. In this event, you will have to reconvene after the market research is completed. Market research should be circulated prior to the next meeting in a position paper for open discussion. You should not proceed with any strategies until the market data are collected and analysed.

   After considering the opportunities, what are the strategies needed to convert them? Will these market plans achieve the objectives by building on the company's strengths and reducing or neutralizing the weaknesses?

8. What market plans are needed to realize the business opportunities? After discussing the market research, you need to create market plans to convert the opportunities (see relevant questions and plan format in Chapter 7).

9. What resources are needed to convert the opportunities? Each participant in open discussion should agree what is needed in the way of people, funds and technology. Individual participants should be assigned to make proposals for each need which can be reported back to the management committee and board for discussion and approval.

10. How will these resources be obtained? After discussion and agreement on where and how to obtain specific resources, each will be assigned to an appropriate participant or be handled by the chief executive and/or financial officer.

11. What are the critical risks, threats and responses to strategies? Each participant in open discussion will suggest critical threats and risks. Collective responses will decide how the company can respond with each scenario and agreed response be recorded.

12. What actions need to be taken? An action list will emerge from the planning session. Actions need to be recorded by priority and each one should be assigned to a participant for implementation.

Corporate plan review

Each year the corporate plan will be reviewed formally. The same rules apply for the first planning session as noted above. People who participated in the first session should be invited for the review session, as well as any other individuals who emerge as important factors during the implementation phase.

A different set of questions should be used as discussed in Chapter 14. A key question is: have the strategies helped achieve the objectives by building on the company's strengths, reducing the weaknesses and dealing with the threats? Position papers are very important to the review process and should be encouraged or required by the chief executive.

References

1. Arthur Bloch, *The Complete Murphy's Law: A Definitive Collection*, Price, Stern, Sloan, Los Angeles, 1991.

2. Daniel Gray, 'Uses and misuses of strategic planning', *Harvard Business Review*, **64**(1), January/February 1986.

The model revisited

Delay is the deadliest form of denial.

PARKINSON'S LAW OF DELAY[1]

Let us revisit NAP's strategic planning model and see if it makes more sense now.

THE STRATEGIC PLANNING MODEL

1.0 How did we get here?

    1.1 Successful factors

2.0 Where do we want to go?

    2.1 Vision

    2.2 Objectives

        (1) Internal evaluation:
        Strengths and weaknesses

    2.3 Goals

3.0 How do we get there?

    3.1 Strategies

        (1) External evaluation:
        Opportunities and threats

4.0 How do we make it work?

    4.1 Structure

    4.2 Implementation

        (1) Action programmes

    4.3 Review

The diagram will help show how the various parts are interconnected.

THE STRATEGIC PLAN FLOW DIAGRAM

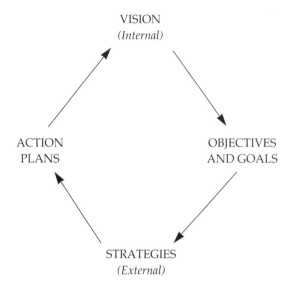

Final word

I have taken you through my model, looking at the problems and pitfalls in strategic planning. We have touched on other related subjects, surveying the contemporary landscape and noting good management practices. You now have a solid introduction to strategic planning.

You now stand at a crossroads. Straight ahead is easy, just continue as you are. The fork to the left or to the right is the turning towards a future of your own choosing. The choice is yours.

Reference

1. Arthur Bloch, *The Complete Murphy's Law: A Definitive Collection*, Price, Stern, Sloan, Los Angeles, 1991.

Bibliography

Ansoff, Igor H., *Corporate Strategy* (rev. ed), Penguin, London, 1987.

Argenti, John, *Practical Corporate Planning* (rev. ed), Unwin Hyman, London, 1989.

Asch, David and Bowman, Cliff (eds), *Readings in Strategic Management*, Macmillan, London, 1989.

Bloch, Arthur, *Murphy's Law and Other Reasons Why Things Go Wrong*, Methuen, London, 1979.

— *Murphy's Law Book Two: More Reasons Why Things Go Wrong*, Price, Stern, Sloan, Los Angeles, 1980.

— *Murphy's Law Book Three: Wrong Reasons Why Things Go More*, Price, Stern, Sloan, Los Angeles, 1982.

— *The Complete Murphy's Law: A Definitive Collection*, Price, Stern, Sloan, Los Angeles, 1991.

Bloch, Sidney, *Money Talk: A Lucrative Cocktail*, Buchan & Enright, London, 1986.

Bowman, Cliff, *The Essence of Strategic Management*, Prentice-Hall, London, 1990.

Green, Jonathon, *The Cynic's Lexicon: A Dictionary of Amoral Advice*, Sphere, London, 1986.

Hanan, Mack, *Fast-growth Strategies: How to Maximize Profits From Start-up Through Maturity*, McGraw-Hill, New York, 1987.

Handy, Charles, *The Age of Unreason*, Arrow, London, 1991.

Harvey-Jones, John, *Making it Happen: Reflections on Leadership*, Fontana, London, 1988.

Holtje, Herbert F., *Theory and Problems of Marketing*, McGraw-Hill, New York, 1981.

Johnson, Gerry and Scholes, Kevan, *Exploring Corporate Strategy*, Prentice-Hall, London, 1989.

Lawson, Michael K., *Going for Growth: A Guide to Corporate Strategy*, Kogan Page, London, 1987.

Ohmae, Kenichi, *The Mind of the Strategist: Business Planning for Competitive Advantage*, Penguin, London, 1983.

Pascale, Richard T. and Athos, Anthony, G., *The Art of Japanese Management: Applications for American Executives*, Warner, New York, 1981.

Pearson, Barrie, *Common-sense Business Strategy: How to Improve your Profits and Cash Flow Dramatically*, Mercury, London, 1987.

Sharplin, Arthur, *Strategic Management*, McGraw-Hill, New York, 1985.

Taylor, Bernard and Harrison, John, *The Manager's Casebook of Business Strategy*, Heinemann, Oxford, 1990.

Williams, Allan, Dobson, Paul and Walters, Mike, *Changing Culture: New Organizational Approaches*, Institute of Personnel Management, London, 1989.

Wing, R. L., *The Art of Strategy: A New Translation of Sun Tzu's Classic The Art of War*, Aquarian, London, 1989.

Index